TECHNOLOGICAL DIFFUSION AND INDUSTRIALISATION BEFORE 1914

A.G. KENWOOD AND A.L. LOUGHEED

T0382883

Routledge
Taylor & Francis Group

LONDON AND NEW YORK

First published in 1982 by Croom Helm Ltd

This edition first published in 2018
by Routledge
2 Park Square, Milton Park, Abingdon, Oxon OX14 4RN

and by Routledge
711 Third Avenue, New York, NY 10017

Routledge is an imprint of the Taylor & Francis Group, an informa business

British Library Cataloguing in Publication Data
A catalogue record for this book is available from the British Library

ISBN: 978-1-138-50336-6 (Set)
ISBN: 978-1-351-06690-7 (Set) (ebk)
ISBN: 978-0-8153-8572-1 (Volume 24) (hbk)
ISBN: 978-1-351-17987-4 (Volume 24) (ebk)

Publisher's Note
The publisher has gone to great lengths to ensure the quality of this reprint but points out that some imperfections in the original copies may be apparent.

Disclaimer
The publisher has made every effort to trace copyright holders and would welcome correspondence from those they have been unable to trace.

ROUTLEDGE LIBRARY EDITIONS:
THE ECONOMICS AND BUSINESS OF
TECHNOLOGY

Volume 24

TECHNOLOGICAL DIFFUSION AND INDUSTRIALISATION BEFORE 1914

Technological Diffusion and Industrialisation Before 1914

A.G. KENWOOD AND A.L. LOUGHEED

CROOM HELM
London & Canberra

ST. MARTIN'S PRESS
New York

© 1982 A.G. Kenwood and A.L. Lougheed
Croom Helm Ltd, 2-10 St John's Road, London SW11

British Library Cataloguing in Publication Data

Kenwood, A.G.
    Technological diffusion and industrialisation
    before 1914.
    1. Technology transfer—History
    I. Title   II. Lougheed, A.L.
    338.9'009   T174.3

    ISBN 0-7099-1508-X

First published in the United States of America in 1982
All rights reserved. For information write:
St. Martin's Press, Inc., 175 Fifth Avenue, New York, N.Y. 10010

Library of Congress Cataloging in Publication Data

Kenwood, A.G.
    Technological diffusion and industrialisation before
1914.
    1. Industries—History.   2. Diffusion of innovations
—History.   3. Technology transfer—History.   I. Loug-
heed, A.L.   II. Title.
HC51.K43   1982   338'.06'09   81-14332   AACR2
ISBN 0-312-78795-2

Printed and bound in Great Britain

CONTENTS

PART ONE: THE PROCESS OF INDUSTRIALISATION
AND THE DIFFUSION OF TECHNOLOGY

1 TECHNOLOGICAL DIFFUSION AND NINETEENTH-CENTURY INDUSTRIALISATION

I

As a distinctive epoch in the economic organisations of society, modern industrial growth is dated from the eighteenth century, when its beginnings in western Europe, and more particularly in Britain, can first clearly be discerned. Its characteristic feature for industrialising countries was the application of factory production, based on the increasing use of modern scientific knowledge, to the satisfaction of human wants, and, compared with output increases experienced in previous times, its economic consequences were a *rapid* and sustained rise in *real* output per head of the population accompanied by revolutionary changes in the structure and organisation of the economy and of society.

Because the *per capita* output of a country is arrived at by dividing the country's total output by its population, and because a country's workforce consists only of those members of the total population available for employment, a rise in *per capita* output usually means an even larger rise in output per worker. This improvement in the efficiency or *productivity* of labour is made possible partly by the application of new knowledge to production, a fact that focuses our attention on the economic and technological transformation of society that has accompanied modern economic growth. This transformation has encompassed wide-ranging changes in the techniques of producing, transporting and distributing goods, in the types of output produced and consumed, and in the occupational and spatial distribution of productive resources. Together with attendant political and social changes modern economic growth in this sense embraces innovation in almost every aspect of individual behaviour and social organisation.

II

Amongst these innovations in economic and social behaviour and organisation, technological progress has a major role to play in bringing about the sustained increase in output per head that is the distinctive feature of modern economic growth. The technology

3

existing at a given point in time sets limits on how much can be produced with given amounts of labour, capital and other productive resources. Given the level of technology, there is generally a wide range of possible methods of producing a particular good or service. Some require little capital and much labour, some require much capital and little labour; some are old techniques, some are new; and so on. Which of these technically feasible methods of production will be used—which one will minimise the costs of production—will depend upon the prices and therefore upon the available supplies, of the various factors of production.[1] For example, if there were only two inputs, capital and labour, Figure 1.1(a) might show the production function for a particular product (X) at a particular point in time.[2] As the diagram indicates, the given level of output can be produced with varying combinations of the two inputs depending upon the relative prices of labour and capital. Thus, if the supply of labour is relatively less abundant than that of capital, and its price therefore relatively more expensive than capital, we would expect this to result in the choice of a more capital-intensive method of producing X (combination A, say, rather than combination B).

Figure 1.1(a)   **Figure 1.1(b)**

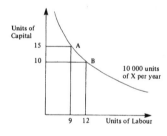
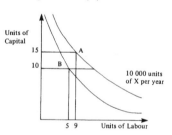

Technical progress also results in a change in the combination of inputs required to produce a given level of output. In this case, however, as the result of the introduction of a new and superior method of production it becomes possible to produce the given output with a *smaller* amount of inputs than previously. This situation is depicted in Figure 1.1(b). Because of technological progress, the given output of X can now be produced using smaller amounts of both labour and capital. This represents an improvement in total resource productivity and it is shown diagrammatically by an inward shift of the production function from A to B. It is productivity improvements of this kind which were largely responsible for the sustained rise in *per capita* output and incomes characteristic of modern economic growth. This, in short, is the role that technological change has played in modern economic growth.[3]

Thus an immediate effect of technical progress was to change the combination of factors used in production. If the new technique was capital-saving, it resulted in a greater proportion of labour to capital per unit of final output. If it was capital-using, it resulted in a greater proportion of capital to labour per unit of final product. Over the long run, technical progress tended to be capital-using, since labour became the relatively expensive factor, and attempts were made to economise on its use. In one industry after another the capital coefficient increased. This increase in capital, in turn, raised the productivity of labour which was the root cause of rising real incomes. By enabling the production of the same output with a smaller input of resources, technical innovations set free resources that could then be used to increase the supply of the commodity in the production of which the innovation occurred, or to increase the supply of other commodities. In either case, the innovation increased real income by allowing a given supply of resources to be used efficiently.

III

The process of developing a modern technology and applying it to economic production has a distinctive pattern of its own, involving not only scientific discovery and invention, but also innovation, technical improvement and the spread of the innovation through extensive imitation. Whereas innovation, defined as the application of a new invention, whether social or technological, to economic production, is a key element in the process of economic growth, the rapidity of the spread of an innovation is obviously extremely important in determining how quickly a new technique is capable of raising the general level of productivity within an industry or within the economy as a whole, thus bringing about a rise in total and *per capita* real incomes.

When we look at the historical evidence of the spread of modern technology before 1914, apart from the fact that the diffusion was confined to select geographic areas, mainly in Europe and North America, and to a relatively small number of technical changes, the available evidence suggests that the diffusion of technology both across national frontiers and within nation-states was much faster in the nineteenth century and after than in any previous period in human history. The historical evidence also suggests that the spread of technology across national borders was much faster than its diffusion within national boundaries. Thus Watt's steam engine, patented in Britain in 1776, was introduced into France in 1779, into Germany in 1788, and into Italy in 1816. Yet its use was not widespread in Britain until the 1830s and 1840s, and until even later in France, Germany and Italy. A similar experience is found in the spread of the techniques basic to the modernisation of the textile and iron and steel industries. Certain other technological developments of the nineteenth century, such as machine tools and the use of interchangeable parts, spread at an even slower rate, so that in these instances even larger technological gaps came to appear between nations.[4] Moreover, in respect of some of the later technological developments, Britain, a pioneer in the field of early modern industrial technology, fell behind Continental and American innovators, and failed to adopt many of the new techniques readily. These observations raise a number of questions concerning the diffusion of technology. Why, for example, are some innovations diffused internationally faster than others? Why is diffusion often faster between countries than within them, and why do diffusion rates within countries differ? And, finally, why is one nation a leader in one area only to be a laggard in another? In order to answer questions such as these, what have to be studied are the conditions and circumstances that favour the diffusion of technical knowledge between persons and geographical areas, and the mechanisms facilitating the spread of modern industrial technology that have emerged in the recent past.

IV

As a first step in any study of this kind, it is obvious that the process of technological diffusion has to be studied in terms of two stages: the spread of technology *between* countries and its spread *within* a country. Fruitful analysis also demands the setting up of an appropriate framework within which such a two-stage study can be conducted. One such framework suggested in the recent literature on diffusion emphasises the fact that the diffusion process is essentially a learning process involving demonstration and imitative activities as its key elements. Learning by imitation is an intellectual feat of which, apart from man, only the highest vertebrates (e.g., monkeys, dogs, etc.) are capable. *Demonstration* and *imitation* form the basis of human development, both drives being innate in us. A diffusion model based on the concepts of demonstration and imitation has obvious attractions.

However, another possible framework of analysis, which is the concern of this chapter, is that based on an analogy with the spread of a disease. If the manner in which a disease spreads is examined, it is found that epidemics and pandemics result from the conjunction of three essential conditions:

(i) an available store of organisms causing the disease;
(ii) effective transmission of these organisms in sufficient numbers;
(iii) other individuals with tissues susceptible to the organisms.

Given the existence of sources of infection, the spread of a disease can be broken down into two distinct proceses: the *transmission process*, which is concerned with the *mechanisms* whereby diseases are transmitted between persons and carried over long distances. In epidemiology the mechanisms involved are referred to as the vectors or *carriers* of the disease. The *contagion process*, on the other hand, examines the spread of a disease from the point of view of the susceptibility of the individual to the disease. In other words, whereas the transmission process is concerned chiefly with the *methods of spread* of disease between infected and non-infected individuals, the contagion process involves a study of the determinants of *the rate of spread* of the disease within a newly-infected population. In respect of the latter problem, it should also be noted that to speak of an individual's susceptibility to infection implies, as its alternative, the existence of different degrees of human *resistance* to the spread of disease.

When we turn to the fields of economics and economic history and examine the recent literature on technological diffusion in terms of the framework just outlined, we find that the problem of technological diffusion has been studied mainly at the micro-economic level, and that research has been largely concerned with a study of the rate of spread of modern technology.[5] These studies tend to show that the diffusion of new techniques is generally a slow process, and that the rate of diffusion varies widely between countries and regions within countries. They also tell us much about the economic and technical determinants of technological diffusion at the national and international levels. Broadly speaking, these determinants reflect either market conditions or supply conditions of complementary factors of production in the country or region receiving the new technology, and it is perhaps the supply side of the economy that has received most of the treatment in the literature.

V

Turning to the international diffusion of technology, it is a well-established fact that the international economic system played a major role in promoting the spread of modern economic growth. The flows of trade, capital and labour which linked countries together were not only the means whereby the benefits of economic growth in the form of higher real incomes, could be transmitted from country to country, but they were also the mechanism by which the technological and social innovations which are the essence of modern economic growth could be diffused. It is a matter of general observation that the diffusion of technology is closely related to the problem of mobility—of goods, people, ideas and behaviour. It is also apparent, from the available evidence, that mobility in this sense was greatly enhanced during the nineteenth century by innovations in transportation and communications and in the field of international finance which greatly helped the large-scale movement of goods, men and capital between countries. These international flows of economic resources were in turn important channels for the diffusion of the new industrial technology, since physical capital embodied it, immigrant artisans and entrepreneurs possessed the required technical skills and knowledge, and imported goods provided opportunities for demonstration and adaptive imitation.

While diffusion at the international level leads naturally to an examination of economic relations between countries, some economic historians have argued strongly for a study of diffusion at the regional level. Sidney Pollard has argued that, although industrialisation spread across Europe regardless of national boundaries, within individual countries only certain regions experienced industrial development, with the result that much of European industrial activity came to be concentrated in a few select areas.[6] An American economic historian has put the same argument in the following way:

> If historians studying the diffusion process would consider environments, or regions, as well as nation states, the problem of diffusion might be more clearly defined . . . water wheels and turbines . . . were not diffused from Switzerland to the United States; they were diffused from water power regions in Switzerland to the Niagara region in the United States . . . that the Watt steam engines . . . were diffused to Philadelphia and St. Petersburg, not to amorphous abstractions, the United States and Russia. To put it differently,

technology diffusion may occur most rapidly and with the greatest ease between regions or environments where the complex mix of factors is similar; therefore, the unit of study for diffusion should be regions rather than— or certainly as well as—nations.[7]

This stress on the regional aspects of the diffusion is obviously important. Thus, if in the case of personal face-to-face contact, which still remains the single most important method of transmitting new knowledge, the exchange of knowledge is made all the easier if the communicator and the receiver speak a common (technical) language, then equally the introduction of a new method of production into a region is all the more likely to succeed if the recipient region has a somewhat similar set of economic resources available to that in the region already using the technology.

Having said that it is as well to remember, however, that there are very powerful reasons for continuing to examine the process of industrial diffusion in the context of the nation-state. To begin with, the nation-state represents a body of people imbued with common aspirations, one of which may be a desire for economic growth. The fact that nationalism has acted as a prime mover in the process of modern industrial development further strengthens the case for adopting the nation-state as the appropriate unit of study. As Supple has pointed out:

> The determined aspirations for economic growth on the part of the inhabitants of (a country) is not and cannot be a function of economic appetite alone; it is in fact found in conjunction with pervasive and powerful ideology and the ideology which historically in many instances and almost invariably today is most strongly associated with the desire for economic expansion is some version of nationalism. It is a yearning for an increase in the income and power and prestige of a particular country which . . . goes far to explain the current concentration of effort on the tasks of development . . . [8]

The fact that individual countries achieved industrial take-off at different points in time during the nineteenth century has considerable significance for the process of diffusion because it meant that there were considerable differences in the objective conditions which faced them on the eve of industrialisation, differences determined by the current state of industrial technology, by how many countries had industrialised before them, and by their economic relations with these other countries. Thus while during the early nineteenth century newly-industrialising countries grew on the basis of textiles and iron, with both activities for the most carried on in relatively small enterprises, after 1850 the course of technical change widened the range of 'modern' industries to include steel, shipbuilding, chemicals and electrical and heavy engineering, with a consequent increase in the relative size and captial intensity of the typical firm. This meant that late industrialisers not only had a much wider technological base on which to develop an industrial economy, but it also meant that greater demands were made on the country's capital and human resources. These variations over time in the stock of available industrial technology, as well as variations in different countries' capacities to absorb the available technology, largely explain why industrial growth was not uniform between countries: why in some countries, such as England and France, the process of industrialisation was spread over many decades, while in others, for example Germany and the United States, rapid industrialisation occurred within three or four decades.

The existence of a number of already-industrialised countries undoubtedly had some influence on the pattern and process of industrialisation characteristic of late industrialisers in the nineteenth century. The presence of these countries had a positive as well as a negative impact on the spread of industrial technology. Thus small countries could develop industries based either on the availability of semi-manufactures produced by large industrial nations, for example the use of rough forgings and steel plates imported from Germany by the highly-successful Dutch shipbuilding industry, or by developing specialist products for use partly by the industries of larger nations, for example the high quality steel forgings produced in Denmark and used in the British shipbuilding industry. On the negative side, one can cite the spread of protectionism after 1870 in Europe and elsewhere, which was in part a consequence of the desire by newly-industrialising countries to offset the advantages enjoyed by foreign manufacturers in the domestic markets of these countries. However, the obstacle to the spread of industrialisation posed by the existence of a bloc of highly-industrialised nations, both in terms of its relatively high efficiency in production and its control of the major markets for industrial products, is a far greater problem for late industrialising nations in the second half of the twentieth century than it ever was during the same period of the last century.

Conditions in the international economy also changed over time, thereby creating differences in the circumstances facing countries industrialising at different times. Thus, for example, the rapid expansion of the cotton textile industry, which was a leader in Britain's early industrialisation, was based not only on an expanding domestic market but also, just as significantly, on a large export to India, which was secured at the cost of displacement of much of the traditional Indian hand-textile industry. Such opportunities for displacing traditional production and thus gaining an initial market tended to decline both at home and overseas for each country trying to industrialise. Even so, the extremely rapid growth of world trade after 1850 helped to alleviate the problem to some extent for those countries industrialising later in the nineteenth century. Here, too, therefore, it appears that this problem has had a more adverse effect, for fairly obvious reasons, on those countries industrialising during this century.

Two features of the international diffusion process require further comment. First, at what stage in the local adoption of an innovation developed in one country does that innovation become available for diffusion to other regions of the world? The conditions for this to happen are still not clear. Presumably the results of the application of a major innovation must reach some minimum threshold before the process of spread may be expected to begin. What is equally certain, however, is that diffusion of the innovation will also be partly a function of the receptivity of other regions and peoples to the new knowledge, and partly a function of the availability of adequate and effective means of transmitting the new knowledge abroad. The second problem of some importance for the analysis of the overall process of technological diffusion concerns the stage at which the international diffusion of a new technology ceases and national diffusion takes over. If we define the end of the process of international diffusion as that point in time when the nationals of the technology-receiving country are themselves capable of using and do use the new technology in production, then the length of time taken for a technology to diffuse internationally will vary considerably as between different countries. Some host countries will possess the resources and institutional structure needed to absorb the new technology readily, others will not. In the case of countries lacking the domestic capacity to absorb modern technology, the early stages of the international diffusion of the technology may be marked by the importation of the new techniques into these countries via the activities of foreign firms and artisans. In such countries, therefore, the process of international diffusion will be complete only when domestic firms in the recipient country have themselves become capable of using the new techniques.[9]

VI

If the adequacy and effectiveness of the channels of spread were the only determinants of the rate of technical diffusion, then the problem of transmitting technology would not be as complicated as it actually is. What also has to be considered is a quite different set of factors, namely, those which determine the rate of spread of technology at both the national and international levels. These often co-existent and sometimes overlapping determinants of technical diffusion include:

(i) *demand factors* (there may not be sufficient demand to support local production);

(ii) *capital factors* (local producers may lack or cannot obtain the capital to utilise the technology);

(iii) *natural resource factors* (a nation's available natural resources may be inappropriate for the effective use of the technology);

(iv) *labour-cost factors* (low labour costs relative to other costs may discourage the application of a particular technology);

(v) *technological factors* (local producers may not have the skills or education to absorb the technical knowhow);

(vi) *scale factors* (foreign producers may have economies of scale that cheapen costs *vis-à-vis* host nation producers; without government protection, national producers may have little hope of meeting foreign competition);

(vii) *infrastructure factors* (there may not be sufficient supporting services, such as transport facilities and banks, or complementary techniques to warrant diffusion);

(viii) *cultural factors* (there must be values and norms of behaviour conducive to the absorption of technology); and

(ix) *language barrier factors* (most easily overcome, language barriers, which may retard diffusion).[10]

What all this implies is that the successful introduction of a new technology means that financing must be arranged, productive capacity built, intermediate materials and components obtained, and labour trained and employed. At any stage in the process of introducing a new technology bottlenecks may appear because of shortages of particular inputs, thus emphasising the need for people with the ability to redesign the production process to overcome these shortages, or at least to minimise their retarding effects on the overall industrialisation process. There is also the need for adequate markets to absorb the greatly expanded output of modern industry. The importance of limited and fragmented markets as an explanation of the slow rate of industrial development in western Europe during the first half of the nineteenth century has been clearly put by Landes in his classic work on the subject.[11] How these market limitations were eventually overcome—through a combination of political (unification of Germany and Italy, protectionism, and government-centred demand for goods, as in Russia), technical (improved transport and communications), and economic factors (such as the formation of the Zollverein)—focuses attention on the fact that the determinants of the rate of technical diffusion just outlined are but a short-hand description of a complex bundle of interrelated factors, each of which has some influence on the speed of the diffusion process.

The existence of certain political requirements for successful industrial growth reminds us that to understand the diffusion process we must regard it as a cultural, social, political and psychological process, as well as an imitation of artifacts. The introduction of a new technology into any country is a challenge to stability, and to facilitate its adoption, existing institutions and the social and political structure must be capable of absorbing the potential disruption to established value systems and ways of doing things. In the circumstances, therefore, it is hardly surprising to find groups in an industrialising society which resist change. Such non-economic barriers to technological progress many be an important determinant of the speed of diffusion of a new technology both between countries and within them. At the same time, the available evidence on European industrial development suggests that the resulting degree of resistance to industrial change declined with the passage of time. The reasons for this are fairly obvious. To begin with, as more countries industrialised, the competitive economic pressures on the non-industrialised became more and more intense. Moreover, since growing industrial power meant increased political and military power, the threat of political intervention on the part of already-industrialised nations was ever present. Again, some of the new technology, for example the railway, offered benefits of a kind that could not be forgone. Finally, no country could completely isolate itself from the economic changes going on around it. Inevitably, some sectors of the 'resistant' economy came to experience the impact of the new technology.

VII

If international political and economic pressures were often necessary to bring about the desire for industrial change in some countries, equally powerful promotional institutions were also often needed to diffuse within these countries the technology which would make this goal realisable. At this point in the diffusion process it is useful to look at Alexander Gerschenkron's model of nineteenth-century European development in which the concept of *substitutes* for the prerequisites of economic growth plays such a vital role. Gerschenkron argues that the existence of certain preconditions are for the most part neither necessary nor sufficient for successful economic growth. A few may be necessary, such as the abolition of serfdom in Russia which was crucial for increasing labour mobility in that country. In the main, however, the missing ingredients of economic growth could be substituted for, and this is in fact what did happen in Europe during the nineteenth century when a series of such substitutes became visible. Furthermore, Gerschenkron claims that these substitutes can be organised into a meaningful pattern according to the degree of economic backwardness of the countries concerned. Thus he argues that the organisational drive for development in the early stages of European industrialisation was provided by firms, investment banks, or governments, depending on how backward the country was when it entered the industrialisation process.[12]

Although Gerschenkron's thesis has been much criticised in recent years, the validity or otherwise of that thesis is not a point at issue here. For irrespective of whether or not a meaningful pattern can be established between the degree of economic backwardness of a country and the organisational drive for industrial development provided by firms, investment banks, or governments, there is no doubt that these institutions were important mechanisms for diffusing modern industrial technology during the nineteenth century. As has already been argued, the successful spread of modern industrial techniques within a country depends not only on the presence of a set of conditions conducive to technical diffusion, but also on the existence of mechanisms capable of diffusing the new techniques

between persons and through space. In favourable economic circumstances, the free market mechanism—firms operating in the market
under stimulus of the profit motive—was sufficient in itself to provide
a means of spreading modern technology and thus bringing about a
process of 'spontaneous' economic growth. In less-favoured areas,
however, owing to shortages of markets, capital, skilled labour,
entrepreneurial ability, or some other ingredient of importance to the
successful diffusion of modern technology, new institutions, such as
investment banks, or governments had to susbstitute for the free
market mechanism. Thus, on the one hand, investment banks were a
novel means of overcoming the shortages of capital and entrepreneurial
skills so vital to the adoption of large-scale technology. On the other
hand, governments not only provided a possible substitute for a lack of
a domestic market through their purchases of goods and services, but
they also provided capital funds out of taxation, entrepreneurial skills
from amongst the ranks of government officials, as well as a variety of
other aids to technological diffusion. In any of these ways, and in the
absence of a freely-functioning market economy, investment banks
and governments could provide a set of preconditions that were
conducive to the adoption and spread of modern industrial technology.

VIII

It has been the purpose of this chapter to suggest a framework within
which to analyse the spread of modern industrial technology. Broadly
speaking, the rate of spread of this technology is determined by the
presence within a country of a set of conditions, economic, political
and social, influencing its willingness and ability to undertake
industrial change. Technological diffusion is also a function of the
adequacy and efficiency of the mechanisms for diffusing technology.
Narrowly conceived, these consist of the means of communication
that link the transmitter of the new knowledge and its receiver, such as
migrant artisans, industrial exhibitions, trade journals, and the like.
But obviously the transmission of new technology takes place within a
broader institutional framework than is described by these channels of
communication. In the nineteenth century, the spread of technology
between countries took place in the context of an expanding international
economy, and within countries, the growth of certain institutional
arrangements, whether the result of spontaneous development or
more deliberately conceived, served to assist in spreading the new

technology more widely and effectively. In this connection the Gerschenkron theory of organisational substitutes for spontaneous growth is particularly useful. Conceived of as a means of overcoming a country's deficiencies in the set of economic and social prerequisites of growth (and, by definition, of technological development), institutions like investment banks and governments provided alternative mechanisms to the free market for diffusing technology.[13]

NOTES

1. The claim that producers will use that production method which will minimise costs is based on the assumption that producers are motivated by a desire to maximise profits (i.e. the difference between production costs and selling price).

2. The production function defines the *technical relationship* between the amount of output capable of being produced by each and every set of specified inputs (or factors of production). It is defined for a *given* state of technical knowledge.

3. Technical progress also involves the production of *new* commodities. In many cases, the availability of new products can be regarded as a change in the production function since they are merely more efficient ways of meeting old wants, if these wants are defined broadly enough.

4. With the exception of an innovation specific to a one-firm industry (i.e. a pure monopoly), a single case of the taking-up in one country of a technological innovation perfected in another country does not constitute the completion of the international diffusion process. Further adoption of the innovation by other firms and industries is necessary before the process of national diffusion takes over.

5. See, for example, Mansfield's article on the spread of 12 major innovations within the US bituminous coal, iron and steel, brewing, and railway industries between 1890 and 1958, and Griliches's article on the adoption of hybrid corn by US farmers since the early 1930s. Both articles are reprinted in N. Rosenberg (ed.), *The Economics of Technological Change* (London, 1971).

6. S. Pollard, 'Industrialisation and the European Economy', *Economic History Review* (November 1973).

7. L.P. Hughes, commenting on a paper by E. Robinson on 'The Early Diffusion of Steam Power', *Journal of Economic History* (March 1974), p.129.

8. B. Supple (ed), *The Experience of Economic Growth* (New York, 1963), pp. 43-4.

9. See M. Wilkins, 'The Role of Private Business in the International Diffusion of Technology', *Journal of Economic History* (March 1974).

10. Wilkins, loc. cit., pp. 172-3.

11. D.S. Landes, *The Unbound Prometheus* (Cambridge, 1970).

12. A. Gerschenkron, *Economic Backwardness in Historical Perspective* (Cambridge, Mass., 1962), pp. 353-64.

13. A parallel set of institutional arrangements for diffusing modern techniques is apparent in agriculture. In Britain, for example, the landlord-tenant relationship provided an adequate means of promoting agricultural improvement. In other countries, however, owing to inadequate social arrangements, lack of capital, fragmentation of land-holdings, etc., co-operatives or the government played a much more important role in diffusing the new agricultural techniques. But see Chapter 3.

2 THE SPREAD OF INDUSTRIALISATION BEFORE 1914

I

To explain why individual countries entered the industrialisation stakes at different points in time is the central concern of this book. Before we can proceed to analyse this problem, however, we need to establish in broad terms the spatial pattern of industrialisation that emerged in the period before 1914.

The industrial revolution, which began in Britain in the late eighteenth century, and which spread first to Europe, then to the United States, and later, to Japan during the nineteenth century, was relatively limited in the extent of its geographical spread. Within this limited area, however, the diffusion of the new industrial technology was relatively rapid. By 1850 it had penetrated into France, Belgium and Switzerland. Half a century later it had reached Germany, the United States, Sweden, Russia and Japan. Apart from the timing of the entry of a country into the industrialisation process, the pattern of the spread of industrial technology displays a number of other interesting characteristics. To begin with, the first European countries to follow Britain's industrial lead, France and Belgium, were those continental countries geographically adjacent to Britain. Furthermore, although industrialisation spread across Europe regardless of national boundaries, within individual countries only certain regions experienced industrial development, with the result that much of European industrial activity came to be concentrated in a region running roughly through northern France and southern Belgium down through the Ruhr and the Rhine valley into Switzerland and through to northern Italy. Other heavily industrialised regions also developed in parts of Germany (Silesia), Austria-Hungary, Russia, Sweden, Denmark and Finland, but by 1924 the greater part of Europe's industrial development was concentrated along a line running from northern France through to northern Italy. Finally, over time, the spread of industrialisation was, broadly speaking, from the more-advanced economies to the less-advanced. In other words, other things being equal, the later a country entered the industrialisation process the more backward economically and socially it tended to be.[1]

In reviewing the spread of industrialisation during the nineteenth century it is convenient to make use of Rostow's concept of the *take-off*, which, in terms of his theory of the stages of growth, represents the crucial stage in a country's industrial development.[2] According to Rostow there are five stages in the process of modern economic growth. The starting point of the growth process is the *traditional* (pre-industrial) *society* in which the social structure is hierarchical, and the value system is geared to long-run fatalism. But the essence of the traditional society is that it possesses a low ceiling of attainable output per head because of the backward nature of its technology. As Rostow says, its production capabilities are based on pre-Newtonian science and technology and pre-Newtonian attitudes towards the physical world.

The second stage of growth, during which *the preconditions for take-off* are developed, involves important non-economic and economic changes. In the non-economic sphere what is significant is the emergence of a new elite who regard economic modernisation as being not only possible but also highly desirable. In the economic sphere the preconditions stage involve such fundamental changes as a rise in the rate of capital accumulation above the rate of population growth, and the exploitation of existing innovational opportunities as well as the creation of new ones, particularly in the agricultural sector, where a surplus emerges that can be used to finance industrial expansion. Similarly, substantial investment in transportation facilities and other forms of social overhead capital is undertaken during this period.

The crucial stage, however, is *take-off*, the decade or two when the economy and society are changed in such a way that growth becomes built in to the economy. In practical terms, take-off is characterised by a rise in the rate of investment to over 10 per cent of national income, the development of one or two major manufacturing sectors with a high rate of growth, and the emergence of a political, social and institutional framework conducive to economic growth. After take-off follows the *drive to maturity*, during which growth is transmitted to all parts of the economy. Finally, the economy moves into *the age of high mass-consumption* when the leading sectors shift towards the production of durable consumers' goods and services.

Rostow's concept of industrial take-off has been subjected to much criticism. Considerable doubt has been cast on his hypothesis that this stage in a country's industrial development was compressed into a relatively short period of time. There is little evidence, for example, to support Rostow's assumption that the rate of net capital formation doubles (rising from 5 to 10 per cent of national income) during the 20- to 30-year period designated by him as the take-off stage for a variety of countries. In nearly all cases, the period necessary for the investment rate to double was longer, often considerably longer, than that postulated by Rostow. On the other hand, whatever one's views on the assumptions made by Rostow concerning the nature of industrial take-off, the economic histories of today's advanced economies all feature a period, of varying length, during which an acceleration in the rate of industrial growth occurred. Moreover, this acceleration was associated with the introduction of modern technology into a number of industries which very quickly emerged as major growth centres in the economy as a whole. These developments were also accompanied by a rise in the rate of capital formation. Given the existence of these periods of industrial acceleration in a country's economic development, which in effect launch it along a path of sustained economic growth, it becomes possible to describe in diagrammatic form the chronological and geographical pattern of the spread of industrialisation in the nineteenth century. This has been done in Figure 2.1 and Table 2.1. While there may be some disagreement amongst economic historians as to the precise dates used to designate the period of industrial acceleration for the

Table 2.1: Industrial 'Take-off' Dates prior to 1914

Country	Dates of Industrial 'Take-off'
Britain	1783–1830
France	1830–1870
Belgium	1833–1870
Germany	1840–1870
United States[a]	1843–1870
Sweden	1868–1890
Japan	1885–1905
Russia	1890–1905
Italy	1895–1913
Canada	1896–1914

Note: a. New England regional 'take-off'—1815–1850.
Source: W.W. Rostow, *The World Economy. History and Prospect* (Austin and London, 1978), pp. 365-455.

individual countries included in the figure and table, the broad pattern of industrial spread which it describes is not likely to be a matter for dispute.

Figure 2.1: Industrial 'Take-off' Dates Prior to 1914

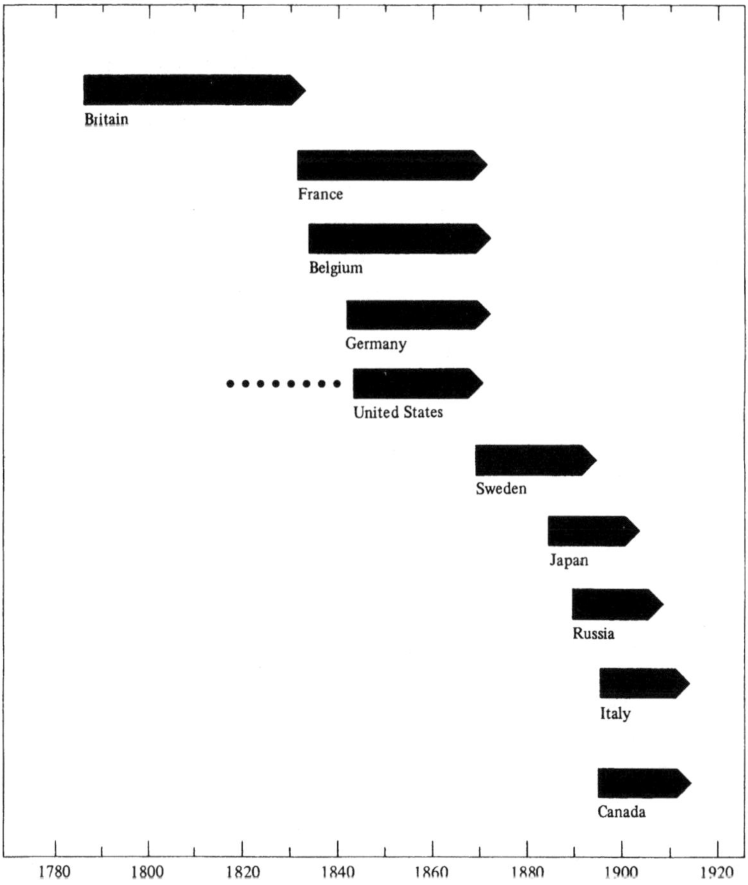

II

According to Rostow, industrial take-off is characterised, amongst other developments, by the emergence of one or two major manufacturing sectors with high rates of growth. Whereas in Britain after 1780 there was an expansion of output in a number of industries, including agriculture and woollen textiles, it was the cotton and iron industries that acted as the leading sectors in the early stages of Britain's industrial revolution. It was in these industries that the most significant clusters of technological innovations appeared, taking the form of new machinery and new processes which multiplied the output per worker several times and produced better-quality products. Contrary to the experience of later industrialising countries, the impact of railway technology on British industrial production occurred late in the country's industrial development. In its early stages, however, the country had been well-served by an excellent system of canals and roads.

Given the gradual nature of French industrialisation, it is difficult to choose the industry or industries which predominated during the period of take-off. Silk production was important from 1800 to 1850, cotton textiles from 1800 to the 1830s, and the metallurgical industries after 1830. Railways became important after 1850. Taking the period of industrial take-off as 1830–70, coal, iron, engineering and, from the late 1840s on, railways, appear to have constituted the leading sector complex of industries that carried France through this vital stage in its industrial development.

Coal, iron and steam power were three crucial factors in Belgium's industrial development after 1820. Coal was cheaper than in most other continental countries at the time and several innovations in the 1820s involving the use of steam power rapidly increased coal output which reached two millon tonnes by 1846. The iron industry, which had its origin in Liège and Charleroi in the eighteenth century, expanded rapidly in the 1820s. During these years the achievements of the coal and iron industries constituted the key element in the country's industrial development, and their continued growth, along with expansion of the textiles, chemical and glass industries, made Belgium one of the most industrialised nations on the continent by 1840. Thereafter, railway construction, which gave the country one of the most comprehensive railway systems in the world, played a critical role in stimulating what industrial development took place during the next decade or two.

Germany's take-off was based on an acceleration of coal production in the 1830s, and, more importantly, a burst of railway building during the 1840s which was on a larger scale than that in France. There was also by 1850 considerable mechanisation of the textile industry. Coal production expanded faster in the 1850s with the development of the Ruhr coalfield, and pig-iron production, which had stagnated in the two previous decades, now began to grow quickly. The modernisation of the textile industry continued with the rapid acceleration in mechanical weaving in the 1850s and 1860s. Along with the growth of the railway system, this expansion of the coal, iron and textiles industries provided the basis for industrial take-off in Germany during the period 1840 to 1870.

Industrialisation in the United States took place against a background of territorial and agricultural expansion. In the early stages of its industrial development household manufacturing was widespread, and the only highly-localised manufacturing activities were those like shipbuilding, flour milling, and lumbering which depended heavily on locally available resources. Textile manufacturing did flourish in the north-east, and provided the leading sector in New England's industrial take-off in the years between 1815 and 1850. Industrial growth became more vigorous and general from the 1840s onwards, however, and American manufacturing activity became more diversified with the expansion of the domestic output of machinery, iron manufactures, textiles, boots and shoes, and so on. This increased industrial output was encouraged by a growth in domestic demand which stemmed, in part, from the spread of a railway network throughout the country which definitely solved the problem of creating an efficient national market, although canals, turnpikes and river steamboats had earlier contributed significantly to improving the market linkages.

Sweden was one of the smaller countries in Europe to reach a high level of industrial development by 1914. In 1850 it was still a predominantly agricultural country with an embryonic industrial sector based mainly on iron manufacturing. In the 1850s, an improvement in agricultural productivity, which supported an expansion of grain exporting, was accompanied by increases in the production of iron, timber and textile products. When another burst of industrial development began in the 1870s, agriculture's dominance of the Swedish economy remained unchanged, and although there was no marked increase in the relative importance of manufacturing industry in total output until the 1890s, the changes which occurred in the 1870s represented a turning-point in the development of the economy. In industry, the value of production of the capital goods sector rose by more than 100 per cent up to 1875, and total industrial investment by more than 80 per cent. During these years extensive investment occurred in virtually all sectors of manufacturing industry, as well as in housing and railway construction.

Japan was the one country outside Europe and North America to experience industrial take-off during the nineteenth century. It was following the Meiji Restoration in 1868 that the first steps were taken to provide Japan with a modern industrial base. Adopting quickly the technological discoveries and institutions which had been developed in Europe in earlier decades, Japan entered a take-off stage within an industrial framework which, like that of Britain, was based squarely on the production and export of textiles. In the case of Japan, however, silks as well as cottons, were of major importance. At the same time, the Japanese government's demand for defence equipment, the growth of the shipbuilding industry, even if largely dependent on imported raw materials, and the expansion of the metallurgical industries also played a part in Japan's industrial take-off.

The modern stage of industrialisation in Russia commenced slowly in the 1850s and the 1860s and later accelerated in two big 'spurts' in the 1890s and after 1904. The Russian effort is an example of how an economically backward country, a latecomer to modern economic growth, can achieve a substantial industrial structure with the use of foreign technology and funds while the agrarian economy remains virtually stationary. What economic development took place in Russia after 1850 was aided substantially by capital inflow and by state encouragement of industry. Foreign capital and entrepreneurship were particularly evident in the big spurt of the 1890s, when foreign capital favoured the coal, iron and steel, and petroleum industries. At the same time, government loans floated abroad did much to assist railway construction. Moreover, in addition to providing direct state encouragement in industry, the government also protected the home market by means of high tariffs, placed orders for railway materials with domestic firms, and transferred taxation receipts, obtained largely from agriculture, into manufacturing, and thus contributed more to the emergence of a large manufacturing complex than most other European governments during the nineteenth century.

Italy was another latecomer to modern economic growth, achieving a high rate of industrial growth only in the period after 1895. From the unification of the country in 1861 to 1895, the average rate of growth of real product was around 0.7 per cent and from 1896 to 1914 it was 2.7 per cent (being at its highest from 1897 to 1906). The major leading sectors which produced the upswing in Italy's industrial output were textiles (chiefly silks and cottons), electricity, engineering products, chemicals, steel and shipbuilding. The introduction of hydro-electric generation played an important part in the entry of this country into modern economic growth. Being a latecomer to modern economic growth, Italy was able to take advantage of the most recent technological knowledge developed in other industrialising countries. Thus, in addition to the expansion of old industries such as textiles, new industries were adopted readily. Electricity generation, the manufacture of bicycles, motor cars and typewriters are cases in point, and these industries were well established in Italy by 1914.

Finally, Canada moved into the phase of industrial take-off during the second half of the 1890s. By that time, however, the country had already developed a considerable industrial base which had been expanding rapidly since the middle of the nineteenth century. The processing of agricultural raw materials, including flour-milling, leather tanning, and boots and shoes, and the working up of other natural resources in the form of log and timber products, were the important manufacturing activities in this early industrial development. After 1890, this convergence between agricultural and industrial expansion was carried further with the development of meat packing and dairy products as new major forms of manufacturing activity. In addition, the steel industry as well as modern cotton textiles expanded rapidly after 1900, as did pulp and paper, farm machinery, motor vehicles and other activities linked to them.

III

What did all this development mean in economic terms? The index in Table 2.2 purports to show the rate of growth of primarily modern industry over the period 1820 to 1913. Although the industrial output and pricing data on which these growth rates are based are necessarily rough approximations, particularly in the earlier years, the rates of growth of output depicted in the various sub-periods are consistent with the picture of industrial spread described in Table 2.1. The rise in the growth rate in the period before 1860 reflects the acceleration of industrial development in Germany and the USA after 1840, along with the continued industrial growth of Britain, France and Belgium. Railway construction also became significant in the years after 1840. The subsequent period of accelerating industrial growth between 1860 and 1913 is also consistent with the continued rapid industrial development of Germany and the USA, particularly after 1870, and the successive entries of Sweden, Japan, Russia, Italy and Canada into industrial take-off.

Table 2.2: Index of World Industrial Production 1820–1913 (Annual Average Growth Rates)

Sub-period	Growth Rate %
1820–40	2.9
1840–60	3.5
1860–70	2.9
1870–1900	3.7
1900–1913	4.2

Source: W.W. Rostow, *The World Economy. History and Prospect* (Austin and London, 1978), Table II-1, p. 49.

It has already been pointed out that certain industries, such as textiles, coal, iron and steel and railways, were strategic elements in nineteenth-century industrial development. The figures in Table 2.3 illustrate the growth of these industries in the group of countries listed in Table 2.1. The upper half of the table contains figures of output totals and railway miles opened at 20-year intervals between 1820 and 1900 and for 1913, whereas the lower half of the table shows figures of the increases in total output and the railway miles added during each sub-period between 1820 and 1913. The long-run trends in the output increases and railway miles added were much as would be expected. Output additions got larger and the number of railway miles added increased in each successive sub-period as more countries became industrialised. The exceptions to this generalisation are the decline in the number of railway miles added between 1900 and 1913, as railway development reached saturation levels in some of the more advanced industrial countries, such as Britain and France, and the slow-down in the growth of the cotton textile industry between 1860 and 1880, which was followed, however, by a spectacular acceleration in output after 1880.

IV

From this necessarily sketchy account of the industrial growth of a number of countries it is evident that industrialism spread from one country to another in a reasonaby consistent pattern. Britain was the first country to achieve industrial breakthough. Thereafter it was, in general, the countries closest to Britain which were able and willing, often with the aid of English entrepreneurs and capital, to follow the British example, and industrialism spread across Europe along a reasonably well-defined trail. Outside Europe, the other major countries to achieve industrial take-off were the United States, which had close economic ties with Europe, and Japan, which experienced political and economic penetration by the West. It is also clear that, in addition to the establishment of a modern industrial sector, increased productivity in agriculture was an essential aspect of modern economic growth. Some countries, such as Denmark, Norway, the Netherlands,

Table 2.3: Total Output Growth and Change, Selected Industries, 1820–1913

(a) Total output

	1820	1840	1860	1880	1900	1913
Railway miles opened (000s)	–	5	58	180	343	431
Raw cotton consumption (mn. metric tons)	101	342	940	1383	2717	4278
Coal output (mn. metric tons)	20	47	132	315	709	1225
Pig iron output (mn. metric tons)	0.8	2.7	7.0	17.4	38.1	73.5
Crude steel output (mn. metric tons)	–	–	–	4.2	26.7	71.0

(b) Output increases

	1820–40	1840–60	1860–80	1880–1900	1900–13
Railway miles (000s)	5	53	122	163	88
Raw cotton (mn. metric tons)	241	598	443	1334	1561
Coal output (mn. metric tons)	27	85	183	394	516
Pig iron (mn. metric tons)	1.9	4.3	10.4	20.7	35.4
Crude steel (mn. metric tons)	–	–	–	22.5	44.3

Sources: B.R. Mitchell, *European Historical Statistics 1750–1970* (Cambridge, 1975); M.C. Urquhart and K.A.H. Buckley, *Historical Statistics of Canada* (Cambridge, 1965); *Japan Statistical Yearbook* (various issues); Bureau of Census, *Historical Statistics of the United States, Colonial Times to 1970* (Washington, 1975).

Canada, Australia and New Zealand, were able to achieve relatively high *per capita* income by 1913, largely through concentrating on providing the foodstuffs and raw materials demanded by the industrialising countries. It is also apparent that in some countries that experienced industrial take-off in the period before 1913, for example Sweden and Canada, the relationship between agricultural and industrial development was very close indeed. Before looking at the spread of modern industrial techniques, therefore, it is worth briefly considering the modernisation of agriculture in the years up to 1913.

Notes

1. The chief exceptions to this rule were countries like Canada and Australia, which were late industrialisers because for them primary production continued for some time to be more 'profitable' than manufacturing activities, in the sense that these countries could increase their real incomes more rapily by specialising in agricultural and mining production and exchanging their surpluses of primary products for manufactures produced elsewhere.

2. W.W. Rostow, *The Stages of Economic Growth: A Non-Communist Manifesto* (Cambridge, 1960). Much more is, of course, involved in economic growth and the modernisation of societies than industrial production. Nevertheless, the diffusion of industrial technology is at the heart of the process.

Selected Reading

S. Kuznets, *Modern Economic Growth: Rate, Structure and Spread* (New Haven, 1966)

A. Maddison, *Economic Growth in the West* (London, 1964)

W.W. Rostow, *The World Economy* (London, 1978)

B. Supple (ed.), *The Experience of Economic Growth* (New York, 1963)

PART TWO: THE SPREAD OF MODERN INDUSTRIAL
TECHNOLOGY: PRECONDITIONS

3 THE SPREAD OF MODERN AGRICULTURAL TECHNIQUES BEFORE 1914

I

The process of structural change associated with modern growth is characterised by an increase in industrial and other forms of economic activity relative to agriculture. The rate at which this change occurs, at least in the early stages of a country's industrial development, depends on, among other things, the rate of growth of non-agricultural employment opportunities. Moreover, since in its pre-industrial stage of development the bulk of a country's economic resources are engaged in agriculture or in activities associated with agriculture, the speed with which employment opportunities in the non-agricultural sector grow will depend on the rate at which labour, capital and other resources are transferred out of agriculture into the other sectors of the economy. The sheer size of the agricultural sector in the pre-industrial economy points to its importance as a potential source of captial, entrepreneurial talent, labour and technical skills for industrial development. But resource transfers out of agriculture can take place only if the productivity of the land, capital and manpower left in the agricultural sector rises so as to maintain or even increase existing farm output levels. Increased agricultural productivity is also needed if agricultural production is to keep pace with a growing population and the rising demand for raw materials associated with successful industrialisation. Furthermore, agriculture may make a significant contribution to a country's net foreign exchange earnings through the substitution of domestically-produced agricultural products for imported ones or through expanded exports of agricultural produce. Under favourable circumstances these increased foreign exchange earnings can then be used to purchase foreign capital equipment needed for industrial development or to pay off loans made by foreign investors. Whether the extra foreign exchange comes about as a result of import substitution or export expansion, an improvement in domestic agricultural productivity is a prerequisite for its realisation. Increased agricultural productivity and the higher levels of farm incomes this implies can also mean an increased demand for manufactured consumer goods and for agricultural inputs, such as fertilisers, machinery, farm tools, and so on. In the early stages of

31

economic development this agriculturally-induced demand for industrial goods is obviously an important factor in widening markets and permitting the increased specialisation of labour and diffusion of artisan skills so vital to large-scale industrialisation. Finally, the convergence between agriculture and industry was an important factor in bringing industrialisation to largely agricultural regions. Canada has already been mentioned in this context, as the processing of agricultural products played a significant role in the early stages of that country's industrial growth. Sweden and Hungary were two other countries in which substantial engineering industries developed on the basis of agriculture's demand for modern machinery. Subsequently some of the engineering firms in these two countries broadened their industrial bases by moving into the manufacture of other kinds of engineering products, including railway and electrical equipment.

II

The crucial importance of a rise in agricultural productivity during the early stages of industrialisation is sufficient justification in itself for devoting some space in a book of this kind to a review, however brief, of the spread of modern agricultural techniques, since the rise in agricultural productivity obviously depended to a considerable extent on the use of improved agricultural practices. There is, however, another reason for including such a review. It is to show the broad similarity between agricultural and industrial techniques in the set of factors determining the spread of these techniques and in the manner in which obstacles to the use of these techniques were overcome.

What kinds of agricultural improvements led to the rise in agricultural productivity in the century and a half before 1914? Apart from the introduction of new crops, the first wave of agricultural improvements, which became widely adopted in Britain during the eighteenth and early nineteenth centuries and then spread outward to Europe and North America, involved the gradual elimination of the traditional grain-and-fallow rotation and its replacement by continous crop rotation. Modern rotation agriculture is based in turn on two further improvements: the introduction of the thick-rooted varieties of our present root crops (swede, turnip and beetroot), and the adoption of other leguminous hay crops (lucerne, clover, rye-grass, etc.) as elements of arable farming. Because the increased output of these fodder crops made it possible to feed livestock through the winter when grazing was limited, the main restriction on the growth of animal numbers was removed and an increase in the supply of meats and manure followed, the rise in the latter augmenting the supply of fertiliser available for use on cultivated land. In short, *mixed* farming came to dominate agricultural activity, associated as it was with advances in seed selection and animal breeding. There was also at this time some improvement of traditional farm implements and the introduction of new ones. In the making of ploughshares iron replaced wood and the scythe took over from the sickle in the harvesting of the enlarged grain output. There was an extension of the use of the horse for farm work in place of oxen with their much slower speed of traction, but the use of mechanical or steam-driven machinery contributed little to the increase of agricultural productivity, at least in the period before 1850.

After 1850 there was a second burst of innovations in agriculture involving the use of new agricultural machinery (chiefly threshers and reapers); the development of improved drainage systems; further improvements in traditional farm implements; the first use of non-animal traction; and the introduction of chemical fertilisers. Britain was still an important innovator in agriculture during these years but the centre of innovation in some fields had shifted to other countries, including the United States (farm machinery) and Germany (chemical fertilisers). In the United States the enormous extent of land available favoured farming with power-driven machinery involving the use of steam power, the internal combustion engine and electricity. The growing need for more efficient types of agricultural machinery was also partly the result of the increasing crop yields brough about by the growing use of artificial fertilisers. Before 1870, natural Peruvian guano had supplemented the traditional fertilisers used in Western agriculture. Thereafter, however, superphosphates were manufactured on a commercial scale, and nitrogen and potassium emerged as two new chemical developments of considerable importance for the further growth of the artificial fertiliser industry. In addition to the growing use of machinery and fertilisers, other developments responsible for the increased agricultural productivity characteristic of the period included: better methods of land utilisation, improved drainage and land-clearing techniques, better weeding, soil conservation and the protection of crops against insects and fungi. In the present century many of these innovations have been further improved and their use, particularly of farm machinery and fertilisers, has become much more widespread. What has dominated agricultural innovation in the twentieth century, however, so as to make it possible to speak of a third agricultural revolution, has been the development of scientific plant and animal breeding based on modern genetics, an innovation whose impact on agricultural productivity has been felt mainly since the second quarter of this century.

III

Given the existence of improved farming practices, how were these innovations taken up by the rural sector? Put simply, an effective diffusion of new agricultural techniques requires favourable conditions on three principal fronts. First, means must exist for the effective transmission of the new techniques to the farmers. Second, conditions must be such as to make the farmers willing to adopt these new techniques. This is largely a matter of the presence of incentives and inducements sufficient to make the farmer want to invest in progress— for example, the availability of markets in which to sell the consequent increased output, adequate price and profit expectations, and a land-tenure system which ensures that the farmer reaps the benefits of any improvement he makes.[1] Finally, the willingness of the farmer to adopt new techniques must be backed by the ability to do so. In other words, the farmer's desire to improve his farming practices must not be frustrated through lack of inputs and finance. The rest of this section will be devoted to an examination of a number of major agricultural innovations introduced before 1914 in order to illustrate how agricultural progress in Europe and elsewhere during this period was influenced by conditions two and three listed above. A survey of the means by which this new knowledge was transmitted is carried out in the following section where an attempt will be made to show how the institutional character of these 'transmission mechanisms' was in part determined by the presence or absence of the conditions favourable to the diffusion of agricultural techniques discussed below. Before proceeding with these considerations, however, some brief comments on the need for land consolidation and land reform as a necessary prerequisite for successful agricultural development are in order.

Historically, there are no clear-cut answers to questions about the importance of land consolidation for agricultural progress. It is true that in Britain agricultural improvements in the late eighteenth and early nineteenth centuries were closely associated with land enclosure and consolidation. Yet whereas, in addition to Britain, land consolidation was carried furthest in Scandinavia and parts of nothern Germany (chiefly Prussia), in the rest of Europe land consolidation has been on a very modest scale right up to the present day. Even now, at least one-third, and probably one-half, of the agricultural land in Europe would need to be reallocated or consolidated to do away with the technical disadvantages of scattered holdings and the consequent need to conform with neighbours in farming operations. In short, whatever damage fragmentation of the land has done to the technical and economic efficiency of labour and capital in agriculture, any claim that land consolidation is a prerequisite of the use of modern crop rotations and certain other agricultural innovations has not been borne out by experience. The new and improved crops and changes in the crop sequence in cultivation characteristic of nineteenth-century agricultural progress were not halted or too seriously retarded by the continued existence of the field system throughout much of Europe. Moreover, even where land consolidation did occur, population growth and the absence of the law of primogeniture served to offset this advantage to some extent by encouraging the fragmentation of the land into even smaller operational units.

Changes in the ownership of land were also not enough in themselves to guarantee agricultural improvements. Peasant ownership of the land became general throughout most of western Europe in the first half of the nineteenth century as a result of reforms begun by Napoleon. But supporting changes were obviously needed if the new freedom conferred on the peasant was to be realised in the form of increased agricultural output. In France, for example, the peasants finally gained complete ownership of their holdings in 1793, when the National Convention abolished all remaining feudal privileges. This development, along with the removal of some of the taxes which drained capital away from rural districts, and the decreasing rate of rural population growth, laid the foundations for progress in agriculture. This potential was not realised, however, until the growth of urban industry and the expansion of the railway system in the second half of the nineteenth century gave French agriculture the effective market it needed. Similarly, the emancipation of the serfs in Russia in 1861, while giving the Russian peasant greater security of tenure and title to property, gave him little chance of attaining economic independence. The peasants were not given their land but had to compensate the former landowners by paying a fixed annual sum to the state, the state in turn compensating their landowners with state bonds. Since these redemption payments were based on land valuations considerably above the true market value, they represented a severe financial burden on the peasantry and did much to depress its purchasing power and reduce its ability to invest in agricultural improvements. Moreover, most peasants did not own their land individually since, over a large part of the country, ownership was vested in the peasant commune (the *obshchina* or the *mir*). The absence of private ownership, and the fact that peasant lands were subject to periodic redistribution among the members of the commune, reduced the incentive for peasants to make long-term improvements in their land and invest capital in their holdings, even if they could afford to do so.

The effect on agricultural progress of the differing patterns of land consolidation and land tenure that emerged in Europe during the eighteenth and nineteenth centuries was, in many instances, to limit its spread, by reducing both the capacity and the willingness of farmers to undertake improvements. Thus the continuation of strip farming in many parts of Europe tended to strengthen resistance to change by stressing the common need to cling to traditional practices. In some instances, strip farming was incompatible with agricultural improvement.[2] On the other hand, under those systems of land tenure where a greater degree of individual initiative existed, the inhibiting influence of the exactions of landlords, of the governmental tax system, and of the Church blunted incentives and prevented peasant farmers from rising above subsistence levels.[3]

Turning to examine the diffusion of some of the major agricultural innovations, we find that the spread of some new crops was hindered more by the distrust of things new than by any economic or technical obstacle. Potato cultivation, for example, met with some resistance in those regions where the potato was considered an unusual crop, for instance, in mid-eighteenth-century Sweden, but once it had become familiar, its further expansion was determined mainly by the growing need for cheap food. The fragmentation of the land unit also encouraged the introduction of the potato since it gave a high yield per acre. Likewise, maize required very little promotional effort to make the peasantry of the Danubian provinces see its advantages. On the other hand, a quite different degree of educational effort was needed to make the expansion of sugar beet production a success. This required not only an awareness on the part of the farmers of the crop's profitability and the presence of sugar factories to make the profits real, but it also needed the training of farmers in the use of the right variety of seed and the correct techniques of cultivation to suit local conditions. Indeed, the need for seed varieties and for slight but significant variations in methods of cultivation to suit the soil and micro-climate conditions of particular locations, often constituted major determinants of the success or failure of attempts to diffuse new crops and new agricultural techniques.

Unlike the new food crops grown for local consumption, the widespread use of chemical fertilisers depends on the favourable market conditions for the increased agricultural output as well as an effective demonstration of the usefulness of artificial fertilisers in increasing agricultural productivity. Among the technical problems associated with the use of fertiliers is the need to relate doses to different soil types. Indeed, with the progressive development of various pure or mixed fertilisers more instruction and understanding are needed in each case for their effective use. Literacy, education and training consequently became more important characteristics for a progressive farming community. But if the use of modern fertilisers was conditioned by the farmer's level of education, economically, the use of fertilisers depended upon the ability of the farmer to sell his increased output at prices that would cover their cost. With the exception of Germany and the Benelux countries, farmers in western Europe were slow to make full use of the new chemicals and it was only after the 1920s or slightly earlier that standards of minimum use were achieved throughout the region. While there were many technical and economic conditions favouring the use of chemical fertilisers in Europe, including limited land resources, which placed a premium on high yields per acre, and large, protected and growing home markets for agricultural produce, the cost factor may well have been decisive in causing many European farmers not to use fertilisers, especially when agricultural prices were falling. Cost considerations were certainly overwhelmingly important in eastern and southern Europe, where smallholdings predominated and peasant poverty was widespread. Low educational standards may also have been important here. Consequently, in these parts of Europe there was little progress in the use of fertilisers up to the late 1940s.

Labour supply and labour costs were major factors determining the spread of new tools and, later, of agricultural machinery. Increased agricultural productivity meant greater output and thus the need for more labour to sow and harvest crops. This increased demand for labour could be solved in a number of ways without resort to machinery. The local labour supply could be used more fully by the introduction of incentives, faster work tempo or longer hours, and migrant workers could also be employed. Alternatively, earlier cutting could be adopted to lengthen the harvest period and staggered sowing used to phase out the ripening process. But where the labour problems persisted, the shortage was overcome by the use of improved farm tools. Of crucial importance here was the switch from lower into higher working capacity hand tools, with the heavy hook or scythe superseding the traditional toothed sickle and smooth reap hook as the standard corn-harvesting implements.

The use of the scythe spread rapidly in the Scandinavian countries during the eighteenth century, due apparently to the combined pressures of short seasons and extensions of cultivated land on already scarce labour supplies. Similarly in the United States, a labour shortage and the extensive methods of farming pursued there meant that the cradle scythe progressively displaced the sickle from the end of the Colonial period, to become general in most large grain-growing farms in the eastern states by 1800. Progress in Britain was much more rapid in the 20 years after the 1790s than either France or Germany. In Europe generally, however, the widespread adoption of the new hand tools did not occur until the years 1835–80 and particularly 1850–80. In Russia, the scythe was not taken up until after 1850 and its use was not predominant in the Balkans until the 1930s. As for the spread of faster tools for harvesting, resistance to new methods was always strongest where labour was most abundant and where the incentives to labour-saving innovation were consequently lowest. Moreover, since the scythe required strength and long practice for efficient operation, wherever farmers were dependent for their harvest on female or part-time industrial workers then the adoption of the scythe and heavy hook was predictably slow. The use of migrant workers was also an obstacle to the introduction of new methods, for their hand-tool preferences were much more resistant to pressure for change than those of resident workers.

The introduction of the scythe and heavy hook, which had the advantage of low cost, was partly responsible for the slow spread of reaping machines in Europe. Other factors which prevented the use of these machines included the limitations imposed on their use by farm layout and terrain, and the fact that the effectiveness of the mechanical reaper in saving labour was greater on larger farms and on higher-yielding land. Changing the existing landscape through ground levelling and removing hedgerows to make larger areas of cultivation, thus creating conditions more favourable to machine use, was expensive, however, if only because the rising wage rates, which encouraged the use of mechanisation, also made this kind of preparatory investment more costly.[4] Furthermore, in many areas of Europe, farmers and landowners were socially constrained from introducing work methods which might create unemployment among the resident workforce.

In the United States, too, physical conditions were effective barriers to the early use of the reaper, despite the prevailing high wages in agriculture. From the mid-1850s onwards, however, the reaper was taken up much more rapidly. This change of attitude on the part of American farmers came about mainly as a response to the higher grain prices of these years which, by increasing the demand for farm labour, forced up farm wage rates relative to the cost of farm machinery thus making the adoption of this equipment profitable even on those farms where this had not previously been the case.[5] The greater use of farm machinery was also encouraged during these years by the expansion of grain acreage sown on many existing farms, which was brought about by the rise in grain prices, and by the shift of the centre of grain production from the more confined eastern seaboard to the open spaces of the Midwest.

Threshing machines were altogether quicker to catch on than reaping machines. In 1882, for example, France and Germany had between them 585,000 threshers, but only 55,000 reapers. Why farmers should be prepared to mechanise a winter operation but not a summer one remains a puzzle, but part of the answer, no doubt, is to be found in the fact that the traditional method of threshing, using the flail, was extremely labour-intensive, requiring the services of strong adult males, thus preventing any extensive use of casual and 'inferior' labour, such as was abundantly available for the harvest. But its labour-saving potential was not the only advantage of the thresher. In the United States, for example, its advantage lay chiefly in speeding up the delivery of crops to the market so that they arrived before prices began to fall. The mechanisation of hay-making also involved a substantial saving of labour. By 1860 good mowing machines of modern design were on the market and one man using a mower driven by two horses could cut hay faster than ten men with scythes.

As a source of power horses came to replace men as the mechanisation of agriculture proceeded. Of the three main horse-driven implements (harvesters, threshing machines and sowing machines), threshers, as we have seen, were the first to be adopted on a large scale. But if horses remained the chief source of power on the farm in most countries until well into the twentieth century, other forms of power-driven machinery were soon in evidence. Steam-driven machinery was never widely used on the farm, however, chiefly because it was too expensive to run and needed a large initial capital outlay. Its use in the fields was also limited by the problem of keeping it supplied with water and coal. What revolutionised agricultural mechanisation was the internal combustion engine and the use of electrcity. Stationary petrol-driven engines began to appear on American farms as early as 1900. They were quickly followed by petrol-driven tractors which were being taken up rapidly by the beginning of World War I, especially in the grain belts. By 1918 there were 85,000 tractors at work on American farms. Electricity could also be used to power a wide variety of farm operations, as well as to improve the comfort of farm life. Its use, however, was determined primarily by the pace of rural electrification, which did not become widespread in any country until the 1930s or 1940s.

IV

Mechanisms for diffusing innovations have to perform two main functions. First, they must make adopters aware of the existence of new ways of doing things. This is largely a matter of communicating the new knowledge to its potential user. Equally important, however, is the fact that the mechanism for diffusing modern techniques has to provide a means of overcoming the obstacles to the use of the new knowledge that may exist in different countries. In other words, the institutionalising of the process of diffusion may vary from country to country according to the ease or difficulty experienced in taking up the new techniques.

During the nineteenth century, knowledge of new agricultural methods spread in three ways. First, there was the 'spontaneous' modernisation of agricultural practices which came about chiefly as a response to expanding market opportunities and the ready availability of new methods of production. In this situation landlords, acting individually or through 'enlightened societies', played a leading role in promoting agricultural change. The other two main agents of agricultural modernisation were the farmers' co-operatives and the government, both of which came to prominence in the last two decades of the nineteenth century. Of course, in any given country a combination of mechanisms of diffusion was always possible. Indeed, this tended to become the case as agriculture matured and the farmer found himself confronted with marketing problems and an ever-widening range of agricultural innovations which demanded more capital and more technical knowledge.

One of the first and best organised attempts to extend the use of new agricultural techniques was that undertaken by landlords in England, Scandinavia and some parts of Germany, by means of their lease contracts with tenant farmers. Through the use of contractual obligations, the tenant farmers were encouraged to adopt crop rotations and restrict or abolish the use of fallowing. This in turn led to the desired increase in livestock carried on the land. Once the tendency to cling to traditional practices was broken in a large sector of the farming community, the usefulness of the new practices became evident in the whole region and were more easily accepted by those farmers who owned rather than leased their land. Regions with a dominant stratum of owner-operated farms were in most cases slower in adopting the new techniques. But ownership patterns are not the sole determinant of the rate of diffusion of agricultural techniques, and the greater receptivity of tenant farmers to the new methods may well have been because these farmers were especially numerous in those regions of Europe which experienced expanding markets for agricultural produce at a comparatively early date.

The rate of diffusion of new agricultural methods also depended upon the ability of farmers to undertake the necessary investment. In this respect the division of responsibility for improvement between landlords and tenants which was peculiar to Britain was especially helpful. Most of land in nineteenth-century England was owned by a small number of very rich landlords and most of their tenants were 'tenants-at-will', often with no more right to the land than a six months' lease. In constrast to the Continent, however, the majority of the tenants' holdings in Britain were large enough to need hired labour or machinery, or both, to work them. Yet as the farmer had only a short lease of the land, it was usually the landlord who was responsible for the fixed capital, i.e., for drainage, roads, farm buildings, etc., while the farmer provided the 'removable' capital he could take away with him if he were to quit. This combination of the large and very rich landowner, on the one hand, and the small tenant farmer whose holding was still large enough to permit him to buy the movable equipment he wanted, on the other, in effect put the responsibility for progress in the hands of those who had the necessary capital. The landlords invested in agriculture because by doing so they hoped to be able to increase their incomes from higher rents, and the tenant farmers invested because they could increase their revenues by using the latest innovations. It was on the basis of this institutional arrangement that British agriculture became the most prosperous and progressive in the third quarter of the nineteenth century.

Whereas the British tenurial system appears to have been highly effective in encouraging the spread of agricultural improvements in the period before 1875, after that date it appears to have been less effective as a promoter of change. This was particularly the case with the mechanisation of British farms, where, for some of the new harvesting machines to be used effectively, considerable improvement of the existing farm layout and topography was necessary. Land had to be levelled, sub-surface drainage installed, and hedgerows removed. These improvements were costly, and getting more so as agricultural real wages rose during the third quarter of the nineteenth century. Because the tenant farmer did not own the land he worked, he was understandably loth to invest money in durable improvements, the full benefits of which he would not obtain should his tenancy be terminated, either voluntarily or at the landlord's insistence. As for the landowner, he could not be certain that, having undertaken the improvement, the tenant would take advantage of the opportunity presented to him. In other words, the uncertainties normally associated with the adoption of a new technique were compounded by uncertainties created by the characteristic system of land tenure in Britain.

Information on agricultural innovations spread in a number of ways. In Britain, France and a number of other European countries, agricultural societies offered prizes and medals by way of encouragement, tested new implements, obtained land for experimental plots, published accounts of new things, organised agricultural shows, and sent out questionnaires. Moreover, in Arthur Young, one of the most voluminous and influential agricultural writers of all time, eighteenth-century British agriculture found its greatest publicity expert. In the United States, numerous non-governmental agencies concerned with fostering interest in scientific farming methods and new products were also active early in the nineteenth century. By 1856 there were 912 local and state agricultural societies in the country, most of them in the north and west. These societies were successful in reviving the country fairs; they published statistics of crops and livestock, descriptions of new practices, and in general focused attention on scientific knowledge in agriculture. Many of the societies were followed by state boards of agriculture, and a national organisation, the United States Agricultural Society, founded in 1852, existed for a time. As in Britain, however, most of these societies, as well as the fairs, tended to be dominated by large-scale or 'gentlemen' farmers. Later in the century, with the advent of large-scale production of farm machinery in the United States, the aggressive and imaginative selling techniques of men like C.H. McCormick did much to popularise their use on the farm.

Next to markets farmers needed adequate finance to undertake agricultural improvements. Rarely does a farmer possess sufficient money of his own to defray the cost of buying, improving, equipping and operating his land. The cost of all these tasks tended to rise during the nineteenth century, but the banking system, geared largely to servicing the needs of commerce and industry, gave scant attention to the demand for rural credit, especially the need of the small farmer. He had to rely on the storekeeper or produce merchant or go to the professional money lender. The result was a burdensome debt because of the high interest rates charged for the credit obtained.

Germany was the first country to find a solution to this credit problem, and the two methods involved there were copied throughout Europe and the United States. The first method was tried in 1770 in the form of the Landschaft (Land Mortgage Credit Association). This was an association of landowners who raised money by the sale of land mortgage bonds, which were backed by the property of all the members, and used it to make loans to member borrowers. The second solution to the rural credit problem was the Raiffeisen co-operative bank. The first of these banks, in which the people of the district could deposit their savings and from which the local farmers could borrow, was formed in the village of Anhausen in 1862. By 1910 Germany had 17,000 rural credit banks of the Raiffeisen or similar pattern, with a million and a half members and an annual turnover of close to $1,500 million. These banks were quickly copied throughout Europe. Switzerland had 49 credit co-operatives in 1905; Ireland had 200; in 1906 there were 431 co-operatives in Belgium and 1,461 in Italy. In 1907 France had 1,767 co-operatives of various kinds. Co-operative credit was least popular in Britain, partly because of the land tenure system described above which did much to ease the credit problems of the British farmer, and partly because of the availability of substitute commercial banks. Consequently, only eleven co-operative banks existed in Britain in 1906. In the United States, where farm credit became a pressing problem during the second half of the nineteenth century, nothing was done about the problem until the land mortgage bond was adopted (by the Acts of

1916 and 1923) as a means of raising funds through the Federal Farm Loan system.

The first success in co-operation was in the field of credit, but it was soon extended to cover marketing, purchasing and the processing of agricultural products. The problem of reconciling mechanisation and small-scale farming was also solved by co-operation. Initially some of these co-operatives were concerned solely with the wholesale purchasing for their members of such commodities as manures, seed, cattle cake, insecticides, compressed fodder, and sometimes even consumer goods. Later some of them became involved in the collective purchase of agricultural machinery, which they hired out 'per acre' or 'per day' to members, thus earning back the money originally spent on it. Finally, they ventured into the distributive side of farming, organising the collection, handling and sale of members' products. In performing these functions co-operatives not only saved labour time (going to market to buy and sell) and reduced purchasing and transport costs by buying wholesale rather than in small quantities, but they also made expensive mechanical equipment available to the small farmer. Consequently, along with the co-operative banks and insurance societies, they played an important role on the Continent in promoting and financing improvements in farming, and filled the gap created by the absence of the 'improving capitalist landowners and farmers' who had been in the forefront of progress in Britain.

Both purchasing and production co-operatives were first initiated in Germany.[6] Eventually both types of co-operative activity spread to Ireland, Britain, Switzerland, France, Belgium and Italy, as well as to Scandinavian countries. Producers' co-operatives played a particularly important role in the development of Danish agriculture, where the invention of the cream separator in the early 1880s made co-operation between dairy farmers possible. Previously, butter on a commercial scale had required a great deal of capital and a steady supply of milk which had neither been shaken in transport nor stored for more than a short period of time. Since the new separator worked perfectly well even with stored and shaken milk, large-scale butter production based on milk collected from many farms became a possibility. Within a short period a great number of co-operative creameries came into existence (about 500 between 1885 and 1890), which not only enabled small farmers to benefit from the advantages of economies of scale, but also taught them a lesson in co-operation which made them extend the system to other branches of production, including bacon and egg production, with equally profitable results.

Co-operative activity was also present in the United States, where for almost three decades after the Civil War farmers were in an almost continous condition of revolt. Characterstic of the period was the Grangers movement which was chiefly concerned with combating the result of railways and business monopolies. The railway companies were resisted on the political level, but business monoplies were resisted by the farmers going into business themselves. Co-operatives were organised for the sale of general merchandise and farm implements to members. Granger activities encompassed every phase of the marketing field. Purchasing agents were stationed throughout the Granger states to handle farm commodities, and stores were established in many communities to sell or purchase on a co-operative basis.

Governments were the other important agent active in promoting agriculture improvements in the nineteenth century. Such activities began in the United States in 1839, when Congress appropriated $1,000 to be extended on the collection of statistics and the promotion of agriculture. After 1842 gradually increasing appropriations were made for this purpose, culminating in the setting up of the Bureau of Agriculture in 1862. In 1889 the Bureau was raised to the rank of a government Department. As a result, after the 1860s, the American farmer did not lack aid from either the state or the national government. Amongst this aid the educational and research activities of the Department of Agriculture figured very large and did much to help diffuse modern agricultural methods. Thus the Bureau of Plant Industry, one of the many bureaus into which the Department of Agriculture was eventually divided, engaged in combating plant disease, in studying better agricultural methods and plant acclimatisation, in distributing seed, and in related activities. The Bureau of Agricultural Chemistry and Engineering investigated the chemical and physical properties of soils, fertilisers and agricultural products, and conducted research in farm machinery and equipment. On a much smaller scale most of the states, through departments of agriculture, financial appropriations and protective legislation, sought to aid agriculture after the manner of the federal government.

Scientific farming in the United States was also given tremendous impetus by agricultural education, and this in turn received its greatest stimulus from the federal and state governments. The decade of the 1850s saw a rapidly growing interest in agricultural education and the formation of several state agricultural schools. The Morrill Act of 1862, which established the land-grant college system, constituted the greatest single piece of legislation ever passed in the interests of agricultural education in the United States, and under its provisions agricultural colleges were gradually established in each of the states. Later, the Hatch Act of 1887, which provided funds for experimental stations in the various state colleges, turned the attention of these institutions to research as well as to teaching. Almost as valuable as the actual instruction and research carried on in these schools was the diffusion of information among people not regularly attending them. This was achieved by means of special short-term winter courses and, more importantly, extension work. Agricultural education was also carried on by the United States Department of Agriculture, which engaged in the two-fold task of experimentation and dissemination of information.

Financial and other forms of aid were made available to American farmers in a variety of ways. Because of its heavy capital cost, irrigation as a solution to the water problems of the arid areas of the Great Plains and the foothills of the Rockies, could be provided only by the federal government. This came about finally with the passage of the Reclamation Act of 1902, which provided for the setting aside of proceeds from the sale of pulic lands in 16 designated states, to be used as a fund for irrigation purposes. Under this Act and subsequent appropriations, over $300 million was spent on the examination, construction and operation of projects for the reclamation of arid lands. In the present century the cheap electric power provided by federally-built dams to rual areas may have proved as valuable to farming as these earlier irrigation projects.

European farmers also enjoyed a great deal of government support. Schools and colleges in France, Germany, Denmark and Switzerland, for example, taught practical farming to the peasant, and at the same time operated experimental stations and provided a trained scientific advisory service at a high level. There was also growing government support throughout the nineteenth century for exhibitions, agricultural societies, and the fostering of better breeding techniques and new seed strains. The state system of agricultural education was perhaps most highly developed in Germany, where it stretched from universities at the top through full-time agricultural schools, down to winter schools for agricultural students and agriculturalists, and evening contination schools for the sons of small peasants and labourers from primary school, both of which were open during the winter months when agricultural activities were almost at a standstill. In this way, between 1870 and 1900, the channels were provided through which agricultural knowledge could flow even to the lowest ranks of the independent cultivators.

There was already a tradition of gradual improvement in Japanese agriculture by the second half of the nineteenth century, but after 1870 government activity greatly intensified the awareness of the desirability and the possibility of change. In this respect the Ministry of Agriculture and Commerce, which eventually emerged in 1881, performed a number of important functions, including land reclamation, the promotion of exports and the reduction of imports by the substitution of home-grown products, and the encouragement of agricultural improvements. It achieved these objectives in a number of ways. Foreign plants and seeds were imported and tested for local use. A factory was established to manufacture farm tools modelled on foreign ones. Japanese officials and students were sent abroad to study foreign agriculture, and foreigners were hired as advisors in Japan. German scientists were brought in to adapt new findings in chemicals and fertilisers to Japanese conditions, and Dutch agricultural engineers were used to carry out reclamation and drainage schemes. Foreign strains of cattle, horses, sheep, pigs and poultry were imported, helping to diversify the Japanese diet as well as contributing to traction power and manure supplies. This initial obsession with things foreign brought an inevitable reaction, however, especially when some of the new methods proved unsuitable to Japanese conditions. After 1880, therefore, the emphasis turned back somewhat to the search after improvement within the framework of Japanese agriculture, by developing new strains of traditional crops and by diffusing more widely the best practices of particular regions.

The methods used by the Japanese government to diffuse the new knowledge included: agricultural exhibitions and national prize shows; the promotion of agricultural schools and colleges; and direct promotional and extension activity undertaken by the Department of Agriculture. Other links with farmers were established with the publication from 1874 onward of the Department's Bulletin and the organisation of local agricultural associations to promote agricultural improvement. At the regional level the work of the local government administration in the development of agriculture in early Meiji Japan was similar to that of the central government and at least as important. While the prefectures worked partly in conjunction with the central government, they also took their own initiative in importing and testing seed, in livestock breeding, and in the provision of agricultural education. Moreover, being closer to the mass of farmers, the local official often had a greater impact as a diffuser of new knowledge since, given the traditional respect for authority characteristic of the Japanese masses, the recommendations put forward by these officials were often likely to be taken as orders. While it is difficult to assess the total effect on Japanese agriculture of this central and local government activity, it seems certain that, in the early stages at least, it played an essential organising role which greatly magnified the effect of local individual initiatives. Later, when this activity became routine and complacency set in, this may well have been less the case.

In Europe, where government-inspired land reform had done something towards providing conditions more conducive to agricultural progress, systems of technical schooling for agriculture and government technical advice to farmers were additional benefits conferred on agriculture by government, thus making it more receptive to change. In many countries the government was also active in supporting and encouraging the spread of co-operative activities in the countryside. In some cases, however, government activity of this kind was inadequate to compensate for the weakness in agriculture brought about by land reform which, along with land fragmentation, had served to keep the mass of peasant farmers poor. It could be argued, for example, that peasant agriculture in France could have been made more effective given a more positive government policy in respect to education, credit facilities, co-operation, the marketing of agricultural products and the rearrangement of land holdings. Such a policy, however, was almost entirely lacking or was pursued half-heartedly. It is claimed, moreover, that in the depression years late in the nineteenth century the lack of a positive agricultural policy sponsored by the government was partly responsible for the French farmers' slow response to the growing demand for dairy produce, vegetables and fruit in other industrial countries. In fact, the only policy to which the depression gave rise was the return to protection, notably the Méline Tariff of 1892.

European trade in agricultural products had become even more free than that in manufactures during the free trade interlude of the third quarter of the nineteenth century. After 1870, however, a growing nationalist sentiment and the desire for more rapid industrialisation in many European countries led to a return to protectionism, which was supported by European agricultural interests confronted for the first time by the challenge of overseas competition. Consequently agricultural protection soon became widespread in Europe, having been adopted in Germany, France, Italy, Belgium, Switzerland, Sweden, Austria-

Hungary, Spain and Portugal. Free trade in agriculture persisted in Denmark and the Netherlands, where a successful conversion from arable to dairy farming provided an alternative to protection, and in Britain, where agriculture was sacrificed to the needs of manufacturing industry and the demand for cheap food.

Shielded from the worst of the depression, farmers in European countries where protection was adopted probably suffered a smaller loss of income than those in Britain. On the other hand, the preoccupation with tariff policy diverted attention away from more constructive measures to combat the decline in agricultural prices brought about by the intensification of competition from overseas farmers. In Denmark, the farmers themselves took the initiative in making agriculture more efficient, in particular by building their excellent co-operative marketing system. In Germany, progress was made in several respects, including the Raiffeisen co-operative banks, but the effects on overall agricultural development remained marginal. In general, farmers in France and Germany came to rely increasingly on tariff protection, and their governments did little to encourage them to improve their position through higher productivity, better marketing, and so on.

Notes

1. This statement assumes that the agricultural changes produce a surplus of output over and above the farmer's own immediate needs. It also assumes the existence of a market in which that surplus can be sold. On the other hand, in a largely subsistence economy, the pressure of population increase may serve to bring about some improvement in agricultural practices and output.

2. Communal strip farming in no way hindered the taking up of uncultivated common and waste land, or the introduction of new crops, such as the potato, maize and tobacco, and new crop rotation. On the other hand, improvements, such as selective animal breeding and the laying down of special pasture for animal feed, were of a kind that needed the dissolution of the communal farming system into one of private enclosures in order to be effective. See, for example, A.S. Milward and S.B. Saul, *The Economic Development of Continental Europe 1780–1870* (1973), especially pp. 71-83.

3. For a more detailed discussion of the land management system in Europe at this time, see A.S. Milward and S.B. Saul, op. cit., pp.46-70.

4. P.A. David, 'The landscape and the machine: technical interrelatedness, land tenure and the mechanisation of the corn harvest in Victorian Britain', *Essays on a Mature Economy: Britain after 1840,* D.N. McCloskey (ed.), pp. 145-205. David argues convincingly that the slow adoption of mechanised reaping in Britain is to be explained by the existing form of land tenure, which diminished not only the incentive but also the financial ability of Britain's farmers to undertake substantial improvements of any kind. But see later, p. 42.

5. In other words, the faster adoption of reapers in the United States during the 1850s was partly a response to a change in the relative prices of the inputs labour and capital.

6. The two types of co-operative organisation were first set up in 1860 and 1881, respectively.

Selected Reading

E.J.T. Collins, 'Labour Supply and Demand in European Agriculture, 1800–1880', in *Agrarian Change and Economic Development,* E.L. Jones and S.J. Woolf (eds.) (London, 1969)

P.A. David, 'The Landscape and the Machine: Technical Interrelatedness, Land Tenure and the Mechanisation of the Corn Harvest in Victorian Britain', in *Essays on a Mature Economy: Britain after 1840,* D.N. McCloskey (ed.) (London, 1971)

F. Dovring, 'The Transformation of European Agriculture', *Cambridge Economic History of Europe,* M.M. Postan and H.J. Habakkuk (eds.), Vol. 6, Part II (Cambridge, 1965)

4 THE SIZE OF THE MARKET

Though no single factor can, by itself, explain so dramatic a transformation of the economy as that associated with modern economic growth, an expanding market could of itself, be a powerful means of inducing significant changes in the methods of production. Indeed, the importance of the market for successful industrial growth was fully appreciated quite early on in the era of modern economic growth. Thus, Adam Smith, whose treatise on *The Wealth of Nations* (1776) was published during the early stages of the industrial revolution in Britain, argued that economic growth resulted from the increase of trade and extension of the market, which led in turn to a greater specialisation of labour, greater productive efficiency, invention and the improvement of machines and equipment. According to Smith, specialisation of labour is the key to increased productivity, but since the division of labour cannot take place on a large scale unless workers use specialised machinery and equipment, Smith emphasised the need for an economy to accumulate stocks of these capital goods in order to enjoy the benefits of higher *per capita* income levels. If markets are too small, however, demand will be insufficient to buy the goods produced under mass production methods. Consequently, the division of labour is also limited by the size of the market. In other words, productive efficiency is partly a function of its scale, which in turn is conditioned by the size of the market.

For Smith the size of the market is determined by the amount of capital in existence, and by institutional restrictions that are placed upon trade. One way in which markets may grow is through an increase in the real incomes of the people of a country which enables them to buy more. Thus capital invested in promoting the specialisation of labour and increasing productivity will also result in rising real incomes and expanding market demand. Moreover, capital accumulation may affect the size of the market in another way. Since the major cause of separate markets is the cost of overcoming the distance between them, investment and technological change in transportation and communications reduce this cost and are a prime means of linking and enlarging markets. The size of the market and the productivity of labour are also influenced by the regulation of domestic and international trade. Any restrictions upon domestic trade and free international commerce will of necessity limit the size of the market, and by impeding the national and international specialisation of labour lower domestic productivity and incomes.

It is obvious from what has just been said that the growth of markets is not independent of changes in other economic variables. A growing population, increasing specialisation of labour, rising real incomes, increased capital accumulation, and improvements in transport and communications, are all related in one way or another to the growth of markets. Moreover, increased specialisation and exchange require the parallel growth of the money mechanism, since barter becomes impossible as a means of exchange once a worker becomes responsible for producing only part of a commodity. In modern times, this has meant the growing use of paper money and chequing accounts instead of specie and coin, the evolution of credit instruments to finance more capitalistic methods of production and the holding of stocks, and finally the growth of techniques for regulating the amount of money in the economy. But whereas market growth is the result of the complex interaction of many economic variables, the nature of the relationship between the size of the market and technological diffusion is relatively straightforward. The sources of market demand may vary, and its size may be determined by numerous influences, including the efforts of suppliers of new products to create markets for their output, but unless the demand exists there is little incentive to increase production, and therefore little need to introduce more productive techniques or to search for new products or new methods of production. In the rest of this chapter, therefore, we shall examine the market conditions favourable to the spread of modern industrial technology within Britain between 1750 and 1850. We shall also consider the market limitation that inhibited the spread of modern manufacturing industry throughout Europe and, to a lesser extent, the United States during the same period, as well as look at the manner in which these market limitations were eventually overcome.

II

In Britain the industrial revolution was associated with an expansion of markets both at home and overseas. The expanding domestic market for industrial output was due in part to an absence of internal customs barriers and feudal tolls which in effect made Britain the largest single market in Europe. This economic unity was attained all the more easily because of the geography of the island, with its small size, easy topgraphy and ready access to the sea via its indented coastline. Furthermore, an extensive system of rivers made inland water transport improvements relatively simple. By 1750 there were over a thousand miles of navigable waterways in Britain, and this total had grown to some 2,000 miles by the end of the eighteenth century, chiefly on account of the canals built between 1760 and 1800. Further canal and river development occurred after that date, and at their peak in 1858 the inland waterways of Britain reached a length of about 4,250 miles. Road improvements, which also accelerated after 1750, were also made easier by the shorter distances involved in Britain compared to those on the Continent.

British industrialists benefited too from a population that grew faster than that of any of the other countries on the Continent. From not quite six millions around 1700, the British population rose to almost nine millions by 1800, and to 18 millions by the middle of the nineteenth century. This increase in numbers was associated with rising real incomes, so that within the British market purchasing power per head and the standard of living were significantly higher than they were on the Continent. Moreover, the available income appears to have been more equitably distributed in Britain than it was in other European countries, and although there is a suggestion, particularly in the war years of the 1790s, of some redistribution of income in Britain in favour of the better-off middle classes, this growing middle-class market increased the demand for solid, standard-ised, moderately-priced manufactured products rather than for luxuries produced by more traditional methods of production. Whatever the net effects of the redistribution of income during these years, however, the more equal spread of income in Britain resulted in an expenditure pattern favourable to industrial products.

The demand for British manufactures was also sustained by an expanding export market. In the eighteenth century this expansion was mainly concentrated in two principal periods: between 1735 and 1760, when the value of exports of English produce and maufactures roughly doubled; and between 1785 and 1800, when another doubling in value of domestic exports occurred. In the earlier period it was the expansion of exports to Ireland and to the British colonies, especially those in the East and West Indies and North America, which principally accounted for the rise. After 1785, it was the growth of the North American market which dominated the trading picture, so much so that by the end of the century one-third of Britain's domestic exports went to this region. But whatever the source of this foreign demand, the fact that it was concentrated largely on manufactured goods only served to reinforce the pressures building up in the British economy for a changeover to the production of cheap, machine-made goods.

III

If a growing market, both at home and overseas, exerted a powerful influence on technical innovation and diffusion in Britain before 1850, thoughout Europe and, to a lesser extent, the United States, market limitations inhibited the spread of modern industrial technology during the same period. Geographical obstacles to unified markets were more in evidence on the Continent than in Britain, where many European countries were larger in size relative to their populations, and consequently greater distances, combined with topographical difficulites, made for higher transport costs and fragmentation of markets. Where rivers existed, these were used to their utmost, although they were often icebound in winter and too shallow in the dry season. Their usefulness was further limited by poor communications between the different basins. With few exceptions, roads were bad everywhere in the eighteenth and early nineteenth centuries. Even in France, where thousands of kilometres of good roads were built, they carried little commercial traffic, having been built for political and strategic reasons and consequently having only poor connections with the small towns and villages in which the bulk of the population lived. A few countries, such as Holland, were well served by the sea but others, in particular Russia, had only very poor sea communications with the rest of the world, or none at all, like Switzerland. Moreover, size not only made for long distances and difficulties of transportation, but it also fostered regional differences in language, customs and tastes. This diversity, which meant that some regions in a country could continue to exist with very little economic intercourse with the rest of the economy, obviously added to the difficulties involved in creating a unified and homogeneous market.

Domestic commerce in Europe was also impeded by man-made barriers to trade. Tolls and other charges imposed by princes, lords, towns and market authorities aggravated the geographical handicaps on domestic trade. Political boundaries were a further obstacle. Germany consisted of a patchwork of kingdoms, archducies, duchies, bishoprics, free cities and other forms of sovereignty, each with its own laws, courts, coinage and, above all, customs barriers. To a lesser extent, Belgium and Italy were also politically fragmented. Even France, although unified politically by the end of the seventeenth century, suffered from the division of the country into separate tariff areas, with duties having to be paid on commodities passing from one area to another. Superimposed on these formal barriers to European domestic trade was a network of informal boundaries defining markets and zones of supply for goods like grain, wood or salt, that were vital to local survival. Finally, there was the deliberate use of political power to cripple trade. The worst victim here was Belgium, whose natural route to the sea via the river Scheldt was blocked by the Dutch, at least until 1815, and whose manufactures consequently were compelled to turn to Central Europe for markets.

These geographical and man-made obstacles to trade were compounded by economic, social and institutional limitations on demand. The predominance of subsistence agriculture throughout much of Europe narrowed substantially the market for industrial goods, since the peasants themselves had little to sell and thus could buy little. Most of what they needed could be obtained from village craftsmen, from pedlars, or at the periodical fairs and markets. The prevailing poverty among the rural population of Europe was due also in part to the crushing levels of taxation, both direct and indirect, which further limited the rural income available for the purchase of industrial products. Moreover, the extreme income inequality which tended to be associated with this mass poverty produced societies with deep-seated class divisions that discouraged the consumption of machine-made goods among the wealthier classes. Rather the emphasis was on conspicuous consumption manifested in the purchase of luxury goods which depended more on hand skills than on machinery for their production.

Continental manufacturers were also handicapped in foreign markets. Apart from the high costs of domestic production, due mainly to the transport and other difficulties discussed above, Continental producers were faced with higher charges for all the ancillary commercial and financial services connected with overseas trade, such as shipping, insurance and bank credit. Moreover, Britain had made use of the war years between 1792 and 1815 to capture the foreign markets of her main European rivals and to build up her own

trade connections in South America, Asia and Africa. When the
Napoleonic wars ended, therefore, European producers faced severe
competition in overseas markets, where British manufacturers with
their superior technology were already firmly entrenched. But Napoleon's
Continental System was not all bad, and by the protection it afforded,
it did allow the manufacturing industries of some European countries
to expand into neighbouring markets. This was so, for example, with
high-quality Swiss cotton textile exports, which thrived under these
conditions, aided by improved transport facilites, particularly better
roads, and a growing French market for these goods. Even so, this
successful export trade, which continued in being throughout the
nineteenth century and afterwards, was based on what was to become,
by European standards, a small total output, and a degree of
mechanisation which was far less than that attained by most other
European industrial nations.

As a result of all these limitations on the demand for manufactured
products, the industrial structure of early nineteenth-century Europe
was dominated by small firms supplying a conglomeration of small,
largely self-contained markets. Textiles and other simple consumer
goods were produced everywhere, mainly with locally-produced raw
materials. Iron manufacture was also a scattered and small-scale
affair. Only a few industries, for example chemicals, non-ferrous
metallurgy and porcelain manufacture, were compelled by special
requirements, such as specialist skills, raw materials supply or market
considerations, to concentrate in suitable localities.

In the United States, too, the willingness of manufacturers to take
advantage of the stock of new industrial techniques that Britain was
pioneering was tied up in part with the size of the available market.
With American labour and capital costs higher than those in Britain,
success in manufacturing could be achieved, in the absence of a fall in
factor prices below those in competitor countries, only by a substantial
improvement in productivity. One way in which productivity could be
increased was by the creation of a market large enough to make it
possible for manufacturers to reap the economies of large-scale
production. The 'market difficulty' confronting US industrialists was
thus basically different from that which Continental producers faced.
While the problem of geographical size was common to both regions,
in the United States the basic problem was the creation of a market
large enough to permit not just the use of machine production, but the
use of machine production on a scale big enough to overcome the
competitive disadvantages of the high cost American labour and

capital. Until such a market size was achieved, the American industrialist remained at a competitive disadvantage *vis-à-vis* his British counterpart.

IV

If modern industrial technology was to be diffused throughout Europe and overseas during the ninteenth century, these limitations on market demand had to be overcome. How was the problem solved? One way of overcoming it was by political unification and the removal of internal tolls and duties. In France, for example, the Revolution swept away all existing internal barriers to trade and the movement of people, thus providing some favourable conditions for further industrial development in the nineteenth century, while the ratification of the US Constitution by the member states in 1787 created a potentially huge free trade area on the North American continent. In the nineteenth century the two most important political developments were the unification of Italy in 1861 and the creation of the German Reich ten years later. In Germany, however, economic union had preceded political union. In 1818 Prussia abolished all internal tolls and duties on trade, and a year later it took the first step towards the formation of a free trade area amongst the German states by signing a trade treaty with the tiny principality of Schwarzburg-Sondershausen. This agreement was followed by further treaties with other neighbouring states which enlarged the area of the Prussian Customs Union and which encouraged Bavaria to enter into similar agreements with its neighbours. Finally, in 1834, the Prussian and Bavarian Customs Unions united to form the Zollverein, which came into existence on the 1 January 1834, and which included 18 German states with a total population of 23.5 million people. After its formation new states were admitted to membership of the Zollverein so that by 1852 it included all the states that were eventually to constitute the German Reich.

Improved transport and communications were even more important for the widening of markets. Transport improvements during the half century before 1830 took the form mainly of better and more active roadbuilding, river improvements, and a certain amount of canal construction. Round about 1820 England had nearly 21,000 miles of turnpike roads, as much as France which is three and a half times its size. Despite the inadequacy of the French road system, however, on the Continent only it and the Netherlands possessed what could be

really described as a road network at this time. Across the Atlantic,
the United States possessed, from about the middle of the eighteenth
century, a network that was scanty but comparable in quality to that of
England. Indeed, so effective was the government roadbuilding effort
in the United States that by 1820 most of the important cities in the
north and east were connected by a usable system of surfaced roads.
Despite the flurry of roadbuilding activity that occurred in a number of
countries in the period around 1800, roads failed to provide an
economically feasible solution to the transport problem. This was
partly because of the failure to solve satisfactorily the problems of
keeping the roads in a fit state of repair, and partly because, with an
inland transport technology based upon horse-drawn carts and
wagons, costs remained too high, even on good roads, to compete with
water transport.

In addition to coastal shipping, canals and river improvements
provided the transport network necessary for Britain's early economic
development, and in less than 40 years navigable waterways had been
constructed throughout the greater part of England and Wales. The
success of the English canals did much to encourage their introduction
into the United States, where the construction of the Erie Canal
between 1817 and 1825 at a cost of $7 million touched off a great
burst of canal building. By 1860 there were 4,250 miles of canal in
operation in the United States, involving a total investment of almost
$195 million. In France, where the Revolution had interrupted earlier
efforts at canal building, work began again following a proposal put
forward in 1820 to build 10,000 kilometres of new canals. This target
proved to be too ambitious, however, and though nearly 1,000
kilometres were added to the 1,200 already in existence, canal
building in France remained insufficient to support an integrated
national market. In western Europe generally the great undertaking of
the period was the improvement in the navigability of the Rhine on
which freedom of navigation was recognised after 1815. What
particularly encouraged river improvements here and elsewhere was
the advent of the steamboat, whose use required waterways of greater
depth and dependability. In Russia, the period before 1850 also saw
improvements in water transportation. A number of canals were
constructed in the Baltic provinces at the opening of the nineteenth
century, and by the 1850s steam navigation was development rapidly
on Russia's waterways, above all on the Volga. Although canals and
new improvements did much to stimulate economic growth and
development in those regions favoured by them, a transport network

adequate to the needs of industrialisation materialised only with the coming of the railways. With few exceptions, railways were a cheaper form of transport than canals, and once built they rapidly replaced the canals.

Most of the early work on the railways was carried out in Britain, where the basic network was already constructed by the late 1840s. On the Continent, there was some early railway building in France, Germany and Belgium, but the key connections for western Europe were not made until the 1850s or the 1860s, when the railway mileage opened had risen to over 20,000 miles. In North America and Russia railway developments were on an even grander scale than in western Europe, permitting the economic unification of whole continents, and opening up untapped wealth of virtually empty territories. In the United States the beginnings of railway construction came in the 1830s, and by 1860 the mileage opened had grown to over 30,000, and to 193,000 in 1900. In Russia railway construction was a dominant force in the country's industrial development from the 1860s onward. By 1874 the Russian railway network stood around 11,000 miles, and had grown to over 33,000 miles by 1900.

While the railways had the effect of widening the market and encouraging specialisation, their impact on industry is not to be underestimated. In the short run, the railways opened up a new market for iron, machinery and construction materials of all kinds. If to this we add the general effect of this huge railway investment on the demand for consumer goods it seems fair to say that railway construction constitued an important stimulus to general industrial growth. Later, as a provider of services, the railways drew large numbers of people into wage work in transportation, distribution and services, as well as encouraging the growth of urban populations and a consequent change of social habits conducive to a more standardised pattern of consumption.[1]

In the years immediately following 1850 certain international developments eased communications both within and between countries. Many conventions were signed during these years to facilitate international commincations—railways, canals, telegraph, postal arrangements, and so on. In 1868 the Rhine—a vitally important commercial link in western Europe—was declared a freeway for the ships of all nations. Other agreements liberalised navigation on the rivers Scheldt, Elbe, Po and Danube. In 1857 Denmark and the principal maritime powers agreed to the abolition of the Sound dues. These developments by improving international communications and by allowing countries greater and freer use of existing waterways, permitted the growth of trade and the expansion of markets.

Even when a cheap and efficient means of transport became available, the other conditions conducive to the spontaneous growth of markets of a size sufficient to support modern industry were not always in evidence. In Russia, for example, the primitive state of agriculture and the poverty of the mass of the peasants meant that the rural sector was too backward to consume much by way of manufactures. When, therefore, in the 1890s, the rate of industrialisation began to accelerate, it was supported by state demand for industrial goods. Textile plants made uniforms and blankets for the army, while the iron and steel industry manufactured military weapons and railway equipment. 'Government-created' markets, of a size sufficient to encourage the adoption of modern industrial technology, were also a feature of Japan's industrialisation effort late in the nineteenth century. Even in the United States, where market forces and civilian demand tended to predominate, the manufacture of firearms using interchangeable techniques, a forerunner of modern mass-production methods, owed something to US government contracts and financial advances, which ensured market stability and a major source of capital. In Britain, on the other hand, the government would give no guarantees of regular orders and this attitude, it has been argued, only served to discourage changes in the techniques and organisation of British private arms manufacturing.[2]

More generally, governments could increase the size of the market available to domestic producers by adopting a policy of protection. By eliminating foreign competition and by allowing the substitution of domestic manufactures for goods previously imported, tariffs could play an obvious role in providing demand conditions suitable to industrial development. While it is true that the widespread movement towards increased protectionism that occurred during the last quarter of the nineteenth century had its origins in a variety of causes, there is no doubt that the desire for more rapid industrial development was an important reason for the protectionist policies adopted in many countries. In Russia, for example, the ending of liberal tariffs came in 1877, when duties generally were increased by about one-third. Further tariff increases took place in the 1880s, culminating in the 'monster' tariff of 1891. Behind this growing tariff wall such industries as iron and coal mining, metallurgy, oil production and machine construction developed rapidly, creating the beginnings of a substantial heavy industry sector in the Russian economy. A somewhat similar pattern of development is evident during this period in many other European countries, including, for example, Germany, Austria, Italy and Switzerland. In France the shift to protectionism came somewhat later than elsewhere in Europe, and it was not until the introduction of the Méline tariff in 1892 that protection of the domestic market was re-established. Across the Atlantic, the United States become more heavily protectionist in the period after the Civil War, which also witnessed rapid industrialisation of the economy.

Although the effect of protection on industrial growth in some countries is still a matter for debate, two features of the protectionist situation which appear to be conducive to economic growth and technological diffusion should be noted. First, the erection of tariff barriers does appear to have stimulated direct foreign investment in protectionist countries. Since the aim of protection is to exclude foreign products from the domestic market of the country imposing the tariff, foreign firms can overcome these trade barriers by setting up branch factories in the protectionist country. Although not widespread before 1913, there were occasions when this kind of direct investment was undertaken. For example, the American tariff of 1883 hit certain cheaper cotton exports from Britain severly. As a result, several Lanchashire cotton firms set up branches in the United States. Part of the American direct investment in Canada before 1913 was also due to the existence of the Canadian tariff. High tariff barriers were also partly responsible for the heavy foreign investment in Russia in the period before World War I. While these examples could be multiplied, this type of investment remained comparatively rare before 1913, but when it did occur its importance for the spread of modern industrial technology can hardly be overemphasised, since such investment was often accompanied by foreign technology and by foreign managers and even skilled artisans.

Protectionism may also have facilitated the diffusion of industrial technology within countries by encouraging the growth of large-scale enterprise. Protected by tariffs, producers in the United States and Germany were able to eliminate domestic competition and create oligopolistic markets dominated by a few large firms. Since, logically, one would expect that new knowledge and techniques would spread faster within a given industry the fewer the number of firms that have to be convinced of the profitability of their use,[3] this tendency towards industrial concentration within protected markets may account partly for the progressive character of much of American and German industry before 1913. Moreover, business concentration also meant access to large capital funds which may have facilitated a more rapid adoption of the more capital-intensive technology characteristic of the late nineteenth and twentieth centuries.

Finally, the expansion of the market to include foreign countries has obviously been an important basis for industrial development in the past. Great Britain furnishes the prime example of successful industrial development based first on textile exports and later on expanding exports of coal and iron. But successful industrialisation in a number of other countries late in the nineteenth century was also partly dependent upon the expansion of foreign trade. In Japan, for example, where the creation of a domestic mass market was precluded by the low incomes of peasants and workers, the growth of foreign markets was imperative for the products of the country's new manufacturing industries, in particular, cotton textiles. Thus the existence of foreign markets may encourage the introduction of modern industrial technology by absorbing ouput that is surplus to the domestic requirements of the exporting country. It is in this sense that the growing need for new markets fostered by the spread of industrialis-ation and the growth of protection was in part responsible for the burst of imperialism and 'colony grabbing' in Africa and Asia that occurred late in the nineteenth century. Alternatively, an expansion of foreign demand could put pressure on the productive capacity of an exporting country, thus stimulating technological change and the search for new methods of production. Such pressure could also call the attention of entrepreneurs to investment opportunities, and stimulate growth by raising the level of investment. Expansion of export demand could thus lead to economic growth by stimulating technical change and investment, or by spilling demand over into other sectors of the exporting economy. Finally, foreign trade remained a major source of increased demand for the manufactured goods of those 'small' countries, such as Belgium, Denmark, Sweden and Switzerland, which desired to industrialise but lacked the large domestic market base needed for such development. By successfully tapping international markets, often through the use of high-quality, specialised manufactures, such countries often achieved a high degree of industrial development, even though they lacked any substantial population or resource base.

V

Once through the early stages of industrial development, the very conditions that assist an economy in increasing the productivity of its resources also increase its capacity to raise the demand for goods and services. With the growth of markets and the increased division of labour this makes possible, real incomes rise and, assuming a sufficiently wide distribution of this rise in real income, it is likely to generate a demand not simply for luxury goods, but for the large-scale production of standardised manufactures. Moreover, as incomes rise a greater demand for more and more varied consumer goods develops, thus creating the possibilities for a still further industrial transformation of the entire economy. In this situation of maturing industrialisation a product may require peculiar market conditions present in one country but not others. For example, the mass-production techniques which emerged in the United States after 1850 were relevant only when there was a mass demand for a homogeneous product. Where the standardised product was a relatively costly one, such as the motor car, high average real incomes were also necessary to ensure an adequate demand for such manufactures. Stated more broadly, the new market situation may have emphasised the importance of certain attitudes towards increased consumption. Thus the high rate of growth of the American economy during the past century or so may have been due in part to the general American philosophy of life. As one American economist has put it: 'The essence of the American philosophy of life is that the opportunity of men to develop themselves and to lead the good life and to aquire the physical comforts of life should not be restricted to a privileged few (limited by both education or wealth), but should be open to all members of the community. This philosophy fosters the idea that all members of the community should be encouraged to be ambitious, to try to get ahead, to aspire to live better.'[4] Such considerations, however, take us to the fringes of the problem of market demand in a mass-consumption society and a mature industrial economy. One final, related, point should be noted, however, and that is that the willingness of American buyers to accept standardised products may have had important consequences for the diffusion of modern machine technology. Thus Nathan Rosenberg has claimed that, in the United States, the manufacurers of capital goods, by taking the initiative in machine design, were able to achieve a high degree of standardisation of product which simplified capital goods production and reduced their prices. In Britain, on the other hand, the willingness of capital goods manufacturers to make design alterations to suit customers' needs placed limits on the cost advantages to be reaped from large-scale production and consequently, by making capital goods relatively more expensive, limited their use.[5]

Notes

1. In recent years the researches of some economic historians have tended to play down the contribution that railways made to American and European economic progress in the nineteenth century. While this work has not yet provided a definitive solution to the problem of the part played by the railways in modern industrial growth, it has given rise to an important and continuing debate about methodology and the use of economic theory in history. For a concise and fair survey of this important area of research see, P. O'Brien, *The New Economic History of the Railways* (1977).

2. E. Ames and N. Rosenberg, 'The Enfield Arsenal in Theory and Practice', *Economic Journal* (December 1968), pp. 838-9.

3. On this assumption, technical diffusion would be fastest in the single-firm industry (or pure monopoly), since the decision of only one firm to take up an innovation would be needed for its adoption to become industry-wide.

4. Sumner H. Slichter, *Economic Growth in the United States: its History, Problems and Prospects* (New York, 1963), p. 132.

5. Rosenberg put the same point in the following way: 'A much more widespread phenomenon in Britain as compared to the United States [was] what might be called "customer initiative" as opposed to "producer initiative". That is, in America, the producer of *capital goods* took the initiative in matters of machine design . . . He brought about, in other words, a high degree of standardization in the machinery, which very much simplified his own production problems, and in turn reduced the price of capital goods . . . In England the initiative in matters of machine design was emphatically in the hands of the buyer, and this had serious implications for the machine producing sector both as a transmission centre for the diffusion of new techniques and as producer of low-cost machinery.' N. Rosenberg, *Technology and American Economic Growth* (New York, 1972), pp. 45-6. However, S.B. Saul has pointed out that standardisation and interchangeability were not confined to, or originated by, American manufacturers. The techniques were also widely used by British locomotive and steam engine builders. The importance of the capital goods sector as a transmission centre for diffusion of new techniques is discussed later. See Chapter 8, IV.

5 SAVING AND THE RATE OF CAPITAL ACCUMULATION

I

The size and rate of growth of markets are not the only determinants of the rate at which a new technology diffuses. It also depends on the availability of supplies of complementary resources, including the factors of production, land, labour and capital. A country's capital is its stock of produced or man-made means of production, consisting of such items as plant, equipment, buildings and inventories of goods held in stock. It also includes 'social overhead capital', a term which normally covers such items as housing, transport facilities, communications, public utilities, government buildings and other assets, including educational facilities, essential for providing public services. While this somewhat restricted definition of capital refers to a stock of tangible physical goods which are 'man-made', we should not forget that a broader definition of the term could include a very important kind of intangible capital—the country's accumulated stock of knowledge, skills and knowhow—which may play quite an important role in industrial development. The growth of a country's stock of human capital is obviously an important determinant of the rate of spread of modern technology. It is, however, a matter which will be considered later in this book.[1]

A country's stock of capital will normally increase over time because some part of total output in any year will usually be directed towards this end. Additions to capital stock over time are called capital *accumulation*, capital *formation*, or *investment*. Part of a country's investment expenditure during a given period will represent the replacement of worn-out plant and equipment which has been scrapped. *Replacement* investment, which accounts for the *depreciation* of capital assets over time, constitutes the difference between 'gross' and 'net' investment or capital accumulation, the latter representing the increase in the capital stock that has occurred during the period under consideration.

Capital plays a many-sided role in increasing an economy's output and in raising the productivity of labour. Capital accumulation is necessary to equip a growing population with the tools and implements of production. Where capital accumulation is sufficient only to

65

increase the country's stock of capital in the same ratio as that of the increase in the workforce, we speak of *'capital-widening'*. In such cases there will be no rise in productivity unless technological improvements are effected through replacement investment. If, however, capital accummulation is rapid enough, it may lead to an increased supply of tools and machinery per worker so that *'capital-deepening'* will occur and average output per worker will rise with the increase in capital per worker. Finally, capital accumulation is closely related to the possibilities of effecting changes in the scale or technology of production. In other words, capital accumulation is the vehicle for technological progress. Where technical change is embodied in capital equipment, a country's rate of capital accumulation is all important since, in general, the more investment is undertaken the greater the degree of technological progress. Capital shortage, therefore, may hinder technological diffusion in a number of ways. For example, it will place limits on a country's stock of social overhead capital, especially transport facilities, with all that that implies for the growth of the market. The need for relatively abundant supplies of capital is also stressed where innovations in techniques cannot be introduced singly but require simultaneous development in a number of industries. Moreover, the fact that techniques can rarely be borrowed without the need to adapt them to local requirement further adds to the capital cost of introducing new methods of production. Finally, because industrialisation in the nineteenth century was accompanied by population growth and urban development, there were heavy demands on capital for housing, public utilities and the additional tools and machines needed to equip an expanding workforce. Consequently, the total capital requirements of an economy experiencing rapid population expansion will usually be much in excess of the level of investment needed to promote the spread of a new technology.

II

Ever since Adam Smith, economists and economic historians have regarded capital formation as the key to economic growth. This is not surprising, given that capital accumulation is the vehicle for technological progress and that capital can be substituted for resources and for labour. Moreover, given a capital/output ratio of some sort,[2] capital formation leads to more output, which can provide a surplus for further investment and further increases in ouput. It is for these reasons that some economists and economic historians have argued that a substantial rise in the ratio of investment to national income is necessary for a country to enter the process of modern economic growth. Arthur Lewis, for example, has made the point that increasing the rate of net investment from 5 per cent to 10 per cent or more of the national income is what we mean by the industrial revolution and that, consequently, 'the central problem of the theory of economic growth is to understand the process by which a community is converted from being a five per cent to a twelve per cent saver.'[3] Following Lewis, W.W. Rostow made a doubling of the rate of new investment from 5 per cent to 10 per cent of national income an essential ingredient of his 'take-off' stage.[4] Indeed, he went even further than Lewis in claiming that the acceleration in the rate of capital formation occurred in most industrialising countries during a comparatively short period of time—in Britain, for example, between 1783 and 1802.

To what extent does the available historical evidence support the Lewis-Rostow hypothesis that a sharp rise in the rate of capital formation accompanies, and is indispensable to, industrial 'take-off'? First, the evidence suggests that the rise in the rate of investment was not achieved in the short periods of time postulated by Rostow. According to one estimate the percentage of national income invested annually in Britain was around 5 per cent at the beginning of the eighteenth century, had reached 6 per cent by 1800, and did not rise to 10 per cent until the late 1850s, when heavy railway investment, the mechanisation of the textiles industries, the expansion of the coal and iron trades, and high investment in shipping raised investment levels substantially.[5] A similar picture is presented by developments in other European countries. In France, for example, net capital formation as a percentage of net domestic product rose from an average of 3 per cent in 1788–1839 to 8 per cent in 1839–50 (with the development of the railways), and to 12 per cent in 1852–80, when even more railway construction and extensive urban improvements were being undertaken. For Germany we have no figures for the period before the 1850s but, even so, the ratio of net capital formation for the two decades 1850–70 averaged less than 10 per cent of national income and did not reach 15 per cent until the decade before World War I. For Japan, the ratio averaged between 4½ and 7 per cent in the period 1887–1917, after the exclusion of military expenditures. While the capital investment estimates for most nineteenth-century industrialising countries are

subject to adjustment in the light of new statistical data, it seems
unlikely that the general conclusion stated above will be modified to
any significant extent.[6] For most of these countries the rate of capital
formation appears to have increased only gradually, and a 10 per cent
rate was achieved only after industrialisation had been proceeding for
some time.

On the other hand, as the above investment figures suggest, some of
the experiences of the industrialising countries do seem to meet the
Lewis-Rostow requirement of a doubling of the rate of investment as
an accompaniment of industrial take-off. In Britain, a doubling of the
investment ratio had certainly been achieved by the end of the period
conventionally designated as marking that country's industrial revolution.
Rapid industrialisation in Germany late in the nineteenth century was
also associated with a marked upturn in investment, as was the case
around the turn of the century or early in the twentieth century for
Denmark, Norway, Sweden and Italy. The United States, however,
seems to have experienced a relatively high investment ratio soon
after the middle of the nineteenth century. On the other hand, only
modest increases in the ratio of capital formation were recorded for
Japan and Canada. The general conclusion to be drawn from all this
evidence is fairly obvious. While the experience of individual
countries supports the basic idea that the investment ratio doubled
during industrial take-off, we have to reject Rostow's thesis that a
change of this magnitude was compressed within the space of a couple
of decades. During most industrial take-offs the rise in the investment
ratio appears to have been very gradual and capital does not appear to
have played a 'strategic role'. Industrialisation in most countries got
well under way with an average net investment of under 10 per cent.

III

An acceleration in technical progress or the emergence of a major
innovation (such as the railways) in a stream of minor ones is bound to
increase capital requirements in advance of output and consequently
disturb the existing equilibrium between savings, income and the rate
of capital accumulation. Given the acceleration in technical progress
that occured in the nineteenth century, therefore, the question still
remains to be answered why the rate of capital accumulation rose so
slowly during these years. A number of reasons can be put forward to

explain this phenomenon. To begin with, improved techniques can be introduced into an industry through the replacements made necessary by the scrapping of obsolete and worn-out equipment. In other words, technical progress can take place without any new(net) investment, although obviously improvements and changes can be effected more quickly if there are positive additions to the existing stock of capital. Furthermore, technological progress does not always involve high net investment. This is particularly the case with manufacturing industry. Given the nature of the technology at the beginning of the industrial revolution, fixed equipment was relatively simple and cheap, for example, the cost of a spinning jenny in Britain towards the end of the eighteenth century was £6, of a mule £30, while the cost of a large steam-driven mule was only a little over £50. Indeed, by 1800, Britain had established a modern cotton industry on the strength of a total investment of less than £10 million.[7] Even by 1914, when the textile industry in Britain was quite a large-scale business in terms of numbers employed and volume of output, the capital per man in the industry was £200 compared with £2,000 per man for railways.[8]

Furthermore, technical progress may permit a reduction in the stock of capital in the sense that it will always be 'capital-saving' to some extent. For example, improvements in transport and communications permitted a more economical and productive use of existing capital resources by freeing capital for other uses in a number of ways: by economising in traders' and industrialists' stocks through ensuring greater regularity in the supply of goods and raw materials, by freeing horses for agricultural purposes, by saving entrepreneurial time and by facilitating credit negotiations. Again, some innovations do not involve the creation of new physical capital, for example, a rearrangement of the layout of the plant and equipment on the factory floor; whereas others call for only very small amounts of capital, as with the purchase of improved seed or a new hand tool.[9] Moreover, some capital formation can take place without the need of investment in the conventional sense. Thus land clearing and reclamation, enclosures and road building could be undertaken by underemployed farmers and peasants with the spare time to devote to these capital-creating activities. Finally, increased technical progress in one sector of the economy, such as manufacturing, maybe supported by reducing or limiting capital formation in another direction, for example housing. In this way saving may be concentrated in the 'progressive' sector of the economy.

IV

Because technical progress does not generally take place without simultaneous investment in fixed capital, and because innovations have to be embodied in new equipment, economists and economic historians have recently stressed the yearly *rate of increase* in the stock of capital which is not measured by investment ratios and for which they are a poor substitute. This approach to the problem of capital formation emphasises the importance of the annual increment to physical capital, especially as it is revealed in the rapidly expanding sectors and industries of an industrialising country. From some figures for Britain, it would appear that fixed capital investment in the cotton industry increased at an annual average rate of 12 per cent from 1783 to 1802 and, in the iron industry, at a rate of 6 per cent per year from 1791 to 1806.[10] While these figures suggest a high rate of capital formation in the modernising sectors of an industrialising economy, the fact remains that the largest part of the increase in investment that took place in the early stages of a country's industrialisation went into sectors of the economy outside the direct context of manufacturing industry. In Britain, for example, well over three-quarters of gross fixed domestic capital formation undertaken during the period of the industrial revolution went into agriculture, into transport facilities, into house-building and into other social overheads, and less than a quarter into more directly productive forms of plant and equipment. The provision of this basic infrastructure of a highly industrialised and urbanised economy was, however, vital to the diffusion of technology and the progress of industrialisation.

Apart from investment in the agricultural improvements needed to increase output to feed a growing pupulation, housing and transport facilites made the heaviest demands on the available capital resources in the nineteenth century. The main impulse to capital accumulation over the years before 1913 came ultimately from the steam engine, especially the railway and the steamship. While housing constituted in most industrialising countries the largest claim on new capital throughout the period, railways used more capital per man employed than any other industry.[11] In other words, in the nineteenth century the demand for capital was dominated not by the expense of introducing a new manufacturing technology but partly by demographic factors— the growth and resettlement of population at home *and* overseas— and partly by the major innovation of the steam engine with all its repercussions on transport and on the distribution of population between and within countries. The diffusion of this new transport technology was, however, crucial to economic growth in the nineteenth century, because the diffusion of modern manufacturing techniques depended on expanding markets, increasing supplies of industrial raw materials, and a growing mobility of men and goods. For this reason alone a lack of capital, by limiting transport developments, could have had a serious retarding effect on a country's industrial development in the nineteenth century.[12]

Despite the relatively limited capital formation in manufacturing industry, one aspect of nineteenth-century industrial development must be noted. As the century progressed, manufacturing industry tended to become more capital-intensive. In shipbuilding, for example, the changeover from sail to steam found many shipbuilders with yards too small to cater for the new technology and lacking the capital needed to extend their operations. Increased size was also a feature of the iron and steel industry once substantial economies of scale became possible through the integrated working of plant and after the discovery of new methods of steel-making increased the optimal size of plant. Apart from heavy investment in equipment, the tendency to apply increasingly larger sums of money to research into new products was a feature of the chemical industry. It was, for example, the Badische Anilin und Soda Fabrik (BASF) that in 1897 solved the problem of the artificial production of dyes after 20 years of research and the expenditure of some 20 million marks. Apart from the need to mobilise larger sums of capital to finance capital-intensive techniques, their 'lumpiness' was often a serious obstacle to their spread within an industry. Thus the Norwegian fishing industry found it difficult to switch from supplying salted and dried fish to low-income markets in southern Europe, West Africa and South America to supplying the rapidly growing demand for fresh frozen fish from high-income European markets because it required larger boats for deep-sea fishing and considerable investment in freezing plant. The lack of an intermediate technology made the changeover all the more difficult to achieve.

This growing capital intensity of production was associated with the tendency of late industrialisers to adopt the most modern techniques available. By 1914, for example, blast furnace practice was more capital-intensive in Germany than in Britain and more so in Russia than in Germany. By the same date, Russia also possessed some of the largest and most modern cotton textile mills in the world. Why late developers should display this tendency to make greater use of capital-intensive techniques is a difficult question to answer. In part, no doubt, it was because foreign industrialists who were familiar with the latest technology played a large part in the early industrialisation of countries like Russia. In part it reflected an attempt to adjust production methods to the available supplies of complementary factors by substituting capital (machinery) for skilled labour, which was in short supply, and using greater quantities of abundant semi-skilled labour to work each machine. Larger units or production may also have permitted some economies in the use of scarce managerial skills. In short, the heavy use of capital involved in adopting modern techniques could be offset by the lower costs of operating the plant. Non-economic reasons, such as the desire for prestige, may also have been partly responsible for the adoption of the latest technology in some countries.

The existence of one country with capital equipment technologically superior to that of another has its parallel within individual industries within a country in the co-existence of firms using modern techniques alongside others using old-fashioned equipment. Whether technological diffusion is considered nationally or internationally, the reasons for the divergences in the level of technology used are partly economic and partly non-economic. Given the availability of capital funds, firms will replace their old equipment with the new only if it is profitable to do so. For replacement to be profitable, the reduction in cost due to the introduction of the new technique has to be sufficiently large to pay for the capital cost associated with the replacement. In other words, replacement will take place only when the operating cost of using the old equipment is larger than the total cost (that is, operating cost plus capital cost) involved in using the new equipment. In these circumstances diffusion depended heavily upon the gains to be expected from the new technology as well as the certainty of these gains. Where the gains were substantial, as with the Héroult process of making aluminium, which was developed in the 1880s and which reduced costs immediately by some 75 per cent, the old technology was overwhelmed and disappeared overnight. On the other hand, in those industries where the gains from using the new technology were smaller or less certain, diffusion depended upon the age composition of the existing plant—in the sense that the older the machines the closer they were to 'obsolescence' and to replacement by technologically superior equipment— and upon the speed with which the costs of new techniques (including the price of the new capital equipment) were reduced.[13] The rate of replacement of old techniques by new in an industry will also depend to some extent on the scrap and second-hand value of existing machines, the replacement rate being higher the higher the prices fetched by the old equipment. Finally, non-economic considerations, such as ignorance, inertia, social rigidities, and particularly resistance to change, will have played some part in bringing about the divergences in the level of technology to be observed within industries or between countries. For all of these reasons, individual firms within an industry may exhibit wide differences in the up-to-dateness of the technology which they are using. Only very rarely is an industry converted quickly and wholly to a new technology.

V

The general conclusion to be drawn from this discussion so far is fairly obvious. Even if the first stages in the industrialisation process did not put any great strain on the supply of capital of most countries in the nineteenth century, this should not blind us to the fact that, in so far as innovations are embodied in equipment, technical progress generally cannot take place without a simultaneous investment in fixed capital. Consequently, a shortage of capital may hinder or limit the spread of modern technology. Indeed, it is possible that the rate of technological diffusion is itself controlled by the volume of investment, not merely because capital formation is generally the means by which new techniques are adopted, but also because high investment creates an atmosphere (expanding markets, etc.) favourable to diffusion. A shortage of capital may also make itself felt through its impact on the various services that are an essential prerequisite of industrial growth. If transport facilitites are limited, for example, the market is automatically restricted and the scope for the use of mechanical power and machinery suffers correspondingly. Since these transport facilities are also needed to feed industry with raw materials, it can be claimed that good transport is perhaps the most powerful single means for accelerating the spread of modern industrial techniques. The fact that innovations tend to cluster together over time suggests that often improvements in techniques cannot be made one at a time but require simultaneous action by a number of industries. The greater the 'chain reaction' of supporting innovations triggered off by an improvement in the industrial field, the larger the amount of capital needed to realise them individually and collectively. Stated even more broadly, successful industrialisation may require the balanced development of both industry *and* agriculture, which is all the more difficult to achieve when capital is in short supply. Finally, techniques can rarely be borrowed without adaptation to suit local conditions. This is certainly so with agricultural improvements for fairly obvious reasons and it is often the case with industrial techniques when, as in Russia for example, a more capital-intensive technology was used to overcome problems of labour supply. Quite clearly, the need for adaptation adds to the capital cost of introducing new techniques and new methods of production.

Yet even when the rate of technological diffusion is slow, it does not follow that that is brought about by a lack of capital. As following chapters will show, the problem is often one of improved organisation and changed attitudes quite as much as of capital formation. Industrialistion may be slow because of the problems associated with training management and men, because of the difficulties in creating new attitudes towards industrial employment, and because of a lack of entrepreneurial ability capable of taking advantage of innovations that need little capital and using the resulting gains to finance further investment.

VI

Irrespective of the amount needed, how is capital accumulated over time? To increase the capital stock of a country it is necessary that some part of its national ouput (income) be diverted towards investment. In other words, some income must be saved and not spent on consumption goods and services if resources are to be released for investment purposes. It is possible, therefore, that an additional factor limiting capital formation is the volume of saving since capital formation will proceed only as long as saving takes place.

From the available evidence it would appear that the problem of generating adequate savings hardly troubled west European countries as industrialisation proceeded. Although marginal amounts were borrowed abroad, and total intra-European investment absorbed about 27 per cent of total foreign investment in the period up to 1914, domestic savings financed all but a relatively small proportion of capital formation in most countries. Internal financing of the growth of the firm through the ploughing back of profits played a central role in the expansion of maufacturing industry while, in the early stages of industrial development, the provision by the banking system of circulating (or trade) capital for the financing of stocks and the production and distribution of the finished product was substantially larger in amount than the volume of fixed capital investment and consequently crucial to the success of industrialisation. Much personal saving, on the other hand, went into agriculture, transport developments and urban expansion, all of which tended to favour the emerging manufacturing sector. In addition, the greater part of the foreign investment undertaken during these years went into providing the basic infrastructure needed for successful industrial development. The same pattern of saving and investment is to be observed in the United States and Canada, where foreign capital played a key role in financing social overhead capital.

There seems to be no reason to doubt that the nineteenth century witnessed a genuine rise in the level of thrift. This is apparent in the gradual acceleration in the rate of capital accumulation throughout the period. It is also apparent from the massive export of capital from Britain after 1820, and later still from a number of other European countries, that foreign investment occurred once saving began to exceed the profitable investment opportunities available in these countries. It is also to be seen in the long-run tendency for the rate of interest to fall, the growth of investment and financial intermediaries of every kind, and the improved organisation of the capital market. All that was necessary in the circumstances was a new perception of the importance of capital formation and a new willingness to accord it priority over other, non-productive, uses of investible funds. Thus the absence of large-scale wars in the nineteenth century released resources for more productive employment, while there was a tendency to reduce the rate of growth of outlay on ceremony and ostentatious display once the possibilities and advantages of modernisation became more widely realised.[14]

Moreover, once economic development got under way, new income was created out of which new saving could be made. The rate of growth of new saving depended in part on the manner in which the newly-created income was distributed. In so far as this extra income accrued to people with high savings potential, to that extent the savings rate would rise. Some of the extra income also passed to governments by way of taxation and consequently became available, at least potentially, for investment in development projects; while the unequal distribution of capital also ensured that interest and dividend income passed to persons whose propensity to save was high. Finally, a larger and growing income provided business firms with a larger fund out of which to finance further capital accumulation. In these circumstances the development problem was not so much one of the adequacy of the current or future level of saving as the need to mobilise saving effectively for productive use in industrial development. In short, the need was often not for more saving but for the creation of effective means of channelling investible resources between savers and investors. Consequently, the manner in which this problem was solved in the industrialising economy in the nineteenth century forms the subject matter of the next chapter.

Notes

1. See Chapter 6.
2. The capital/output ratio relates the value of capital stock (K) to the value of output (O) in a given period. Alternatively, the incremental capital/output ratio relates the amount of new investment (the net increase in the stock of capital) to the increase in output that that investment brings about.
3. W.A. Lewis, *The Theory of Economic Growth* (London, 1955), pp. 208, 225-6.
4. W.W. Rostow, *The Stages of Economic Growth* (Cambridge, 1960), p. 8.
5. See, for example, Phyllis Deane, 'The Industrial Revolution in Great Britain', in C. Cipolla (ed.), *The Fontana Economic History of Europe* (London, 1973), Vol. 4 (1), pp. 198-200.
6. More recent estimates of capital formation in Britain suggest that, in *gross* terms, the total domestic investment/GDP ratio increased from 8 per cent in 1761/70 to 12 per cent in 1781/90 and 13 per cent in 1791/1800. Total investment rose from 8 per cent to 13 per cent and 14 per cent during these periods. For both series no further increases occurred up to 1851/60 at the latest. See C.H. Feinstein, 'Capital Formation in Great Britain', in P. Mathias and M.M. Postan (eds.), *The Cambridge Economic History of Europe* (Cambridge, 1978), Vol. VII, Pt. 1, p.91.
7. One estimate puts the total investment in the fixed capital of the cotton industry at £2.5 million in 1795 and a little over £6 million in 1811. See S.D. Chapman, 'Fixed Capital Investment in the British Cotton Industry 1770–1815', *Economic History Review*, Vol. XXIII, 1970, pp. 235-66.
8. In the early life of a firm large outlays on fixed capital could be avoided by renting factory space. Machinery, and even steam engines could also be rented, or bought.
9. It should also be noted that the relatively inefficient use of much of the existing capital stock in the pre-industrial conditions led to high capital/output ratios wherever this situation existed. There was, therefore, a tendency for capital/output ratios to decline in such cases under the conditions of modern industrial growth when efficiency improved. See S. Kuznets, *Modern Economic Growth: Rate, Structure and Spread* (New Haven, 1966).
10. F. Crouzet (ed.), *Capital Formation in the Industrial Revolution* (London, 1972), p. 28. Crouzet notes that it is not clear if these figures refer to the actual sums invested between the years stated or to the value of capital stock at the years stated. He quotes from P. Deane and W.A. Cole, *British Economic Growth, 1688–1959: Trends and Prospects* (1962), p. 252.

11. One estimate of the construction costs of the world's railways up to 1914 is $100,000m (over £20,000m). See H. Heaton, *Economic History of Europe* (New York, 1948 ed.), p. 577.

12. It should be noted, however, that Japan achieved substantial industrial growth while economising in social overhead capital. This came about because of her well-developed coastal shipping service, which reduced the need for heavy investment in railways, and because of her continued use of the rural 'putting-out' system as an adjunct to factory production, which reduced the need for heavy investment in urban development.

13. Competitive pressures from a new technology could act as an incentive to reduce the costs of existing production techniques. This happened with the Leblanc process of soda manufacture in the face of competition from the Solvay process. Cost reductions of this kind would obviously slow up the diffusion of the new technology.

14. Much of European foreign borrowing before 1850 was spent on the suppression of internal rebellions and on the upkeep of courts and armies. After 1850, however, foreign investment in Europe was almost wholly devoted to economic development.

Selected Reading

A.K. Cairncross, *Factors in Economic Development* (London, 1962)

R. Cameron, 'Economic Development, Some Lessons of History for Developing Countries', *American Economic Review,* Vol. LVII (1967), pp. 312ff.

F. Crouzet (ed.), *Capital Formation in the Industrial Revolution* (London, 1972)

P. Deane, 'Capital Formation in Britain before the Railway Age', *Economic Development and Cultural Change,* Vol. IX (1961), pp. 352ff.

P. Deane, 'The Role of Capital in the Industrial Revolution', *Explorations in Economic History,* Vol. 10 (1973), pp. 349ff.

J.D. Gould, *Economic Growth in History, Survey and Analysis* (London, 1972), pp. 132-57

P. Mathias and M.M. Postan (eds.), *The Cambridge Economic History of Europe,* Vol. VII (Cambridge, 1978)

6 THE FINANCIAL ENVIRONMENT

I

The financial environment encompasses all types of financial institutions which manage the money supply of a country, which mobilise the savings accumulated within a country, which attract savings from abroad, and which offer the funds received to those requiring them for investment purposes. An efficient financial sector ensures that rates of interest are acceptable to both savers and investors by offering different types of institutions as depositories for savings and as sources of loans. The financial environment of a country refers also to the prevailing attitudes of the population to financial instruments and financial institutions and within the financial sector to the rest of the economy. In this respect, the rapidity with which innovations are accepted by the general public, the readiness of savers to deposit their savings with such institutions rather than to hoard them, the efficacy of financial houses in attracting personal savings, the nature of their lending policies and the relations between banks and other institutions and investors, all affect the degree of efficiency of the financial sector in promoting economic growth.

Domestic savings are accumulated by the government and by the private sector. The former can amass savings by recording a surplus budget in which total revenue exceeds current expenditure. Private savings represent the excess of disposable income over current consumption of goods and services. Such funds can be used by savers for financing their own investment expenditures or can be lent privately to others; they can be deposited in financial institutions which lend them to investors directly or indirectly through the capital market; they can be invested directly in company shares and other types of securities; and they can be used to hoard currency. The second and third of these represent savings held in the form of financial assets while the last represents a withdrawal of funds from the money supply. One of the early functions of financial institutions was to attract funds out of hoarding so that they could be used productively.[1]

It is an historical fact that, as an economy develops and *per capita* incomes rise, the ratio of financial assets to national wealth[2] increases rapidly. For example, it has been estimated that this ratio for the United States rose from around one in 1800 to about 4.5 in the mid-1960s; for Japan it rose from 0.1 in the 1880s to over 1.5 recently; while in Russia the increase was from 0.1 in the late 1920s to 0.35 in the mid-1960s. The most highly developed countries now have the highest ratios of financial to real assets, the United States over 4.5, Japan 1.5, and Switzerland and the United Kingdom just over 2.0. France, West Germany and several other developed countries have ratios between 0.8 and 1.0. At the other end of the scale, some of the less developed countries have ratios as low as 0.1 to 0.15, although some in this group, for example Argentina, Brazil, Guatemala, Mexico, Korea, Venezuela and Yugoslavia, have relatively high ratios around 0.5 to 0.6. India's ratio is about 0.35, close to that of Russia.[3] With economic growth there is also an increase in the size of the banking sector relative to the whole economy, as measured by the ratio of bank assets to national income. This ratio for England and Wales rose from 28 per cent in 1800 to around 50–60 per cent by 1900. Over the same period the ratios for the United States were 5 per cent and 63 per cent and, for France, 1.5 per cent and 16 per cent (in 1870). In Japan the ratio averaged 16 per cent over the period 1878–82 and 41 per cent over the years 1898–1902.[4] While there is a suprisingly wide range in the ratios of bank assets to national income of the countries for which data are available, what is equally obvious is that countries with the highest ratios at the end of our period were also the countries that experienced the most rapid spurts of industrialisation. If the experience of England and Wales is taken as the norm then Japan and Russia, both latecomers among the industrial nations, achieved a relatively high ratio in a very short time. While some doubts remain about the accuracy of the data used, the increase in the French ratio is at least consistent with the relatively slow rate of growth of the economy throughout the nineteenth century.

If bank assets are to grow faster than national income, and financial assets generally accumulate faster than national wealth during the process of industrial development, then the financial sector of the economy must undergo a rapid transformation in its structure and policies. This transformation, which was achieved in the nineteenth century by the introduction of a number of important financial innovations, involves changes of attitude towards both the mobilisation of capital and lending to industry and commerce. Put another way, the character of the transformation required is dictated by the contribution the financial sector has to make for a country's industrial development to be successful. This contribution includes the expansion of the money supply at a rate sufficient to accomodate the growth of marketable output brought about by the use of mechanised means of production and where it exists the gradual monetisation of the subsistence sector of the economy; the provision of increased short-term credit facilities to finance the expansion of trade, both domestic and foreign, resulting from the growth of output, and to finance the use of more roundabout methods of production; and the provision of intermediation facilities between savers and potential borrowers, so that credit facilities can expand and capital formation can proceed rapidly enough for technological improvements to be taken up without the threat of a capital shortage developing. Moreover, given a high degree of efficiency in the financial sector of the economy, the cost of borrowing may be low, and may induce the undertaking of many investment projects which, given high interest rates, would not otherwise have been contemplated.

II

While variations between countries were apparent, in most countries the financial sector was largely unorganised in the pre-industrialisation stage of their development. It is true that money markets existed in a number of large centres, for example London, Paris, Amsterdam and several Italian cities, and that by the eighteenth century these financial centres had achieved a fair degree of diversification in their activities. But outside the large cities money markets remained highly unorganised. In these local money markets, characterised by private money lenders who were mainly landlords and merchants, high interest rates were the rule, largely because a high demand for loans was associated with a relatively inelastic supply of funds due to the limited financial resources available to private lenders who lacked opportunities for mobilising funds for lending purposes. As industrial development got under way in a number of countries, however, and with improvements in internal communications, these unorganised money markets were gradually replaced by a variety of financial institutions concerned primarily with the problem of mobilising capital and channelling it into productive uses.

Commercial banking played a particularly important supporting role in the early stages of industrialisation in many countries in the nineteenth century. Two conditions encouraged the rapid growth of this type of banking activity. These were freedom of incorporation, that is freedom to take up this form of economic activity, and freedom of note issue, which obviously acted as a great inducement to entrepreneurs to enter the banking field. Restrictions on entry did exist in some countries. This was the case, for example, in France where the privilege of incorporation was reserved to a very few institutions specially chartered and regulated by the state. Even more harmful to the development of French banking was the restriction placed on the right of note issue which, in 1848, was conferred on a single monopolistic institution, the Bank of France. In Britain, the privileges of the Bank of England effectively prevented any but very small partnerships (fewer than seven persons) from engaging in banking operations. The freedom of note issue, however, enticed many people into banking and the resulting proliferation of small-scale banking firms, especially the 'country banks', led the English system to instability and periodic breakdown. After 1826 the legislation of joint-stock banks eliminated the artificial restriction on the size of banks without, however, completely remedying the instability of the system.

The first banknotes appeared in Sweden around 1650 but the experiment was short-lived. About the same time, London goldsmith bankers began issuing deposit receipts which, being payable on demand, were a form of banknote. From the commencement of its operations in 1694 the Bank of England also issued banknotes but, in Britain as a whole, it was the Scottish banks and the English country banks which, by introducing notes of one pound and lower denominations, accelerated the spread of the habit of using banknotes throughout the country. This habit received a check in England in 1826, however, when the issuing of notes with a face value of less than five pounds was forbidden. In addition, the Bank of England received a virtual monopoly over the issuing of notes under the banking legislation of 1845.

A number of other countries, such as Denmark and the United States, became accustomed to the use of banknotes as a supplement to specie money in the late eighteenth century. The abortive experiment with *assignats* (treasury notes) in France during the Revolution and the Empire, when vast quantities of these notes were put into circulation, depreciating their value in terms of specie, set back the acceptability of paper currency for many years, not only in France but also in other European countries, such as Belgium, in which the *assignats* circulated. Although the issuing of notes was readily adopted by Belgian banks in the 1830s, banknotes were not widely used until after 1850. In France, on the other hand, the Bank of France obtained the monopoly of note issue in Paris in 1803, and throughout the country in 1848. As only notes of high denominations were issued by the bank until the 1870s, the use of paper currency in France spread very slowly and, late in the nineteenth century, there were no notes at all in circulation in many rural districts. Whereas in Germany, Norway and Denmark the central bank alone was responsible for the note issue, Swedish banks had the right of note issue from the 1830s up of 1897 when the *Riksbank* was granted a monopoly. Other European countries quickly acquired the note-issuing habit in the nineteenth century. Paper currency was also introduced into Japan shortly after the Meiji Restoration of 1868. Commercial banks were able to issue their own notes, convertible into gold on request, from 1872 on but in 1882 the monopoly of the note issue passed to the Bank of Japan. Finally, in the United States, the use of private banknotes was widespread in the first half of the nineteenth century. In 1863, however, national banks were required to back their note issues with government bonds and government deposits and limits were placed on the issuing of notes.

Although in most countries the right of commercial banks to issue banknotes was relatively short-lived, while the right existed it did enable the banks to perform a number of functions, including expanding the money supply and increasing the opportunities for borrowing, that were of vital importance for the industrialisation of the economy. Apart from inducing a dishoarding of metallic currency, the use of banknotes enabled the commercial banks to *create credit* on the basis of their enlarged liabilities, which now included the notes they had in circulation. The establishment of a central banking monopoly of the note issue may have somewhat reduced the ability of the commercial banks to create credit but, by the time this restriction on the banks' activities had become widespread, the commercial banks, through the use of bank deposits, had already introduced a further innovation in the field of money supply.

Bank deposits also have a long history, having existed in ancient times. In northern Italy, the payment of interest on deposits which could be withdrawn on notice was firmly established by 1200. By the seventeenth century the transfer of deposits from one account to another had also become accepted as a banking practice. Bank

deposits, withdrawable on demand by the depositor or easily trans-
ferable by means of cheques, become a feature of English banking
practice in the mid-seventeenth century but was largely restricted to
London, where a clearing house for cheques was established in 1773.
Outside London, however, the negotiable 'inland' bill (of exchange)
provided an alternative method of payment to the cheque-deposit
system well into the nineteenth century. A clearing house for cheques
was not established in Scotland until 1856.

On the Continent, deposits in the form of *giro* accounts, by means
of which funds could be transferred from one depositor to another in
the same bank or be withdrawn at will, existed in Italy and parts of
Spain in medieval times. Except in Amsterdam and a few other
commercial cities, however, they were not widely used before the
nineteenth century. In Belgium in the 1830s the early investment
banks adopted deposit accounts as a means of mobilising domestic
savings and the use of cheques and overdraft facilities became
increasingly important in Belgian banking procedures in the second
half of the nineteenth century. The result was a rapid increase in
private bank deposits. In France, interest-bearing time deposits were
accepted by *la haute banque parisienne* (a group of the major private,
family, merchant banks including Rothschilds) as early as the 1800s
and a number of investment banks set up in the 1850s were also
permitted to accept deposits subject to certain restrictions imposed by
the state. But until 1865 private banks generally in France were
prevented from accepting demand deposits, from using cheques, and
from offering overdraft facilities to the public. Even after 1865, the
habit of demand deposit banking and the use of the cheque spread only
slowly in France. The German approach to commercial banking
differed from that followed in Britain and several other countries in
that the bill of exchange and the *giro* transfer were more commonly
used than banknotes, demand deposits and the use of cheques.
Nevertheless, the 'dry bill', a bill drawn on a banker against deposit or
overdraft accounts, played an important part in the creation of bank
credit even before 1815, because of the similarity between the dry bill
and a cheque which bears interest. The bill of exchange remained an
important money substitute for many decades in the German banking
system. Germany was also responsible for the innovation of 'mixed
banking' in the 1850s when several deposit and discount banks were
established.

Elsewhere in Europe, the spread of the practice of deposit banking
after 1850 was largely the outcome of the activities and influence of a

number of French banks, more particularly, the Crédit Mobilier and, later, the Société Générale de France. In Japan, moreover, demand and time deposits had become well established in banking practice by the last quarter of the nineteenth century. Finally, in the United States, deposit banking was fairly common early in the nineteenth century and from the 1840s demand deposits and the use of the cheque became widespread.

The use of banknotes and the growth of deposit banking, as well as the opportunities for credit creation afforded to the banks by these two financial innovations, represented highly flexible means of expanding a country's money supply. The need to increase the money supply became pressing once industrialisation got under way in a country since, for a number of reasons, the demand for money to finance business transactions and to hold in a liquid form for precautionary purposes was likely to grow faster than national income. The ability of the banking sector to innovate in such a way as to foster a rapid growth of the money supply while simultaneously improving the mobilisation of domestic saving, was consequently a major factor in promoting industrial development in the nineteenth century.

III

Apart from those developments which helped expand the money supply, financial innovations in the nineteenth century took the form of novel means of granting credit. In the early stages of industrialisation an expanding supply of credit was needed to finance the expansion of trade, both domestic and foreign, which was a natural outcome of the growth of industrial ouput, and to finance the production of output itself. Indeed, for the industrial firm starting up in business, ready access to short-term credit to finance the purchase of raw materials and to pay wages was often of crucial importance to its long-run success. Moreover, as long as capital equipment remained relatively simple and small-scale, a firm's working capital was often substantially larger than its fixed investment. Access to cheap short-term credit, therefore, solved a difficult financial problem for the firm and allowed it to concentrate its own financial resources on the purchase of fixed capital equipment.

Loans on mortgage, which had the disadvantage of tying up resources for long periods, and promissory notes, which often lacked sufficient guarantees of repayment, were already in use as a means of granting credit by the late eighteenth century. Self-liquidating bills of exchange became the most favoured instrument of credit in the nineteenth century, however, because they could be used as a means of current payment as long as the commercial banks were prepared to act as the ultimate source of credit by discounting the bills.

The bill of exchange as an instrument for financing short-term transactions has a long history and was used in medieval times for foreign as well as domestic transactions. But it was not until the seventeenth century that the negotiability of the bill was assured (in England c. 1700), with a subsequent rapid rise in their use. As a result, a complicated but flexible credit system emerged which allowed for acceptance of bills and which provided discounting facilities and a reasonable degree of security against financial loss. Such a system developed in Britain during the eighteenth century, where the growth of the country banks provided a means of mobilising the surplus funds of agricultural districts to discount the bills of industrialists and traders through bill brokers in London. Merchant firms provided another important part of the credit mechanism through their willingness to accept bills from clients. Underpinning the whole credit system, however, were the commercial banks which used their resources for discounting bills of exchange and for offering credit facilities to merchants who were either suppliers of materials to or purchasers of the output of industry. The growth of joint stock banks after the early 1830s with no right to issue banknotes, soon led to the practice of extending loans by means of the overdraft system which was more flexible than the bill of exchange and the latter declined in importance in internal transactions although it remained an important instrument for the financing of international transactions. While there is some evidence that the English commercial banks were not always averse to offering long-term loans, their role of supporting the short-term capital market allowed industrialists greater flexibility in the use of their own personal funds.

IV

The problem of raising long-term capital for large investments in fixed capital equipment was eventually solved by the reintroduction of the joint stock company with limited liability. The joint stock company had existed from the fifteenth century at least, the best known of these earliest prototypes, such as the East India Company, being concerned with the monopolisation of foreign trade in certain parts of the world. Towards the end of the seventeenth century joint stock companies were also being promoted to undertake river improvements, water supply and banking operations. But the company form of business organisation fell into ill repute with several failures in England and France in the 1720s. In England, government regulation ensured that joint stock companies could only be formed by royal charter or a private act of parliament and in France a charter was required. While several companies were formed on the Continent around the 1730s, often under the patronage of the state, few succeeded, and business organisation as in Britain remained essentially personal, family, or in partnership form until well into the nineteenth century.

The growth of joint stock organisation was partly the outcome of the limitations associated with the partnership, in which each partner had unlimited liability with respect to the debts of the organisation (or limited liability for 'sleeping' partners under the *société en commandite* in France from 1809). Under joint stock legislation the liability of the shareholder was limited. The major reason for the growth of the joint stock organisation was the need to provide finance for large capital-intensive projects in manufacturing and transport. In the first half of the nineteenth century the provision of canals, waterworks, gas and railways (from the 1830s) proved to be beyond the resources of existing forms of financing. In addition, in the second half of that century, the need for the establishment of large plants to obtain the most efficient methods of production was created by the rapid advances in technology. While joint stock organisations came into being in several countries, incorporation was a slow and costly process. In Britain, a parliamentary act facilitated the formation of corporations but it was not until 1856 that general limited liability status was granted to limit the liability of shareholders should the company fail. Company law became established in Britain in 1862. Other countries followed the British example. Limited liability status, for example, was introduced in France by 1867 and in Germany by 1870.

The growth of company formation in the 1860s and 1870s enhanced the importance of stock exchanges as mobilisers of domestic savings and the volume of shares changing hands increased very rapidly. This new financial organisation became suited not only to railway financing, banking and other mercantile businesses but also to the new emerging manufacturing industries, such as iron and steel, petroleum, chemicals and electricity. Nevertheless, joint stock organisation in industry was not as popular on the Continent as it was in Britain and was adopted later than in Britain.[5] In addition, investment banks played an important role in the mobilisation of savings for large-scale industrial ventures and for the formation of public companies.

Another important financial development, in the promotion of which commercial and investment banks played an active role, was the expansion of international investment. Many banks showed an early willingness either to transfer funds to other countries or to attract surplus savings from abroad. For example, in France, where there was an over-supply of savings relative to her domestic needs, investment banks were responsible for these funds being used to finance railway construction, mining and industrial ventures in most other European countries. British savings were also attracted abroad in large quantitites, first to Europe and then to overseas countries in North and South America and Australasia, where a shortage of investible funds existed (see Chapter 11 below). In addition, in a number of countries in which the supply of savings was insufficient to meet the needs of investors local financial institutions and governments actively solicited funds from other countries through the banking system or the capital market. Britain alone was able to enter modern industrial growth without recourse to foreign capital. In France, Germany and Finland, capital inflow performed only a small role in financing industrial development in the first half of the nineteenth century. In the United States, Canada, Norway, Denmark, Sweden, Italy and Russia, however, access to foreign capital markets was an essential aspect of the financing of economic growth for, in concentrating largely on transport and communications, foreign investment facilitated the opening up of the national markets and allowed local savings to be used for other kinds of capital formation.

V

To conclude this chapter we may consider the proposition that industrialisation may be stimulated in a period of inflation. This topic is linked to the financial sector of the economy because inflation may occur as a result of, or be intensified by, the attitude of the banking system towards the creation of credit and thus to the expansion of the money supply.

During the last two decades a lively controversy has arisen concerning the effects of inflation on the process of economic growth.[6]

Those who advocate the use of inflation to promote industrial growth argue that it allows the transfer of resources from consumption to investment by increasing profits, that it produces an increase in the demand for labour and thus reduces unemployment and under-employment, that at the beginning of the process a 'money illusion' effect may encourage more intensive work on the part of labour and entrepreneurs, and that the period of inflation may be relatively short because of the effect of increased investment on total output, some of which may then be saved for further investment. On the opposite side it is argued that inflation creates distortions in the pattern of investment and upsets the efficient allocation of resources; adversely affects exports, increases imports and tends to reduce capital inflow, thereby creating balance of payments difficulties; reduces the incentive to save voluntarily, thereby reducing the resources available for investment; and creates difficulties for the government in its attempts to prevent the deleterious pressures of inflation from becoming progressively more severe. To a large degree the controversy centres around the extent to which inflation occurs. In most cases a modest degree of inflation in the price level may be one of the results of rapid economic growth. On the other hand, high rates of inflation would probably give rise to the undesirable effects outlined above and produce a situation in which real economic growth is lower than what it would have been if price stability had occurred.

As far as the period before 1914 is concerned, it has been argued that in certain countries, such as Britain in the late 1790s, the United States in the 1850s, Japan in the 1870s, Italy in the 1880s, rapidly rising prices may have played an important part in accelerating industrial growth and in encouraging innovation by shifting resources from consumption to profits, thereby providing funds for investment purposes.[7] In other words, in the absence of controls over prices and wages excess demand for commodities led to higher prices and lower real incomes for consumers. But to the extent that producers could keep costs down, their profits and real incomes would rise, thus promoting further investment and even higher profits.

It is also evident that the discoveries of large deposits of gold in California and Australia between 1848 and 1855 led to a substantial increase in the circulation of gold coins in Europe and elsewhere. This large boost to the money supply and its implications for the creation of credit by the commercial banks are said to be at least partly responsible for price increases in a number of countries and for accelerated economic growth during the 1850s and 1860s.[8] The upturn in prices in the mid-1890s and the upward trend which continued into the 1900s has also been attributed largely to the large discoveries of gold in South Africa, Western Austrialia and the Klondike between 1887 and 1896.

In assessing the importance of inflation for industrial development, two aspects of nineteenth-century economic experience should be noted. First, despite the previously cited examples of inflation, the long-term trend in the price level from 1820 to 1896 was downward and only during the years 1851 to 1854 and 1872–3 were prices increasing rapidly. Second, the evidence suggests that it was during periods of declining prices that investment/income ratios were increasing most rapidly. In other words, the effect on prices of productivity increases brought about by industrial innovations was to reduce them. By the mid-1890s, however, although a new cluster of innovations, including electricity, chemicals and synthetic materials, and the internal combustion engine, had been taken up by the industrialising nations, it needed time for producers to reach a cost-reducing and therefore price-reducing stage. Thus new gold supplies and other inflationary forces were able to sustain an increasing price level until World War I. It is by no means certain, however, that economic growth was accelerated during these years as a direct result of inflationary forces. Indeed, as a general conclusion it can perhaps be argued that if price increases were maintained at a rate of around 2–3 per cent per annum as a result of the creation of credit by commercial banks, this inflationary trend could have been more than offset by increased productivity brought about by commercial bank lending to highly productive enterprises. To the extent that this is what did happen in the industrialising economies of the nineteenth century, a stable or declining price level was to be expected.

VI

Modern industrial development and its spread from country to country require a flexible financial sector capable of increasing the available money supply to allow a smooth flow of output and resources within the goods and factor markets. It must also be capable of mobilising domestic or foreign savings and of offering them to industrialists as working capital or for investment in fixed capital equipment. As for the relationship between industrial development and financial innovation, this can take a variety of forms. In some countries, for example England, the financial sector tended to adjust to the needs of the industrial sector and consequently it played a passive role in that country's industrial revolution. On the Continent, on the other hand, investment banks played an active role in promoting industrial development and their growth and development necessarily preceded the onset of industrialisation in a number of countries. In a few countries, such as France, the slow growth and diversification of commercial banking may even have hindered economic growth although one is inclined to the opinion, based on the evidence offered by the experience of most other industrialising countries, that had France developed more rapidly than she did in the nineteenth century, the necessary changes in the financial sector to accommodate this development would have been forthcoming.

Notes

1. In addition, there is 'forced' saving which may occur during a period of inflation.
2. National wealth (or capital) covers the total value of farm land and buildings, crops, livestock, horses, implements and tools, houses, industrial and commercial buildings, urban land, industrial machinery and equipment, non-farm stock-in-trade, ships, vehicles, railways, buildings, rolling stock, mines gasworks, water supply, roads and bridges, docks and harbours, and public works and buildings. (see C.H. Feinstein, 'Capital Formation in Great Britain', in P. Mathias and M.M. Postan (eds.), *The Cambridge Economic History of Europe* (Cambridge, 1978), Vol. VII, Pt. 1, pp. 80-1.)
3. For a full description of the problems and developments discussed in this chapter, the reader is referred to Rondo Cameron et al., *Banking in the Early Stages of Industrialisation* (New York, 1967); and Rondo Cameron (ed.), *Banking and Economic Development* (New York, 1972).
4. Cameron *et al.,* Table IX.1, pp. 301-2.
5. Indeed, Cottrell argues that there was some reluctance on the part of many British firms to adopt limited liability status after this became possible and some only adopted it to avoid bankruptcy. See P.L. Cottrell,*Industrial Finance 1830–1914. The Finance and Organization of English Manufacturing Industry* (Andover, 1979).
6. See G.M. Meier, *Leading Issues in Economic Development,* 2nd ed. (New York, 1971), Part IV.
7. See W.W. Rostow, *The Stages of Economic Growth* (Cambridge, 1960), p.48 for example.
8. See R.A. Church, *The Great Victorian Boom 1850–1873* (London, 1975), pp.16-20, for a discussion of these points.

Selected Reading

Rondo Cameron *et al., Banking in the Early Stages of Industrialisation* (New York, 1967)

Rondo Cameron (ed.), *Banking and Economic Development* (New York, 1972)

P.L. Cottrell, *Industrial Finance 1830–1914. The Finance and Organization of English Manufacturing Industry* (Andover, 1979)

Bertrand Gille, 'Banking and Industrialisation in Europe', *The Fontana Economic History of Europe* (London, 1970), Vol. 3

R.W. Goldsmith, *Financial Structure and Development* (New Haven, 1969)

Tom Kemp, *Historical Patterns of Industrialisation* (London, 1978), Ch. 6

W.H. Parker and B.H. Beckhart, *Foreign Banking Systems* (London, 1929)

7 INDUSTRIALISATION AND LABOUR SUPPLY

I

An inescapable condition of successful industrialisation is the existence of an expanding, mobile and adaptable labour supply. Technical progress can be expected to require either some increase in the numbers engaged in productive activity, or some movement of workers between occupations or both. Even where technical change is capital-intensive (or labour-saving) in its effects, the increase in investment and output to which it gives rise promotes a considerable net increase in the demand for labour. Equally important in the early stages of industrialisation is the existence of skilled labour in sufficient quantities to develop and/or accept technical change, as well as some minimum level of training and education for the mass of the workforce. Moreover, the continuous use of modern technological knowledge in economic activity requires a labour force in whom that knowledge is embodied through experience, education and training. What may pose at least as great a problem as the formation of the required technical skills in the early stages of industrial development is the inculcation of work discipline, co-operation within the factory, and other work habits, which are taken for granted in a mature industrial society. While there is obviously a wide range of alternative means available, both for dividing up and imparting the knowledge requirements among the members of the labour force and for inculcating the required work attitudes, the speed and efficiency with which these ends are achieved will have a significant influence on the rate at which a country industrialises.

II

An abundant supply of labour cannot of itself initiate the process of modern industrial development. The availability of labour in sufficient quantities and of a sufficient quality becomes a problem only when the demand for an industrial workforce emerges. It makes very little difference whether this demand for industrial labour is brought about by increased consumption, investment, exports or government spending, or by technical change itself. What is important is that once the process of industrialisation has started in a country, its rate of industrial growth is determined in part by the rate of growth of the country's industrial workforce, and by the absence of labour bottlenecks which would seriously impede the pace of industrial advance.

The expanding labour supply needed to support industrialisation in the nineteenth century came from a variety of sources. These included population growth which, after an appropriate time lag which will be shorter the earlier the age at which people enter the workforce, must lead to an increase in labour supply. Most industrialising countries in the nineteenth century were favoured with high rates of population growth and a low age of entry into the workforce. Child employment was widespread at least until the 1870s, when the introduction of universal elementary schooling in most industrialising countries considerably restricted the use of child labour. The labour supply was also increased by a more intensive use of the existing workforce. This involved an increase in the average number of hours worked per day and per worker, and came about partly because factory employment involved regularity and steady intensity of effort in place of the irregular spurts or work associated with the cottage industry and with the seasonal pattern of agricultural employment. In this respect, the factories gave full-time employment not only to men but also to women and children, groups which had rarely enjoyed more than seasonal or part-time work for pay in the pre-industrial era.[1] The demand for industrial workers was also partly met by a transfer of labour out of agriculture. Such transfers were not always necessary in the early stages of industrialisation, however, since the existence of an underemployed urban workforce was often sufficient in itself to satisfy the newly-created demand for industrial labour. Only when industrial advance became general within a country and when the continued rapid growth of the rural population, coupled with the gradual use of more capital-intensive agricultural techniques, created a large rural labour surplus, did these transfers occur on a large scale. Then the rural workers moved, not only into the nearby industrialising towns and cities but also overseas to countries like the United States, where industrial growth was accelerating in the second half of the nineteenth century. Immigration of workers thus provided another source, and for some countries an extremely important source, of increased labour supply.

In considering the problem of the recruitment of labour for modern industry in the nineteenth century, it is worth remembering that the technological innovations of the day were often directly related to the kinds of techniques which had preceded them. This suggests that the degree of adaptation of the labour force necessary in Europe and elsewhere to operate the new machines and processes might have been less abrupt than what is needed now for the adoption of modern industry in underdeveloped countries. Thus apart from the availability of craftsmen and other skilled workers in urban centres, there were few trades in nineteenth-century Europe which were not linked with the land. Peasant iron workers, peasant miners and quarrymen, peasant spinners and weavers, peasant woodworkers, and so on, besides providing a potential source of workers for modern industry, were sufficiently numerous to ensure that rural industries remained an appreciable part of the total industrial effort in many European countries. For this reason, few, if any, countries industrialising during the nineteenth century suffered from a general shortage of industrial labour. However, an interesting and widely held view blames the slow rate of industrial expansion in France before 1914 on the failure of agriculture to release sufficient labour to industry because of the prevalence of the family farm and the French peasant's deep attachment to the soil. While this argument has some substance during the period 1830–50, thereafter, as Kindleberger has shown, the position is more complicated. Labour supply in Paris, Marseilles, Lyons and most of the industrial north was adequate throughout most of the second half of the nineteenth century, and there were some rural areas, such as the south-west, out of which peasant labour moved freely. Moreover, while there were undoubtedly some industrial regions and manufacturing industries where labour shortages appeared from time to time, the rate of industrial growth in France was never so intense as to create a general labour shortage, which, by forcing up industrial wage rates, would have brought about a cut back of industrial expansion.[2]

A somewhat similar conclusion applies in the Russian case, where there is little evidence that the formal commune regulations introduced along with the emancipation of the serfs in 1861, restricted the supply of labour to urban industry. Passports to enable members to work away from the communal villages were issued in substantial numbers, and complaints of labour shortages were met with mainly in the newly-industrialising regions of south Russia where the population was relatively sparse and where agriculture was buoyant because of expanding export opportunities. In such areas the industrial workforce included a substantial migratory element with its attendant problems. Industrial output came to depend on the magnitude of the summer exodus which was in turn linked to the results of the harvest. The slow growth of a permanent Russian industrial workforce was attributable only in part to the problems associated with emancipation and migratory rural labour. It also came about because of the slow growth of opportunities for industrial employment.[3]

While the presence of some minimum amounts of labour of various qualitities is obviously essential to the adoption of modern industrial technology, the historical evidence suggests that both relatively abundant *and* relatively limited supplies of labour are consistent with rapid technological diffusion, although the technology adopted will almost certainly vary with the differences in the relative costs of labour in the differing labour situations. Thus access to an abundant supply of labour at a relatively cheap price was an important factor in explaining the rapid expansion of the British cotton industry during the industrial revolution. The presence of an elastic labour supply meant that British cotton manufacturers were able to increase output and manufacturing capacity without correspondingly increased costs due to a rise in the real wage rate.[4] Consequently, the productivity benefits of mechanised cotton manufacture were largely shared between entrepreneur and consumer in the form of rising profits and falling prices, a situation that acted as an incentive to the continued expansion of the industry. As cotton textile prices fell, demand rose and this widening of the market for cotton manufactures—along with the increasing profitability of the industry—stimulated further investment and a further demand for labour. This increased rate of capital formation raised the rate of technological diffusion, by encouraging the greater use of the new machinery and the improved productive techniques, and this in turn meant more output for less input of either labour or capital. Thus abundant cheap labour promoted new investment and so encouraged the adoption of the new technology which, by economising in both capital and labour, generated a cumulative self-reinforcing expansion in cotton production. A somewhat similar state of affairs, but on a wider industrial scale, appears to have existed in the United States from 1880 to 1913, when a massive migrant inflow provided an abundant supply of relatively cheap labour to manufacturing industry.[5]

This process of technological diffusion and economic expansion obviously depended on something more than just a plentiful labour supply for it to be sustained over time. Thus the demand for cotton textiles at home and abroad had to be highly responsive to a fall in their price so that total expenditure on these goods grew in spite of the fall in price. Furthermore, a continued expansion of investment in cotton machinery and factories depended on the willingness of entrepreneurs to plough back their profits into their businesses. As for labour supply, to say that English factory workers were relatively 'cheap' in the late eighteenth and early nineteenth centuries does not imply that they were relatively poor either in relation to workers in other occupations in Britain or to workers abroad. Indeed, to attract into the new factories, cotton manufacturers had to offer workers a higher wage than they could get elsewhere. Given the existence of underemployed or unemployed labour, however, the wage differential needed to lure workers away from other occupations need not have been very great and, quite clearly, the lower the increase that was necessary to attract an adequate labour supply, the more profitable was investment in the new cotton technology. Once the wage level for factory workers was established, moreover, a number of circumstances combined to maintain it at a relatively stable level, despite the rapidly expanding demand for labour. First, the changeover from water power to steampower allowed the cotton factories to shift into the towns, where labour was more freely available than in the countryside. Second, in the early stages of the industrial revolution in Britain the labour force was largely unskilled (or at best semi-skilled) and was therefore relatively homogeneous. This fact, which also accounts for the ease with which women and children were accommodated within the early factory workforce, helped to make the labour supply relatively elastic at a low price. Finally, workers were unable to enjoy the fruits of their increased productivity in the form of rising wages because of their lack of joint bargaining power. Trade unionism among unskilled workers has always been difficult and it was made even more difficult during this stage in Britain's industrial development by the mere abundance of labour, which meant that the labour reserve was large enough to permit most employers to dismiss their discontented workers out of hand and engage new men on the spot.

If industrial labour was cheap and in elastic supply in Britain in the years before 1850, in the United States it was dear and in short supply. American manufacturers therefore had a greater inducement than their English counterparts to adopt labour-saving devices, not only because the dearness of labour reduced the rate of profit (interest) and therefore made more capital-using methods of production profitable, but also because the shortage of labour made the choice one of either expansion by highly mechanised methods or virtually no expansion at all. Labour costs were higher relative to capital costs in the United States than in Britain for a number of reasons. First, natural resources were more easily substituted for capital than for labour in the United States. This was reflected, for example, in the greater use of wood in American machinery than in British equipment, which was built largely of iron. Since timber was abundant and cheap in the United States, it reduced the cost of machine-building there, even if the machinery was more flimsy in its construction than that produced in Britain. Second, it was easier, initially, to get machines and capital funds from abroad than labour, because of the cost of moving labour and the lag in labour's response to the growing wage differentials brought about by boom conditions in the United States. Finally, the fact that land was available in large quantities in the United States set a floor to the industrial wage. In other words, labour was relatively dear in the United States because industrialists had to pay workers something over and above what they could earn in farming on virtually free land. But labour was not only dear in the United States, its supply was also less elastic than in Britain. This came about because of the difficulty of drawing extra workers off the land at anything like the going wage, because of the difficulty of drawing workers from distant parts of the United States, and because of the difficulty of obtaining labour from overseas. In the circumstances it is not hard to explain one widely-commented-on feature of the American industrial situation which helped the spread of technology, namely, the absence of widespread industrial unrest in the face of the growing use of labour-saving techniques. Since labour was scarce, machines did not generally displace workers, but rather increased their earnings. Increased productivity due to mechanisation provided the source of these extra earnings, while the ever-present threat of a loss of labour to agriculture ensured that part of the fruits of these productivity increases were passed on to the factory workforce in the form of rising wages.

This explanation of the high rate of adoption of capital-intensive techniques by American manufacturers before 1850 can be challenged in a number of ways. It might be disputed, for example, whether labour was more expensive in the United States than in Britain at this time, both generally and, perhaps more importantly, between different types of labour skill. Indeed, even if money or real wage rates were higher in the United States than in Britain at this time, this did not necessarily mean that it was more expensive, given its high level of skill and educational attainments, its faster work pace,and its greater degree of 'technical ingenuity'. It could be argued, moreover, that since a labour shortage would have been enough in itself to induce employers to adopt labour-saving techniques, the dearness of labour as such hardly mattered. Another criticism centres on the question why American industrialists wanted to save labour costs more than capital costs, since presumably what they were interested in was reducing *total* costs. In a sense, of course, even when the American employer was endowing his workers with more capital equipment per man than his English counterpart, he achieved in fact a relative 'saving' in capital through the use of more flimsy capital equipment and a higher rate of depreciation. Another reason advanced for the American willingness to adopt labour-saving devices is based on the assumed ignorance of employers concerning their costs of production and their expectations as to the future prices of labour and capital. Given the primitive accounting techniques of the day, it is argued, employers knew their labour costs accurately but had only the haziest ideas of their capital costs. Added to this was the fact that, while the future price of capital remained uncertain, wages were subjected to a constant upward pressure, not only because of the ever-present pull of agriculture but also, and perhaps more importantly, because, unlike the European worker, American labour sought to improve its position in society and was indeed encouraged to do so by the prevailing system of social attitudes and values. In these circumstances there was a bias present in favour of saving on the known factor, which was expected to get more expensive, by adopting techniques which were not labour intensive.

After 1870 the labour supply situation in Britain and the United States began to change. By this time, however, recourse to bigger and better machines had become habit-forming in the United States as had reliance on cheap labour in Britain. In Britain, therefore, when the labour supply became relatively less abundant than earlier in the century, British employers were still thinking in terms of 'keeping wages down' and British trade unions were still resisting technical change so as to avert unemployment. Neither attitude augured well for the rapid adoption of the new labour-saving technology which was becoming increasingly more available.[6] The labour situation in the United States changed, too, with the mass migration of Europeans to the United States after 1880. As a result unskilled labour became more abundant, but technological progress of a labour-saving character had already been set in motion and continued, partly through inertia.

Wage rates for unskilled labour were held down, however, profits were maintained, and the adoption of modern technology through high rates of investment continued unchecked. In other words, the availability of abundant supplies of labour, which had played such an important part in sustaining technological diffusion in Britain before 1850, was also in part responsible for the sustained economic growth experienced by the United States during the second half of the nineteenth century.

Despite the changed circumstances in the labour supply, the American domestic market for manufactured goods continued to expand rapidly. A high rate of growth of the labour force due to immigration, even with a relatively slowly rising real wage rate, meant a faster growing demand for consumer goods of all kinds. Immigration also appears to have favourably affected the *per capita* incomes of the native population, when one might have expected it to lower real wages. Native-born workers, as managers, supervisors and skilled workers, shared in the benefits of increased productivity, along with investors and entrepreneurs, largely because unskilled foreign labour formed a non-competing group in the labour market. The competion from immigrant workers tended to reduce or hold relatively constant wages in the unskilled and semi-skilled occupations, while the expansion of the workforce brought about by the migrant inflow increased the demand for supervisory and managerial skills which the American-born workers were able to provide. If native labour was not in competition with immigrants, which was certainly true for the later immigration from southern and eastern Europe after 1880, if not for the earlier inflow from Britain, Germany and Scandinavia, wage differentials would be expected to widen, and native wages to increase rather than be lowered or maintained at a constant level. Whatever the explanation of its rising level of average income, however, America's rapid industrialisation after 1870 was based in part on a vast growth of market demand and an abundance of natural resources.

III

An industrial workforce can be created only if people are prepared to change their jobs and, often, their place of work and residence. Consequently, one of the most important characteristics of an industrialising economy is its mobility. As applied to labour, mobility has many dimensions, social as well as occupational and material.

Since change is a necessary condition for economic progress, not only must people and goods move more quickly and cheaply, but information, ideas and patterns of behaviour also have to be more mobile. In practice, labour is mobile only so far as it is dependent on wage employment. It is, for example, very hard to develop an industrial workforce in a community where everybody has all the land he needs to satisfy his requirements. This sort of situation was, as we have just seen, partly responsible for the difficulties of industrial labour recruitment in the United States before 1850. In France, too, the peasant's attachment to the soil played some part in limiting the growth of an industrial workforce in that country. Somewhat similar conditions existed in Russia late in the nineteenth century. Widespread ownership of the land was not the only restriction on labour mobility, however. The existence of institutions which limited people to particular occupations or employers, such as serfdom, caste, racial prejudice or social and religious discrimination, and of institutions which blunt the incentive to seek remunerative employment, such as the extended family system or generous social security provisions, have a similar restricting effect on mobility. In Britain, for example, it is claimed that, in so far as the Speenhamland system did influence the supply of labour in the early nineteenth century, it was more likely to have been through its effects, when taken in conjunction with the settlement laws, on the mobility of labour.[7] Fortunately for Britain, the problem of labour recruitment in the early stages of the industrial revolution appears to have been overcome by the high rates of natural increase of population in the industrialising areas, supported by a migration of workers over comparatively short distances from the rural hinterland of the industrial towns.

In part the prevailing restrictions on labour mobility were a carry-over from the mercantilist era, when the productive population had to be retained within a country in order to increase its national wealth, and population movements across borders and overseas were controlled to prevent the loss of skills and technology to competitor countries. Throughout the nineteenth century, however, these restrictions on the movement of population between and within countries were gradually relaxed, thus facilitating the process of industrialisation and economic change. The laws prohibiting the emigration of British workmen (and the export of machinery) were repealed in 1824 and British labour, like British capital, was free to move to any country willing to receive it. The removal of restrictions on emigration from Germany and Sweden followed shortly afterwards. Labour mobility within other countries was facilitated in a number of ways, including the abolition of serfdom in Russia in 1861 and the further relaxation of controls on movement that followed subsequently, and the freeing of entry into the professions and trade in Japan in 1869. On the other hand, transport improvements, like the railways, both encouraged and facilitated the movement of population. Whatever its cause this increased labour mobility not only facilitated the industrial transformation of largely agricultural communities, but it also provided an important channel for disseminating knowledge, new technology and skills.[8] It could also have been a potent cause of enterprise and improvement, especially in countries like the United States, which lacked the rather rigid social stratifications so characteristic of European communities. In such highly mobile societies as the United States, the absence of social constraints on a person's pursuit of material improvement complemented market forces in bringing about the spread of new techniques. It is true that one important element of this high degree of social mobility was education, but thrift and hard work were also important. In short, a society of weak class lines, rapid economic expansion and abundant opportunities was bound to develop a highly dynamic type of social mobility which contributed a great deal to sustaining the pace of economic progress.

IV

Technological diffusion depends as much on the relative *qualities* of the available labour force as on its relative *quantities*, since a shortage of particular types of skilled worker may well limit a country's ability to take advantage of the available technology. Yet one can easily exaggerate the problem of labour skills, and we must be careful not to attribute too many of the difficulties of industrialisation in the nineteenth century to problems of this kind. There were many industries which came into prominence during this period in which the level of skill demanded of the workforce remained relatively low. In textiles, for example, skilled labour formed a relatively low proportion of the industry's total labour requirements. Indeed, probably more than any other industry, textile manufacturing lent itself to adjustment according to the qualities of labour available to it. Expansion of the workforce in coalmining was also a relatively easy matter for most countries. In the iron industry, puddlers formed a select group on account of their strength and skill, but above all because the puddling process was a difficult one to mechanise. Their importance declined only when steel came to replace iron after the 1870s. Engineering required a wider range and higher degrees of skill than most other industries at this time. Even so, the skill required of the ordinary workers in engineering activities was no rare commodity even in the nineteenth century. Later in the century the growing use of machine tools, such as milling machines, turret lathes and grounders, made it possible for relatively unskilled workers to produce small engineering components in large numbers with a high degree of accuracy. As for the chemical industry, it never made large demands on the available labour supply. Even in Germany in 1907, for example, it employed only just over one per cent of the total workforce. More crucial to the long-run success of this industry was the ready availability of technically-trained specialists capable of carrying our research and development in this rapidly expanding scientific field. Finally, we should not forget the fact that more than one half of the capital formation undertaken in industrialising countries consisted of work in building and construction. Here the problem was often less one of shortage of skills, of masons, carpenters, etc., as one of concentrating these hitherto geographically-scattered craftsmen in the emerging industrial growth centres. Moreover, much of the workforce in construction consisted of little more than 'pick and shovel' men.

For much of this 'modern' industrial and constructional work rural skills were more than adequate. Indeed, the industrial careers of rural migrants were often largely determined before migration. Thus in Germany, rural-born workers comprised just over 50 per cent of city masons and carpenters but only 25 per cent of painters, plumbers and glazers, for whom training opportunities were limited by the greater simplicity of rural housing. Even in Russia, where the contribution of the urban population to industrialisation in numbers and above all in skills was limited by the relative underdevelopment of city life, the rural village coped adequately as the major reservoir of labour for factory industry. Within the village cottage (*kustor*) workers, both those working independently and those involved in the putting-out system or as hired hands in rural workshops, were a major source of labour supply, with some skills and occasionally some discipline. Moreover, many of these *kustor* skills had little to do with ancient rural crafts, but owed their existence to the estate factories which came into being in increasing numbers from the early eighteenth century onwards, as landowners sought out ways of processing their own produce—as in distilling, in cloth and linen manufacture, and later in sugar-refining. These pre-Emancipation factories, it is maintained, apart from disseminating new skills to 'cottage' or 'family' industries, also produced a true hereditary worker, whose descendants continued to work in post-1861 factories.[9] Furthermore, the Russian peasant was much more than a primitive cultivator. He had to be very versatile and handy with the axe, hammer and chisel, a fact which many foreign observers stressed. The German writer, Otto Geobel, even maintained that in his skill with tools the Russian worker of peasant origin was superior to his German counterpart.[10]

In the textile industries the labour force was predominantly female. In the British cotton industry, for example, the proportion of women in the workforce rose from 54 per cent in 1835 to 62 per cent by 1907. The Russian experience was similar to that of Britain's. Between 1902 and 1914 the number of women in the cotton industry rose from 195,000 to just over 318,000, and as a proportion of the industry workforce from 48 per cent to just over 56 per cent. The dependence on women workers was even greater in Japan, where the proportion of females in the textile industries' workforce was as high as 69 per cent in 1920. Indeed, the modern sector of the Japanese economy, with its bias towards light consumer goods industries, was notable for its heavy reliance on female workers, some 59 per cent of its factory operatives in 1914 being women. The rapid expansion of modern textile production in most industrialising countries during the nineteenth century suggests that they experienced little difficulty in recruiting the needed female labour. Occasionally, as in Japan between 1887 and 1893, the rapid growth of cotton production could create a labour shortage so that new mills 'stole' workers from older mills in numbers large enough to start their operations and train new recruits. But shortages of this kind were rarely more than temporary, and could generally be overcome by more intensive recruitment activity in the countryside or by some slight improvements in living or working conditions in the mill towns. Moreover, population growth was an ever-present force replenishing the supply of unskilled labour in most countries.

Where a particular type of skill was needed in the early stages of industrialisation it was often readily available. In the better-off western European countries at least there was a substantial reservoir of skilled labour in the existing craft trades and in the local joinery shops or jobbing works where the repair and maintenance of wooden and metal equipment, particularly of agriculture, were normally carried out. In almost every country, moreover, there were armament factories, which provided an important source of skilled labour as well as technological 'spin offs' in the form of safer and better explosive, new metals and more accurate machining techniques. Even when there was a local shortage of particular types of skilled labour, it could be overcome in a number of ways. Bringing in foreign workers was one obvious way in which to solve the problem. The use of mechanical methods, particularly the development of automatic 'special purpose' machines designed for a single operation, and dispensing largely with skilled labour, was another. Yet, while the further subdivision of work into simpler processes followed by their subsequent mechanisation provided one means of overcoming a lack of technically-skilled labour, it does create a correspondingly greater need for supervisors and managers to co-ordinate what is subdivided. In some countries these supervisory and managerial skills were in even shorter supply than technical skills. It should also be noted that a scarcity of skilled labour was not the only reason for the trend towards increased mechanisation. The existence of trade unions amongst skilled workers, with their restrictive practices, high wage demands and threatened strike action, was another powerful force directing energies in search of ways of economising in the use of skilled labour. Thus Richard Roberts's self-acting mule was invented in Britain in 1825 as a result of a strike by the skilled and highly independent mule-spinners of that country. Similarly, the engineering strike of 1851–2 in Britain was followed by the more rapid introduction into the industry of 'self-acting' machine tools, which displaced craft engineers and could be worked by boys and labourers at much lower wages. By the use of machines of this kind not only could the shortage of skilled labour be overcome, but also its recalcitrance in accepting the discipline and the terms of factory employment.

Where specific skills were lacking, shortages could be overcome by importing workers with the necessary training. Skill shortages plagued most pre-industrial economies, but even when industrialisation got under way in these countries, the diffusion of new techniques often needed to be backed up by foreign skills. Thus in Germany in 1861, Dundee workers were hired to teach the techniques of jute manufacture to the natives, and Ludwig Löwe brought American workers to operate his American machine tools in 1869. A similar problem of finding the proper quantity of skilled labour to work with imported technology was also apparent in the establishment of the Yokosuka shipyard in 1865. Initially there were 45 French engineers and mechanics connected with the projects, but as the supply of Japanese engineers and technicians grew, the number of Frenchmen employed in the shipyard decreased to 25 in 1876, and to one or two by 1885. Shortages of managerial and other organisational skills were often acute, particularly in the more backward economies. Though there is evidence of replacement of foreign foremen by Russian personnel trained on the job, foreigners continued to be employed right up to 1914. As late as 1913 Russian employers in the by then thoroughly russified cotton industry complained of a shortage of foremen with specialised technical qualifications. Similarly, the Russian shipping and armaments programme before 1913 was being held up by shortages of foremen, and foreign foremen had to be sought from abroad.[11] Examples of imported skills such as these can be multiplied, and something further is said on the matter later in this book (see Chapter 11, section III). The point that must be stressed here, however, is that while foreign skills were available at a price to all countries, in the final analysis a country's successful industrialisation depended upon the speed with which its traditional crafts and skills could be adapted to the requirements of modern industry.

Whereas the presence in a country of a potential supply of skilled labour suitable for industrial employment obviously in large measure depended on the nature and pattern of that country's prior economic development, once industrialisation got under way a body of skilled workers was quickly built up, even in the most backward country. Repair shops for textile machinery and for the servicing of railway rolling stock provided increased opportunities for the acquisition of skills as well as potential jumping-off points for the expansion of activity into the field of machinery manufacturing, including the building of locomotives. Moreover, even in the more backward economies, the manufacture of railway coaches and wagons, which involved a lot of woodworking, and for which wheels and axles could be imported if necessary, was always technically possible right from the start. In most countries the manufacture of agricultural machinery was also quick to catch on once the demand began to build up. Here too, the opportunities for diversifying industrial activity and thus expanding the range of skills and knowledge available to a country were always present. In Sweden, for example, de Laval, the most successful European manufacturer of cream separators, soon developed into a much more widely based engineering concern, while other Swedish firms supplying steam engines, steam saws and other equipment for the forestry industry later formed the basis of railway equipment manufacture. Similarly, Ganz, a Hungarian firm noted for the metal rollers for modern grain mills which it developed and supplied all over the world, had by the end of the century also established a world reputation in the field of electrical engineering.[12]

V

It is not enough to recruit a large industrial workforce and induce it to accept the values of an industrial society. Beyond a minimal stage of development, the major requirement is for foremen, technicians, supervisors, engineers, scientists and managers. Building up productive skills in this wider sense can be achieved in part through experience gained at the place of work. On-the-job training appears to have been an extremely important means of diffusing technical and entrepreneurial skills in the early stages of industrialisation. The fame of outstanding works in training skilled men caused budding engineers, for example, to travel far and wide to work with men such as Maudsley and John Cann in London, and Egells in Berlin. Even more crucial for successful industrial 'take-off' and sustained long-run economic growth was adequate educational provisions for the bulk of a country's population. This is borne out by an examination of the available educational statistics for the eighteenth and nineteenth centuries which suggest the following broad generalisations: first, that many of the countries that successfully followed Britain's industrial lead in the nineteenth century had a higher level of formal schooling than Great Britain at that time; and second, that in most countries which achieved substantial and sustained economic growth, formal education was either already at a high level or was raised to a high level very quickly.[13]

England at the end of the eighteenth century had one of the highest literacy rates in the world at that time. Scotland was even more advanced, and had an educational system that was superior to that of England at every level from primary schools to universities, which was hardly surprising for a country that between 1750 and 1850 converted its economy into one of the most heavily industrialised of the day. As industrialisation proceeded in England, however, there is evidence that educational provisions failed to keep pace with the progress of the economy. During these years large numbers of illiterate or semi-literate children could be found useful employment in the rapidly expanding textile industry. Furthermore, by offering increased openings for the employment of children the industrial revolution raised the opportunity cost of education and therefore reduced the demand for it. The consequence of all this was that in England, until the middle of the nineteenth century, while the economy grew, popular education stagnated. On the other hand, in western Europe, where the state was traditionally given a greater role in national affairs than it was in Britain, public opinion was quick to appreciate the educational problems of a modern society. In France, the German states, Holland, Belgium, Austria, Switzerland and the Scandinavian countries, laws were passed that made elementary education free and, with some exceptions, compulsory. Consequently, once these countries began to experience industrial expansion, laws existed that channelled a portion of their growing wealth into the education of children. In contrast to the English experience, therefore, industrial 'take-off' in these countries was always associated with educational progress.

Around the middle of the nineteenth century, the lowest rates of adult illiteracy (10–20 per cent of the adult population) were to be found in Germany, Holland, Scotland, Switzerland and the Scandinavian countries. England and Wales, along with Belgium, France and the Austrian Empire, occupied an intermediate position, registering rates of adult illiteracy of between a third and nearly one-half of the adult population. The strongholds of illiteracy (75 per cent and over) were to be found in southern and eastern Europe, namely in Portugal, Spain, southern Italy, Greece, the Balkans, Hungary and Russia. The adult illiteracy rate in Russia in 1850 has been put at around 90 per cent. As far as basic education went, the Americans were even more advanced than the Europeans. Thus according to the census of 1850, only 10 per cent of the whole population over 20 years of age was illiterate. Even allowing for some possible inaccuracy in the American figures, it is quite clear that with the possible exception of Sweden, no European country compared favourably with the United States. Literacy rates were also high in Japan where, at the time of the Restoration (1868), 40–50 per cent of all Japanese boys, and perhaps 15 per cent of girls, were getting some formal schooling outside their homes. If these estimates are accepted, they suggest a spread of literacy greater than in many European countries at a comparable stage of development.

Bt 1850, Belgium, France, Germany and Switzerland were well on their way to becoming industrial nations and by 1900 the industrial revolution had spread to other parts of Europe, with the exception of peripheral countries in the south and east, and to North America and Japan. The better educated countries were the first to import the new technology. Education favoured the diffusion of industrial technology in a number of ways. It avoided shortages of skilled and literate workers in those fields in which such workers were specifically required and, on more general grounds, it made people more adaptable to new circumstances and more receptive to new ideas. On the other hand, after the middle of the nineteenth century, and more especially after 1870, when with the growing importance of steel, chemicals, electricity and engineering, economic growth came to be more and more dependent on organised research and organised technical and scientific progress, economic progress greatly favoured the diffusion of education. The result was a rapid expansion in the school population, particularly at the elementary level. In the major industrial centres in western Europe (France, Italy, Prussia, Sweden, England and Wales) the school population aged 14 years and under grew from around 14 million in 1870 to more than 20 million by the end of the century. In these countries school attendance grew almost twice as fast as the increase in the population in the age group 5 to 14 years. A similar pattern of educational development is to be observed in other European countries. In Russia, for example, the number of children attending elementary schools grew from just under one million in the early 1870s to around 2.2 million in the late 1890s. In Japan, where the educational system was completely redesigned after 1868, almost two-thirds of the children in the age group 5 to 19 were getting elementary schooling, and a fifth went to secondary schools by the end of the Meiji period (1912).

In the training of a technical and managerial elite, Europe led the way throughout most of the nineteenth century. France had laid the foundations of advanced engineering training with the establishment of the School of Bridges and Highways in 1744, the School of Engineering in 1749, and the School of Mines in 1783. The great technical high schools were, however, a creation of the revolution, the École Polytechnique, the Conservatoire des Arts et Métiers, and the Écoles d'Arts et Métiers, which trained the lower grades of technical staff, and the first of which was established at Châlons-sur-Marne in 1806. The institution most in line with the needs of the time was perhaps the Central School of Arts and Manufacturers, which was opened in Paris in 1829, and which produced some 3,000 engineers between 1832 and 1870. These different schools gave a technical education of high quality until the beginning of the twentieth century, when they were eclipsed by the German Technical High Schools.

Germany sought a substitute for the 'spontaneous' technological originality of eighteenth-century England in education. Except in the more backward areas of east Germany, illiteracy virtually disappeared among the younger age group by 1850. Whilst agricultural and unskilled workers tended generally to have a negative attitude towards elementary education, at least until after 1860, the skilled artisan displayed an acute awareness of the value of education. At the intermediate levels of German industry, foremen and supervisors were at first recruited from the better workers within existing firms and trained on the factory floor. With time, however, the training of foremen became gradually more systematised, and the first school in Europe for the training of foremen was opened in Bochum in 1882. At a more exalted level, the German technical high schools worked to create a technological elite. These high schools, many of which achieved university status about 1900, grew out of the trade schools and polytechnics established earlier in the nineteenth century. The most famous of these was the Berliner Gewerbeschule, which was opened in 1821, and later (1902) merged with the Berliner Bauakadamie to become the Berliner Technische Hochschule. Karlsruhe boasted the first polytechnic in Germany. Established in 1825, it was reorganised in 1833, and thereafter acted as a model for several other polytechnics set up elsewhere in Germany.

Despite its relative backwardness, Russian was on the whole fairly well catered for as regards formal technical education even before Emancipation, when its universitities and engineering schools were able by 1860 to provide a comprehensive and up-to-date training in the main branches of applied science and technology. With the acceleration of industrial development in the country after the 1860s, educational facilities also expanded, and by 1912–13 there were 661 institutes of commercial and technical education in existence, including 12 higher educational establishments with a student population of close to 20,000. Of greater relevance to the formation of a skilled factory labour force, however, were the 649 middle and lower technical schools, which had an enrolment of 104,000 students in 1912–13.

The examples given above are only illustrative of the general improvement in educational facilities at all levels that took place in those countries experiencing industrial take-off in the period before 1914. Despite these educational improvements, however, it must not be forgotten that the great bulk of the technical and managerial skills built up during these years was acquired by the workforce on the factory or workshop floor. In modern industry of the day, most of the learning was done by doing.

VI

The main conclusion to be drawn from this survey of labour supply and industrialisation in the nineteenth century is that only rarely did a lack of labour or of skills hinder the spread of modern technology in those countries which experienced industrial take-off before 1914. For the most part, the locally-available supply of labour skills proved adequate to the needs of modern industrial development in its early stages, and what shortages of skills did emerge at this time could be met easily by the importation of trained labour. Moreover, once industrialisation got under way a body of skilled workers was quickly built up, even in the most backward country. Of course, the supply of foremen and supervisors continued to be a matter of concern in many industries and in some countries. But then, even today, foremanship remains perhaps the most critical level of management-labour relations in the factory, and the proper selection and training of foremen continue to demand considerable attention and thought.

Notes

1. Female employment was particularly important in the British cotton textile industry and in the Japanese silk industry.
2. C.P. Kindleberger, *Economic Growth in France and Britain, 1850–1950* (paperback edition), pp. 225-38.
3. M.E. Falkus, *The Industrialisation of Russia 1700–1914* (London, 1972), p.50.
4. Elasticity measures the *responsiveness* of one variable to changes in another variable on which the first variable depends. Thus the elasticity of the labour supply to an industry measures the increase (or decrease) in an industry's labour supply resulting from an increase (or decrease) in the price paid to labour (the wage rate). In the context of the above discussion it is argued that only a relatively small increase in the wage paid to workers in the cotton industry was sufficient to bring about a large increase in the supply of labour to the industry. This high degree of responsiveness of the labour supply was due to the low level of skills demanded in the cotton industry.
5. The continued use of capital-intensive manufacturing techniques in the US at a time when labour was becoming relatively more abundant occurred partly because by the 1880s mechanisation had become an integral part of the 'American way' of manufacturing. Moreover, mechanisation in the US reflected in part the progressive subdivision of manufacturing activities into simpler sub-processes which made fewer and fewer demands on skilled labour. This tendency facilitated the absorption of large

numbers of relatively unskilled workers in American manufacturing industries.

6. The 'cheap labour' attitude hindered technological diffusion in two ways: it limited the growth of a mass market for consumer goods and, by slowing up the rise in real wage rates, it removed a potent incentive for the introduction of labour-saving techniques.

7. Under the Speenhamland system, first introduced into Britain in 1795, magistrates began to give outdoor relief according to a scale based on the price of bread and the size of the family. Later the system was extended to make up from the rates the amount by which the wages of labourers fell short of this standard. This supplement to wages destroyed the incentive to raise wages and reduced the pressure on labour to move because of low earnings, always assuming, of course, that alterntive employment opportunities were available. Under the settlement laws, if a man left the parish in which he was domiciled, and remained in another for a full year, he lost his right to relief in the first and established a claim to it in the second. For this reason parish authorities were reluctant to receive outsiders.

8. For example, the mobility of Japanese craftsmen was high during the Meiji period, if only because an aspiring journeyman had to travel widely in order to increase his knowledge and to improve his skills. In so doing, the mobile artisans became agents of technological diffusion because of their wide exposure to techniques and opportunities in different places.

9. Olga Crisp, 'Labour and Industrialisation in Russia', in P. Mathias and M.M. Postan (eds), *The Cambridge Economic History of Europe*, Vol. VII, Part II, pp. 318, 363.

10. Crisp, loc. cit., p. 375.

11. Crisp, loc. cit., p. 399

12. For an elaboration of the points raised in this section, see S.B. Saul, 'The Nature and Diffusion of Technology', in A.J. Youngson (ed.), *Economic Development in the Long Run* (London, 1972), pp. 45-52; and A. Milward and S.B. Saul, *The Economic Development of Continental Europe 1780–1870* (London, 1973), Chapter 3.

13. C.M. Cipolla, *Literacy and Development in the West* (London, 1969), especially Chapter 3.

Selected Reading

C.M. Cipolla, *Literacy and Development in the West* (London, 1969)

H.J. Habakkuk, *American and British Technology in the Nineteenth Century* (Cambridge, 1967)

P. Mathias and M.M. Postan, *The Cambridge Economic History of Europe* (Volume 7, Part 1) *The Industrial Economies: Capital, Labour, and Enterprise* (Cambridge, 1978), esp. Chaps. 3, 6, 9 and 11, and Volume 7, Part 2, esp. Chaps. 4 and 7

S. Pollard, *The Genesis of Modern Management* (London, 1965)

S.B. Saul (ed.), *Technological Change: The United States and Britain in the Nineteenth Century* (London, 1970)

——'The Nature and Diffusion of Technology' in A.J. Youngson (ed.), *Economic Development in the Long Run* (London, 1972)

8 RESOURCE ENDOWMENT AND INDUSTRIALISATION

I

To the extent that the spread of industrialisation is dependent upon natural resources, or geographical size and location, or some other unequally distributed endowment, growth opportunities are unlikely to be equally available to all countries. It has been argued, for example, that French efforts to industrialise suffered from a shortage of raw materials, in particular coal. More generally, Professor Parker, referring specifically to the nineteenth century, when technology had not gone so far as to reduce the importance of natural resources, claims that 'Resources—mineral, agricultural and transport—were largely responsible for the direction and speed of nineteenth century development among western countries.'[1] On the other hand, there is ample evidence to show that the possession of a raw materials base is not a necessary condition of industrial development. Britain, for example, achieved industrial take-off with an industry whose basic resource input, cotton, was wholly imported. More recently, Japan, with only moderate supplies of coal and few other raw materials, has not found this resource deficiency a major obstacle to rapid industrial development.

One problem in relating resources to industrial development is the difficulty of separating land, or natural resources from capital and from technology. The economic value of an industrial raw material in its natural state will obviously depend upon its quality or grade, its transportability and its accessibility to transport facilities, to other raw materials and to markets. For these reasons, investment in cheap transport is often more important than the possession of high-grade minerals for a region's successful industrialisation, since it makes possible either the opening-up of local resource supplies or the importation of raw materials from elsewhere. Conversely, an important feature of land for industrial development is the way it lends itself to transport and communications. Mountains are an obvious barrier to transport developments, whereas plains present few obstacles to transport, whether by road, canal or railway. Rivers and the sea offer a cheap means of carriage, so that a country with a coastline indented with many natural harbours, and having a well-developed river system, is likely to have a ready-made and efficient transport network. Technology, on the other hand, may alter the economic value, if not the physical characteristics, of a given resource, as witness the increased value of coal following the invention of the steam engine and the coking process in iron manufacture, or of petroleum deposits following the invention of the internal combustion engine.

Capital investment, technology and natural resources are related in other ways too. The abundance or scarcity of resources as reflected in their relative costs of production is often an important determinant of the type of technology used in an industry and thereby a determinant of the rate at which new technology spreads within the same industry in different countries. Coke smelting, for example, was slower to catch on in Europe than in Britain for a number of reasons, including the fact that the coke smelting process did not of itself significantly reduce costs over the charcoal process where charcoal was still easily available because of an abundance of wood and cheap labour. In the United States, on the other hand, the lag in the adoption of the coking process in iron manufacture was due initially to the availability of the rich anthracite deposits of eastern Pennsylvania which postponed the introduction of coke while, at the same time, high transport costs prevented the use of this fuel from completely eclipsing pig iron production with charcoal in other parts of the country. Only with the growth of the transport network and the later discovery of high-quality coking coal in western Pennsylvania did the use of mineral fuel in the United States' iron industry become universal. In contrast to the experience with coke smelting, coke refining was quickly taken up on the Continent and in the United States, because the cost advantage of the new technique was very marked, the quality of the coal used was less important than for coke smelting, and the plant easier and cheaper to construct. In these countries, coke refining came before coke smelting, though their invention and use in Britain came in the reverse order. One other example of resource availability determining the choice of technique is to be found in the adoption of woodworking machinery in the United States before 1850 and its comparative neglect in Britain in the same period. These machines were not only labour saving, but they were also very wasteful of wood. This did not matter in the United States, where wood was cheap and abundant. In Britain, however, wood was expensive (and labour cheap), and the longer persistence of handicraft methods there than in the United States is partly explained by the fact that the handicraft processes were generally less wasteful of raw materials than the corresponding machine processes.

Natural resource availability also played an important part in determining the rate of adoption of steam power within the United States, where steam power for *motive purposes* was only slowly taken up. This came about because in the early stages of the country's industrial development, industry was concentrated largely in New England with its excellent and cheaper substitute in the form of water power provided by numerous fast-flowing rivers and streams. The growing reliance upon steam power in the United States was, in fact, closely connected with the westward movement of population and industry into a geographic region which offered fewer sources of water power and where, as a result, the economic significance of steam power was greater.[2] More generally, perhaps the most enduring and pervasive influence shaping the contours of technological development in the United States has been the very high land/labour ratio: the abundance of natural resources generally relative to a small population size. Consequently, innovation in both agriculture and industry has been directed towards making possible the exploitation of a large quantity of such resources with relatively little labour.

Any assessment of the importance of natural resources for industrial development must also take into account the fact that natural resources, capital and technology are substitutes for each other. Thus a country can compensate for a deficiency of natural resources by superior technical capability. In France and some other European countries, for example, a shortage of cheap coal led to a search for ways of reducing fuel consumption in various manufacturing processes. Thus, from the start, steam engines on the Continent far surpassed those made in Britain, while French locomotives were designed to economise on fuel despite the extra construction costs involved.[3] What these countries did in effect was to make 'fuel out of brains', and to the extent that this is possible the concept of natural resources as existing in a fixed quantity given by nature has to be modified.[4] The fact that capital and human skills can be substituted for natural resources does not make the possession of natural resources unimportant, however. Opportunities for substitution are obviously limited by capital availability and by the extent of a country's ability to develop and apply the appropriate techniques. Consequently, the more backward a country, and the smaller its supply of capital and technical skills, the more important the amount and quality of the natural resources it possesses. After a given level of development has been achieved, however, a high price for natural resources can be a stimulus to technological research and development and thus to technological diffusion and growth. Alternatively, a low price for these resources can be a handicap if it leads the country with abundant resources to ignore the technological changes that are taking place, especially those tending to conserve those resources.

Finally, one further aspect of the relationship between natural resource supply and industrial development must be noted. While it is a fact that industrialisation results in big increases in the consumption of many raw materials, this increased demand is often instrumental in bringing about an increase of supply. Indeed, it has been suggested that rather than the existence of resources leading to industrial development, industrial development leads to the discovery and use of a growing range of raw materials.[5] It follows partly from this consideration that, whatever the relevance of a domestic scarcity of natural resources as an obstacle to the diffusion of technology within a country, it must have become less important during the nineteenth century as new sources of supply were developed, and as new technical discoveries began to make alternative processes possible, or make imported resources more effective substitutes for scarce, highly-priced domestic supplies. Thus the Siemens-Martin steel-making process was of inestimable value to small producers and to countries deficient in iron ore because it allowed the use of scrap metal and because even relatively small furnaces remained highly efficient. Using this process a country like Denmark could economically use scrap to satisfy some of its own domestic demand for steel plates, and also produce highly specialised steel forgings of such quality that by 1914 seven and a quarter per cent of the steel forgings used in the British shipbuilding industry were Danish. Generally, differences in domestic resource availability may well have been a greater obstacle to technological diffusion and industrial development in the early nineteenth century than later, primarily because of the high transport costs in the earlier period. With the reduction of transport costs in international trade that occurred during the nineteenth century, however, the possession of specialised energy and mineral resources became less and less important. Trade came to substitute for industrial raw materials as it did for arable land. Improved transport facilities not only increased the output of industrial raw materials, by opening up new sources of supply, but they also provided the means of carrying the output to the centres of expanding raw material consumption.

The main conclusion to be drawn from this brief survey of the relationship between natural resources availability and industrialisation is that lack of natural resources appears to have played little part in hindering the spread of modern industrial technology. Indeed, as with the continued adherence to charcoal smelting on the Continent during the first half of the nineteenth century, an abundance of a given natural resource may just as often act as a barrier to the introduction of a new technology as a deficiency of resources. Even with limited resources much modern industrial development is still possible, given the availability of capital, technical skills and entrepreneurship, as the industrialisation of such countries as Japan and Switzerland has shown. Over time the range of substitutability to overcome an absence of specialised resources has continuously widened, while improved transportation facilities and an expansion of domestic and foreign trade has provided an increasingly more important means of overcoming the natural resource deficiency of a country wishing to industrialise. But, having made the point that resource deficiency was not an insuperable obstacle to industrial development in the nineteenth century, it is well to remember that the presence of resources in a country does help growth to begin and does support the ongoing process of industrialisation.

II

The extent of a country's natural resource endowment is in part a function of the country's geographic size. Consequently, size is one possible determinant of a country's potentiality for economic growth through the diffusion of modern technology. Size in this context can be viewed either in spatial terms or in terms of the industrial structure, that is, the size composition of the firms that make up a given industry.

For 'small' nations the problem of geographic size is reflected primarily in the fact that they tend to possess less-varied natural resources. Such countries, too, often have small populations, which means that their domestic markets are not large enough to support certain industries at the minimum scale of efficient operation. On the other hand, small nations sometimes do have some advantage in the industrial field, whether it is in the processing of locally-produced primary products or in the prior existence of some industry on which further industrial development could be based. As an example of the latter development we may instance Switzerland, where the presence of a relatively advanced textile industry provided a sound basis for an engineering industry through repair and machine building, and for a chemical industry able to supply it with bleaches and dyes.

A limited domestic market could, of course, be overcome by the development of an export trade in manufactures, and here the smaller countries were much favoured by the character of world trade before 1914. Tariffs were generally low, and there were several important industries where the full advantages of large-scale production did not become immediately apparent. Consequently, many small countries were able to build up a highly-specialised export trade in a number of manufacturing fields, including the high-quality electrical machinery, diesels and turbines made in Switzerland, the marine engines of Denmark and Holland, the glassware of Belgium, and so on.[6] Foreign trade could also support a small country's industrial development by allowing it to import manufactured components not produced locally, for example, the rough forgings and steel plates imported from Germany by the highly successful Dutch shipbuilding industry. More generally, however, the growth of a 'small' country's export trade, whether in primary products and/or manufactures, was often essential to its successful industrial development. Thus Sweden, with its small population, had abundant and varied natural resources which provided a flow of exports, in the form of grain, timber products and iron ore, with which to pay for the import of industrial raw materials, such as wool, cotton, chemicals and metal ores and manufactures, amongst others, which were essential to the growth and development of its manufacturing industry. Likewise, in Denmark, the agricultural sector provided the export base for imports of railway equipment, iron and steel, machine tools and machinery in general, and coal, with which to feed local industry. Even in the absence of an industrial demand for markets and inputs, foreign trade will always play a more significant role in the economic development of a small country than of a large one. This follows if only because the small country, whilst having a consumer demand pattern roughly similar to that of a large country, will have a less-diversified output from which to satisfy it. Consequently, the small country will need to import certain types of commodities. Small countries cannot use foreign trade as a complete offset to their productive deficiencies, however. Certain goods and services, such as construction work, transportation and communications networks, medical and educational services, and so on, cannot be imported, although they have to be provided for the community. Therefore these industries may not be worked at maximum efficiency in small countries, and the adoption by them of more sophisticated techniques may suffer as a result.

Finally, it must be noted that for 'small' countries, the ease of attaining unity, whether political or economic, may facilitate decision-making and reduced the problem of communication. This could mean a greater rapidity in adjusting to change and in accepting the introduction of new ideas and new ways of doing things.[7] At the same time, as we have mentioned earlier, certain nineteenth-century technological advances, such as the Siemens-Martin process of steel-making, clearly favoured the small nation. The fact that Martin steel was good for shipbuilding provided a further boost to the industrial development of some small countries, for example Holland and Denmark. As a general conclusion then, geographical size is a mixed blessing as far as industrial growth and the diffusion of technology are concerned. Limited natural resources, limited markets and a limited supply of skilled labour can act as serious obstacles to industrial development, especially when economies of large-scale production become important. On the other hand, 'smallness' undoubtedly confers benefits when the communication of new knowledge becomes necessary, always assuming that the technical innovation is appropriate to the small country's particular economic circumstances, and always assuming that the supporting factors are present—entrepreneurial talent, labour skills, market opportunities, and so on. All in all, however, whatever the advantages conferred on a small country, its economic circumstances force it to specialise heavily in the industrial field and to depend increasingly on the export of a highly-competitive, but limited, range of manufactured products if it wishes to benefit fully from the use of modern industrial technology.

III

Modern industrial technologies exhibit strong tendencies toward the geographic concentration of productive activity. Technical indivisibilities, which dictate very large producing units far in excess of local needs, heavy reliance upon the use of geographically-concentrated fossil fuels as energy resources, regional specialisation of a highly productive agricultural sector: these factors create a powerful trend toward geographic concentration of manufacturing industry. Moreover, since large population centres hold out to industrial firms the added attractions of large markets for their output as well as specialised services which are not available in smaller communities, the trend toward a higher degree of spatial concentration of industry has tended to be reinforced over time. Only with the more recent arrival of the internal combustion engine, new energy sources, such as oil and electricity, and refrigeration has the trend towards concentration been reversed.

The tendency toward the geographical concentration of industry was not new. Even in the pre-industrial economy, the need for fuel and power in certain industries in quantities beyond that provided by human or animal muscle caused the main locations to be where fuel (mainly wood) and power from water and wind were availabile. This was true, for example, of flour mills, fulling mills, iron making and metal working. In the nineteenth century, however, the trend towards industrial concentration was powerfully reinforced with the growing use of coal both as a fuel and as a power source in the steam engine. The effect of this technological development is seen clearly in Europe where modern industry remained concentrated in only a few countries. As late as 1914 the United Kingdom, France and Germany accounted for more than 70 per cent of Europe's manufacturing capacity. The predominance of these three countries was particularly striking in the output of steel, machinery and chemicals. They produced about 80 per cent of Europe's output in each of these industries. Their share in the textile industries was also high and in cotton textiles it reached almost three-quarters of European production. The industrial concentration in these three countries is primarily explained by the distribution of energy in Europe. Of the European countries, the United Kingdom, France and Germany in 1914 produced over 90 per cent of the European coal output. The remainder was mined largely in Belgium and the Austro-Hungarian Empire, both of which countries had industrial structures similar to that of each of the Big Three. The principal heavy industrial region of Tsarist Russia evolved on coalfield in the Donbas region of the Ukraine. On the eve of the 1917 Revolution this area provided about three-quarters of the country's industry, about 50 per cent, was, however, concentrated in the Moscow industrial region, which was largely devoid of fuel and industrial raw materials. But a well-developed transport network and a large population, which provided the country's major mass market and biggest supply of workers of all skills, served as the basis for the region's continued industrial development. The only other industrial region of significance in Russia at this time was centred on St Petersburgh (Leningrad). It possessed advantages similar to those of the Moscow industrial region as well as being the leading port in north-western Russia. At an early date it developed manufacturing based on imported raw materials and industrial equipment.

The direct use of water power continued to be important in industrial location in the Atlantic coast areas of north-east United States for some time after it had begun to decline in Britain, and steam power played little part in manufacturing until the second half of the nineteenth century. After 1850 the pattern of industrial location in the United States began to change. The shift of industry to the Midwest (where fast-flowing rivers were relatively few) increased the cost of water power and led to increased use of wood, and later coal, for energy and fuel purposes. With the growing importance of coal a new industrial region began to take shape in western Pennsylvania and north-eastern Ohio, around Pittsburgh and Cleveland. After 1860, with the development of the Lake Superior iron ore field, this industrial belt was extended on through northern Ohio, northern Indiana, southern Michigan, northern Illinois and south-east Wisconsin, and became the leading industrial region of the United States and of the world. With easy access to coal and iron ore, this region soon accounted for the overwhelming portion of the country's iron and steel output, and along with it a large part of all those industries which used iron and steel in fabrication.[8]

Technical advances, especially towards the end of the nineteenth century, tended to decrease the pull of coal on industry, But the world's major coalfields had by this time further advantages to offer industry in the form of social overhead capital, labour supplies, communications networks and markets. Important economies continued to be obtained in the use of coal both as a fuel and as a power source in the steam engine, especially in those countries with limited supplies of the fuel. New primary sources of energy also came into being. The first oil well was sunk in western Pennsylvania in 1859, and kerosene began to replace whale oil as a source of light. Subsequently, as the techniques of using oil were developed, this new source of energy opened up new industrial possibilities and also began to compete with coal in established transport and industrial uses, encouraging changes in industrial location. The use of electricity has profoundly changed the structure and the role of energy supplies in modern industry, and has had certain important consequences for the location of industrial activity. While the generation of electricity made use of coal, and in this century fuel oil, the tapping of the great potential of hydro-electric power has led to a revival of interest in water power sites. Although, because of its mobility, electricity enables power to be available in new locations, it also enables power to be provided for old locations and centres of manufacturing activity. In this way, therefore, the use of electricity may serve to some extent to reinforce existing patterns of location.

Notes

1. See W.N. Parker, 'Comment', in J.J. Spengler (ed.), *Natural Resources and Economic Growth* (Resources for the Future, Washington, DC, 1961), p. 160.
2. Although the availability of a good substitute slowed the pace at which the stationary steam engine was acquired in the United States, the situation was vastly different in the application of steam power to transportation where, because of the large land area of the United States, the steamboat and later the railway provided a means for the cheap movement of goods, especially bulky agricultural products.
3. See S.B. Saul, 'The Nature and Diffusion of Technology', in A.J. Youngson (ed.), *Economic Development in the Long Run* (London, 1972), p. 37.
4. 'The chemical industry provides a good example both of resources and an endogenous factor in growth and of the stimulus of inadequate supplies of raw materials. It was technological progress which made resources out of previously unnoticed materials, such as pyrites, brown coal, bauxite, and phosphate rock . . . The whole history of the industry . . . is change in technology. And it was most often in response to resource problems that change took place.' See P.M. Hohenberg, *Chemicals in Western Europe: 1850–1914* (Chicago, 1967), pp. 43-4.
5. C.P. Kindleberger, *Economic Growth in France and Britain 1851–1950* (New York, 1964), pp. 34-5.
6. The ability of a small country to develop an export trade in manufactures was helped by the fact that, even when it exported a large proportion of its total domestic output of a particular manufacture, its output (and) export capacity was often small relative to world supply. Thus as late as 1913, Denmark's merchant shipbuilding capacity was only about one per cent of total world output, while the foreign trade capacity of Belgium and Switzerland varied between 2 and 3 per cent of world trade during most of the nineteenth century.
7. This could well have been an important factor in the early industrial development of Belgium and in the modernisation and restructuring of Danish agriculture after 1850, which was so essential to the growth of modern manufacturing industry in that country.
8. Ready access to raw materials was also a feature of another important segment of American industry, that dealing with the slaughtering of animals, the preserving and canning of food and the grinding of grain. Along with the timber industry, these forms of manufacturing were early in evidence in most regions of recent settlement, such as Canada and Australia, as well as in a number of European countries.

Selected Reading

C.P. Kindleberger, *Economic Growth in France and Britain, 1851–1950* (New York, 1964), Chap. 2

S. Kuznets, *Six Lectures on Economic Growth* (New York, 1959)

W.N. Parker, 'Technology, Resources, and Economic Change in the West', in A.J. Youngson (ed.), *Economic Development in the Long Run* (London, 1972)

S.B. Saul, 'The Nature and Diffusion of Technology', in A.J. Youngson (ed.), *Economic Development in the Long Run* (London, 1972)

J.J. Spengler, *Natural Resources and Economic Growth* (Washington, DC, 1961)

N. Rosenberg, 'Technological Innovation and Natural Resources: the Niggardliness of Nature Reconsidered', in N. Rosenberg, *Perspectives on Technology* (Cambridge, 1976)

9 THE TECHNICAL FACTOR IN INDUSTRIALISATION

I

The technical characteristics of innovations also bear on the speed with which they become diffused. Broadly speaking, the more complex the innovation and therefore the more difficult it is to assimilate, the slower the likely rate of adoption. This attribute of complexity covers not only the mechanical and operational difficulties of the technique but also the economic characteristics and consequences of adoption, the ease with which optimum use can be achieved and, in the case of a managerial technique, its mental complexity. The rate of diffusion of an innovation will also be determined by its compatibility with existing techniques. This is partly a technical and partly a cultural attribute. The new technology may well have to be modified to meet local conditions and, because technology is a process, various time-consuming adjustments and preparations may be necessary before the new technique can be fitted into preexisting procedures, habits and work methods. Finally, it has been argued that technological change in the nineteenth century was both generated and, eventually, institutionalised in a very special way.

> It emerged in large measure as an accumulation of solutions to a wide range of technical problems on the part of a group of specialized firms in the manufacturing sector which was uniquely oriented towards these problems. These firms were the producers of capital goods—producers of the machinery and equipment which were used as inputs in other sectors of the economy. Their growing skill in solving problems in specialized machine production ought to be regarded as the basic learning process underlying nineteenth century industrialisation.[1]

Crucial to this process was the machine tool industry which played a central role in the acquisition and diffusion of the skills and techniques required in a modern industrialising economy.

123

II

As the nineteenth century progressed, technological innovation became more complex with the emergence of science-based industries such as steel and chemicals, and the introduction of technical changes which encouraged the growth of firms geared to large-scale production for the supply of mass markets. Until well into the nineteenth century most businesses were small, mainly because technical and marketing conditions were such that there was seldom any advantage to be derived from a larger scale of operations. Lack of capital was a further limitation on the growth of firms as long as they remained almost wholly dependent on internal funds. Where heavy investment in fixed capital was necessary, however, for example in railways, dock construction and public utilities, the one-man enterprise or the partnership could not provide the funds needed to finance such undertakings, and so public company formation became necessary to raise the funds by appeal to the general public. This need of access to personal savings became even more pressing as the course of technical change widened the range of industries—steel, chemicals, electrical and heavy engineering, motor car manufacture—in which heavy investment was possible.

By the end of the nineteenth century the capital and market requirements for successful industrialisation had changed significantly. The size of the effort required to enter an industry had become much larger and the difficulties far greater. The interdependence of the various sectors of the economy had also increased enormously, and growth based on one sector—the textile industry or railways—was replaced by a multi-sectoral advance. Heavy technical concentration, a higher capital intensity per worker, was combined with a need for improvement in the management and organisation of the firm. As the scale of operations increased, managerial responsibilities increased, the risks of failure became greater and the need for more formal and objective decision-making became acute. These developments only served to make industrialisation more difficult for the latecomers to the field. It also meant that when industrialisation did take place in these countries, their tendency to adopt the most up-to-date technology in any particular industrial field almost invariably led to the emergence of industrial structures dominated by large firms.

Nevertheless, if the growing complexity of industrial equipment, capital markets and managerial expertise meant that a country's opportunities for industrial development became more circumscribed as the nineteenth century progressed, the growth in the average size of the firm and the changes in the industrial structure that these developments brought about may have subsequently encouraged the spread of technology. Other things being equal, one would expect the big firm, with its stronger finances and its wider knowledge of markets and production techniques, to be better placed to take advantage of a new technology when it appears. One would also expect technology to diffuse faster in a one-firm industry than in one composed of a large number of small firms, if only because in the former just one firm has to be convinced of the advantages of the new technology for its adoption to become complete for the industry. In general, statistical investigations suggest a link between the size of the firm and the speed of its response to innovations. Large firms tend to respond faster not only because they operate within a more favourable set of financial and market conditions than do small firms, but also because the technical conditions prevailing within large firms often favour the adoption of new technology. Thus the bigger the firm the more likely it is that at any one time there will be items of equipment to replace. Moreover, large-scale and integrated operations are often necessary for the successful adoption of many new techniques. Thus some of the new textile technologies developed in the nineteenth century, such as ring spinning and the Northrop loom, were for technical reasons better suited to the American mills, which combined cotton spinning and weaving, than to the unintegrated British industry. On the other hand, it is presently impossible to draw any firm conclusions about the nature of the relationship between the degree of business concentration in an industry and the rate of technological diffusion in that industry, little research having been done in the field. There is some evidence for this century that suggests that the degree of business concentration in an industry is not a significant factor in the diffusion of technology, but the studies of the relationship carried out to date remain limited in number and extent and, consequently, it is perhaps best to suspend judgement on the matter for the time being.

III

The most obvious point to make bearing on the character of an innovation is that the speed of its diffusion will be faster the greater is the improvement over existing methods or goods represented by the new process or product. Where the new technology represents a vast improvement on the old, so that costs of production and hence price of the product are substantially reduced, the old technology is likely to be swept away overnight. This was the case, for example, with the Hall-Héroult process of aluminium manufacture (1886) which reduced production costs over the older method of manufacture by something like 75 per cent. More generally, however, the cost reductions resulting from an innovation are likely to be less striking and, in these circumstances, the age structure of an industry's capital stock will influence the speed with which new processes are adopted. In this situation diffusion, at least initially, will occur much more rapidly in an industry currently producing a relatively larger proportion of its output with machines of an older vintage. There is, however, one important way in which a relatively high proportion of old equipment is an obstacle to diffusion. This is where the introduction of a new process depends upon the existence of up-to-date complementary equipment. An oft-cited illustration of the simple, yet frequently encountered, problem of technical interrelatedness and incompatibility in manufacturing industry is the claim that the inadequacy of the floor layout, pillar spacing and lighting arrangements in existing factory buildings hampered the installation of new, more automatic equipment in the British cotton textile industry. Another example of this kind of obstacle to the use of an improved technique is to be found in the large investment needed to modify the coal-screens, weighbridges and railway sidings at collieries, as well as later coal-loading facilities at the ports before the railway companies in late nineteenth-century Britain could replace their inefficiently small ten-ton railway coal wagons with wagons of a larger capacity.[2]

The rate of spread of modern industrial technology between regions and countries is also often influenced by the need to modify the technology before it can function successfully in a new environment. Thus the widespread use of the steam engine in a country such as France, which lacked adequate supplies of coal, depended on technical efforts to improve the efficiency of the engine through fuel economies. Such a process of technical modification often involves a high order of skill and ability, and a country's capacity to achieve such modifications and adaptations was often critical to its successful industrialisation. This need for modification if a new technology was to be transferred successfully to a new environment partly accounts for the length of the observed historical lag in the spread of industrialisation between regions and countries. But even when a new technology was fully compatible with a given environment, it usually asserted its advantage over the old only slowly. This is partly because it takes time to eliminate all the 'bugs' from the new system, and partly because time is needed for the capital goods industries to produce the new technology efficiently and thus more cheaply and so making investment in it by user firms more profitable and less open to the risk of breakdown and faulty performance. Moreover, improvement often continues to be made in the old technology, as was the case with the water turbine long after the introduction of the Watt steam engine, thus prolonging its eventual replacement by the new.

IV

Within the manufacturing sector of an industrialising economy the growth and development of the capital goods industries have a key part to play in the diffusion of new technology. Since technological progress is incorporated in the plant and equipment used to produce output, the industries producing this capital equipment are especially important for both successful innovation and the successful diffusion of those innovations. Whether an invention can be put to productive use will depend largely on the state of development of the capital goods industries in the sense that, for example, a well-developed knowledge of metallurgy and the capacity to perform reliable precision work with metals was critical in the construction of the machinery and equipment which typified industrialisation in the eighteenth and nineteenth centuries.[3] Moreover, the spread of the construction and use of this machinery and equipment to other countries through a process of imitation will depend to a significant extent on whether these skills and knowledge are present in the labour forces of these other countries. Technological diffusion between and within countries is also assisted by improvements in the manufacture of capital goods which reduce their prices and therefore encourage their adoption in the industries using them. Obviously the steeper the fall in capital goods' prices the greater the profitability of using them and hence the faster their rate of diffusion. These price reductions have more general effects, however, in that they affect investment activity as a whole, and because they are capital-saving for the economy as a whole. The capacity of the capital goods sector of an economy to innovate and to bring about improvements in existing techniques, both those used within the industry and those manufactured for use in other industries, is also vitally important in overcoming the problem of the *complementarity* in productive activity between different techniques. That is to say, the realisation of the full potential of a given innovation often depends upon *other* innovations that relax or bypass constraints which would otherwise hinder its diffusion. Achieving the full benefits of mechanised cotton spinning techniques, for example, was possible only with the development of mechanised weaving. More generally, improved means of transport, in particular railways, were often crucial to the growth of markets of a size sufficient to make the adoption of mechanised manufacturing economically viable. In short, the ability of the capital goods industry to assimilate inventions, improve techniques and modify them to meet the needs of specialised users, thereby reducing the prices of capital goods, was an important determinant of the rate of diffusion of modern industrial technology.[4]

As we have already noted,[5] the skills and technical knowhow needed to develop the capital goods industries in an industrialising economy came from a variety of sources. In part they were to be found in the indigenous craft industries. A more important source of machine-building skills was the numerous repair and maintenance workshops which had already existed in the pre-industrial economy, servicing agriculture mainly, or those that came into existence with industrialisation as part of the modernising textile industry or the railways. With time, and increased specialisation, these repair shops also built machinery and later hived off from the parent firm to become independent engineering enterprises. As these firms achieved success as producers of machinery they came to diversify their product, extending, say, out of textile machinery into the manufacture of steam engines, turbines, mill machinery and (more important) machine tools, that is, the production of the types of plant and equipment used by the capital goods sector itself. As Rosenberg has shown, the emergence of multi-product engineering firms was possible because nineteenth-century industrialisation was characterised by the invention of a relatively small number of broadly similar productive techniques which could be applied to a large number of industries and to a wide range of products. Thus the machinery requirements and processes of firearms manufacture were broadly applicable to sewing-machine manufacture and to the production of typewriters. Later they were adopted in the manufacture of bicycles. It was this phenomenon of *'technical convergence'*, that is, the tendency for a limited number of manufacturing techniques to have widespread application in the production of commodities, which led to the emergence in the nineteenth century of multi-product firms specialising by process rather than by type of product.[6] In these circumstances quite small workshops could be transformed into machine and machine–tool making establishments in response to the demands of specific customers and, once new skills and techniques were developed in these firms, they became transmission centres for the transfer of new skills and techniques to the entire machine-using sector of the economy. Escher, Wyss and Sulzer in Switzerland, Cockerill in Belgium, Sharp, Stewart and Fairbairn in Britain, Ganz in Hungary, and Koechlin and Schlumberger in France, all followed this course of growth and development while, in the United States, the Baldwin locomotive works, among others, grew out of a firm previously devoted to textile-printing machinery.

In line with Rosenberg, Trebilcock has stressed the importance of the British armaments industry as a source of technical innovation and 'spin-off' in the late nineteenth century. While there is some evidence of 'spin-off', in the sense of a transfer of new techniques from military to civilian uses, in the period before 1870, a *systematic* 'spin-off' had to wait

> until an advanced metallurgical, machine tool, and chemical technology had grown up. A two-way process was involved: arms techniques had to draw upon these disciplines, before, in its turn, it could hand down useful instruction to industry at large. In this respect things began to change in the 1870s and the 1880s when a distinctively modern arms engineering sector started to develop [in Britain]. It was coaxed into existence by the greater availability of government contracts to private firms as the state monopoly of arms production was gradually dismantled.[7]

With the growth of private arms manufacturing, firms like Vickers, Palmer and Armstrong began to play an important role in developing new alloys and new techniques of metal-drawing and cutting which were to prove of great importance in assisting the growth of heavy machine–tool production in Britain. In shipbuilding, improvements in warship design were subsequently incorporated in merchant vessels, and the application of the steam turbine to shipping followed a similar sequence in its use. Of course, not all of these technical advances originated within the arms firms. High-speed machine tool steel was an American invention, and Charles Parsons, a Tyneside marine engineer, was responsible for the invention of the turbine. But other advances, notably the new alloys, were direct products of arms technology. However, even in the case of those techniques which came from outside the armaments industry, the arms manufacturers performed early development work which was hardly less important than the inventor's own contribution. In Trebilcock's own words, 'Above all, the armourers emerged as adepts in the art of giving a lead to the rest of industry ... Their role was to elaborate and popularize as well as to innovate.'[8]

'Technical convergence' was also present in the industry after 1880, particularly in the rifle trade, which made great use of the principle of interchangeability. Given their knowledge of repeat production and standardisation, arms firms were naturally attracted towards the biycle and motor car segments of general engineering where these techniques were particularly appropriate. In companies like Birmingham Small Arms (BSA) rifle, bicycle and motor-cycle products developed side by side between 1880 and 1914. Apart from the link between 'military' and 'civilian' production provided by acquired skills in standardised production, the expansion of arms manufacturers into civilian production was dictated by the need to find alternative lines of manufacture to provide employment in years of slack government orders. For the same reason, shipyards specialising in the construction of warships continued to build merchant ships.

Finally, it must be noted that Trebilcock has also argued that the armament schemes sponsored by British firms in many European countries late in the nineteenth century provided channels through which flowed a technology which represented 'best practice' methods to the highest Western standard. This flow of technology represented a significant contribution to the growth potential of many industrialising economies like Russia, Japan and Italy in the period between 1890 and 1914.[9] The significance of these developments for Japan's industrial growth has been described by Yamamura, who claims that the arsenals and government shipyards which spearheaded Meiji Japan's technological progress were important both because they were large (enterprises) by Meiji standards and because many of them aided private, non-military shipyards and factories. In particular, they provided steam engines, many types of machinery and machine tools which enabled the cotton textile and other industries to take the initial steps towards rapid growth.[10]

Notes

1. N. Rosenberg, *Technology and American Economic Growth* (New York, 1972), pp. 88-9.
2. A more up-to-date example of this problem as it affects British railways today is the heavy investment in new signalling equipment needed to allow the use of the new high-speed trains developed by British Rail.
3. Thus the commercial practicability of the Watt steam engine was realised only with Wilkinson's invention of the boring mill (1774), which made possible the manufacture of reasonably accurate cylinders.
4. In this paragraph we have leaned heavily on N. Rosenberg's article, 'Factors Affecting the Diffusion of Technology', *Explorations in Economic History*, Vol. 10, 1972, pp. 3-33. Within the capital goods sector, Rosenberg singles out the machine tool industry for special mention.
5. See Chapter 7, section III.
6. N. Rosenberg, 'Technological Change in the Machine-Tool Industry, 1840–1910', *The Journal of Economic History*, Vol. XXIII, 1963.
7. C. Trebilcock, ' "Spin-off" in British Economic History: Armaments and Industry 1760-1914', *Economic History Review*, December 1969, pp. 478-9. In the late eighteenth century, as Trebilcock points out, guncasting techniques and material requirements played a significant role in promoting the development respectively of the Watt steam engine and Cort's puddling process.
8. Trebilcock, loc. cit., p.484.
9. C. Trebilcock, 'British Armaments and European Industrialisation 1890–1914' *Economic History Review*, May, 1973, p. 116.
10. Kozo Yamamura, 'Success Illgotten? The Role of Meiji Militarism in Japan's Technological Progress', *Journal of Economic History*, March, 1977, p. 116.

Selected Reading

N. Rosenberg, 'Technological Change in the Machine-tool Industry, 1840–1910', *Journal of Economic History* (December 1963)
—— 'Factors Affecting the Diffusion of Technology', *Explorations in Economic History* (Fall, 1972)
—— *Perspectives on Technology* (Cambridge, 1976)
S.B.Saul, 'The Nature and Diffusion of Technology', in A.J. Youngson (ed.), *Economic Development in the Long Run* (London, 1972)
C. Trebilcock, ' "Spin-off" in British Economic History: Armaments and Industry 1760-1914', *Economic History Review* (December 1969)
—— 'British Armaments and European Industrialisation 1890-1914', *Economic History Review* (May 1973)
Kozo Yamamura, 'Success Illgotten? The Role of Meiji Militarism in Japan's Technological Progress', *Journal of Economic History* (March 1977)

10 INDUSTRIALISATION AND ENTREPRENEURSHIP

I

Entrepreneurs are frequently singled out as the key force that made possible the whole process of modern economic growth. In so far as output growth is dependent on the rate at which opportunities for technical and economic innovation are perceived and exploited, a vital role of economic leadership obviously has to be performed in any country wishing to modernise its economy. There must be what economists call entrepreneurs: men who possess the ability to recognise opportunities for the successful introduction of new comodities, new productive methods and new material resources, and are capable of assembling the necessary plant and equipment, management and labour force and organising them into a going concern. Although on the basis of this definition of entrepreneurship, the distinctive characteristic of entrepreneurs is that they fulfil in one person the function of capitalist, innovator, manager, merchant and salesman, economists and economic historians have tended to emphasise one or other of these functions as being of overwhelming importance in unleashing the forces of modern industrial growth.

For example, Schumpeter saw the entrepreneur as an innovator, whose job it was to introduce a new commodity into the market, use a new productive method, open up a new market, develop a new source of raw material supply, or completely reorganise an existing industry. In performing this function an entrepreneur might supply capital or technical expertise to an enterprise, nevertheless he was neither a capitalist nor a technician. For Schumpeter, the essential function of entrepreneurship consisted in creating something new in the market place.

The trouble with this definition of entrepreneurship is that it is unduly restrictive even when it is the act of innovation alone that is the function under consideration. As we have already argued, in bringing about the spread of modern industrial technology a vital part is played not only by innovators responsible for the introduction of new industrial techniques, but also by those far more numerous people and institutions responsible for the spread of the new technology both within and between countries. In this process of industrial diffusion, besides the clearly exceptional business personalitites, there is always a large number of men who make minor but still important innovations, and many more who are imitators and followers whose activity nevertheless involves a considerable degree of initiative and vigour. Consequently, it is not the appearance of a handful of remarkable 'captains of industry' which has to be explained when we consider the problem of technological diffusion, but the emergence of a large social group concerned with promoting and supporting the spread of industrial activities. Indeed, given the existence of unapplied production techniques and the existence of markets, innovators of the type envisaged by Schumpeter may be largely irrelevant. What is needed in these circumstances is people capable of solving the operational problems of matching a new technology with qualitatively ill-fitting local factors of production, obtaining adequate investible funds, adapting existing techniques and organisations to the demands of the new technology, improvising substitutes for non-available skills and materials, and so on. Finding a solution to these problems will more often than not represent the critical entrepreneurial function in the late-industrialising country.[1]

For some economic historians, however, to assume the existence of markets is to beg the question. To the extent that the introduction of modern industrial technology depends on the size of the market, they argue, successful entrepreneurship owes as much to a grasp of commercial opportunity as it does to a capacity to apply and develop a new technology. British economic historians in particular have tended to stress the importance of the entrepreneurial marketing function, which is not surprising, given that Britain's pioneer industrialists were often under pressure to search out new markets in which to sell their expanding industrial output. On the other hand, entrepreneurs in some following countries were not faced with such acute marketing problems, if only because domestic producers in these countries were often able to substitute their output for imported products, or because the state offered a guaranteed market for industrial output as an incentive to entrepreneurs to adopt the new technology.[2] Where the domestic demand for industrial products was small, however, as in the case of Switzerland, Denmark, Sweden or Holland, industrial entrepreneurs were faced with the need to expand into foreign markets if the use of the new industrial technology was to be profitable. Searching out such markets, often with a view to supplying the demand for some high-quality or highly-specialised product, involved marketing skills of a high degree.

Economists, on the other hand, have stressed the entrepreneur's function as an organiser of productive activity, in the sense that there must be present some element or factor which combines the inputs of land, labour, capital and technology in the right proportions, sets the task and sees to its accomplishment. Of crucial importance here is the capacity of the entrepreneur to lead other men in a common undertaking, for whereas in pre-industrial societies the small trader or handicraft master could operate with few or often without any assistants, an industrial entrepreneur typically must have a group of men whose labour he must organise and direct. Moreover, as industrial development proceeded and the firm grew in size, decision-making, of critical and routine sorts, became more complex while affording at the same time growing opportunities for the specialisation of function within the firm's organisational structure. During the industrial revolution in Britain the entrepreneurial functions of capitalist manager and innovator more often than not were performed by one individual, but during the nineteenth century, as firms grew in size, a splitting-up of these functions took place. To begin with, around the middle of the nineteenth century, following the introduction of limited liability, which made it possible for firms to obtain funds from a growing number of investors, the function of 'capitalist' tended to become a separate one. Later still, with the continued increase in the size of the business enterprise, a second functional split occurred with the growing division between 'strategic decision-making' and the routine management of the firm. In this situation the entrepreneur was the planner, innovator and ultimate decision-maker in the firm, whereas the day-to-day management of the enterprise became the function of salaried company officials. The fact that the basic entrepreneurial function tended to change over time has had obvious repercussions on the nature of the demand for entrepreneurial talent, particularly in those countries that were latecomers to industrialisation. It increased the need for a wider range of managerial abilities as well as a higher level of technical competence than were necessary during earlier industrialisation efforts. Both developments placed increased emphasis on a country's need for educated manpower.

II

Given that the performance of the entrepreneurial function, however defined, is crucial to the process of industrial development, what determines the supply of entrepreneurial ability? The available historical evidence suggests that the supply of entrepreneurs may be limited by economic circumstances, by social structure and by the prevailing social attitudes towards entrepreneurs. In most industrialising countries in the nineteenth century strictly economic limitations do not appear to have been of major importance, and consequently some economic historians consider entrepreneurial supply to have played a largely passive part in the industrialisation process whose major themes were invention, changing factor prices and new market opportunities. In this scheme of things the supply of entrepreneurial services is regarded as being highly elastic, given a favourable economic environment, and given the existence of a strong psychological drive for profit making. Once the assumption of a reasonably well-functioning modernising economy is relaxed, however, and ignorance, fragmented markets, limited mobility of capital and labour, lumpiness of capital investment, government controls and the non-availability of inputs, are brought into the picture, then the possibility of limited supply of entrepreneurial services becomes apparent.

The fundamental difficulty with the purely economic approach to the problem of entrepreneurial supply is that it can neither be disproved nor established unequivocally that economic factors and market incentives alone are its major determinants. It is always difficult to know how much importance we should attribute to the entrepreneur as such, and how much to the economy in which he works, to the nature of the market he supplies, to the quality of the workforce and the extent of the natural resources available to him. How far, for example, was the rapid growth of the American economy during the nineteenth century the result of the existence of a vigorous entrepreneurial class and how far was it the result of an abundance of natural resources and a large and expanding domestic market? Or to take the case of France: to what extent was the relatively slow rate of industrialisation in that country before 1914 the outcome of the conservatism of the family firm and to what extent was it the product of the slow growth of the domestic market, the difficulties in recruiting an industrial workforce, and a lack of adequate supplies of vital industrial raw materials, such as coal? In short, the essential problem is whether entrepreneurship is cause or effect (or partly both) of the social and economic environment with which it is associated. Neither empirical evidence nor theoretical reasoning is likely to settle the dispute. Furthermore, reliance on the profit motive alone may not be enough to get industrialisation under way. Simply holding out the prospect of profit alone will hardly move a trader or money lender to become a modern industrialist or banker if the economic, social and political conditions in a country are broadly inimical to industrial change. In short, a purely economic explanation of entrepreneurial supply, by emphasising only the demand side of the situation, ignores the fact that social and political obstacles to the performance of the entrepreneurial function may well exist on the supply side.

III

The difficulties associated with a purely economic explanation of entrepreneurial supply has meant that the majority of economic historians have shown a preference for a more realistic multi-casual explanation embracing economic, sociological and historical determinants. Sociological factors include the existing social structure which in the United States, for example, was exceptionally favourable to the performance of the entrepreneurial function. Unlike Europe, America had no long established class system to impede social mobility and this made getting to the top all the easier. Once there, however, there were few competitors to business success as a source of social prestige. Consequently ambitious and able men turned naturally to business, not only because it was profitable, but also because it had unusual social prestige. In Europe, on the other hand, the existing social structure both limited social mobility and provided alternative sources of power and prestige to business. Land ownership, the state bureaucracy, the Church, army and the professions were all powerful competitors for the services of able men. This argument, however, is subject to one important qualification. Broadly speaking, European entrepreneurs were drawn from every social group, including the ranks of artisans, labourers, yeomen and farmers. In other words, many of the early industrialists came from the ranks of social classes which were debarred by birth and upbringing from entering those competing fields of social activity open to the nobility and gentry.

The existence of these lower-class aspirants to wealth and prestige is part of the evidence supporting the argument that business leaders and economic innovators tend to be 'outsiders', that is, individuals who for some reason do not feel securely at home in the society in which they live. Foreigners and immigrants are also likely to form part of this group, being less inhibited by customary ways of doing things and having a greater need to establish themselves in their new homeland. Native entrepreneurs, on the other hand, are sometimes found to come predominantly from a socially distinct group. In

Britain, for example, many of the early industrialists were drawn from the several kinds of religious dissent, especially the Quakers, Presbyterians and Unitarians. Their prominence as industrialists came about not only because the Nonconformists constituted the better educated section of the British middle classes, but also because their solidarity as a group provided a powerful means of mobilising financial resources at a time when capital markets were imperfectly organised and business relatively small in size. Or again, Jews, Protestants and immigrants were important sources of supply of industrial and financial entrepreneurship in France. Indeed, immigrant entrepreneurs played a significant role in the early industrial development of Europe and North America. They were of particular importance in Russia, where the prevailing social values system placed severe constraints on indigenous entrepreneurship. The extent to which entrepreneurs are 'outsiders' in society must not be overexaggerated, however, since they must be capable of leadership in the field of business if a new technology is to spread and become widely accepted. This obviously means that whereas the function of entrepreneurs as innovators or their social origins may make them in some sense deviants from the traditional culture, they must at the same time retain membership in their traditional culture and share to some extent its values if their leadership is to be effective.

The idea that important relationships exist between the family system and entrepreneurship figures prominently in the theories of entrepreneurial supply developed by psychologists and some economists. Professor McClelland's analysis of achievement motivation provides one such explanation.[3] This theory can be seen as a further development of Max Weber's Protestant ethic in which an intermediating motive (the need of achievement or *n-achievement*) is introduced.[4] McClelland ascribes the inculcation of the achievement motive to child-rearing practices which stress standards of excellence and training in self-reliance. He also claims that high achievers are attracted into business rather than other occupations or professions because they tend to set themselves moderately difficult goals so as to maximise the likelihood of maximum achievement satisfaction and because profitability gives them concrete evidence of how successful they are. McClelland sees the same psychic phenomena as influencing the activities of both individuals and of societies at large. Consequently, a society with a high level of n-achievement will produce more energetic entrepreneurs who, in turn, produce more rapid economic growth.

As a counter to McClelland's thesis it has been argued that, in so far as successful industrialisation is dependent upon the emergence of a new class of businessmen, what is important is not the level of n-achievement in the total population, but rather the achievement motivation of a group of people who in a particular society for one reason or another are destined to business leadership. Since it is believed by some of McClelland's critics that the normal variation in child-rearing practices and in IQ will produce enough potential entrepreneurs in every society, the critical question relating to entrepreneurial supply is whether the opportunities are available for entrepreneurial endeavour. Put another way, between the need of achievement and achievement itself stands the ability to achieve which is an independent variable. If a high achiever is prevented for some reason from exercising his business talents then the need of achievement will be aborted. Consequently a high n-achievement will not automatically bring about industrial development. In reality, of course, there is so single motive, n-achievement or any other, which determines the actions of men in the economic field. It is true that McClelland does mention two other motives—power and affiliation motivation—as being important in this respect, but as Schumpeter and others have argued the pursuit of status, success and wealth are at least as important as McClelland's three motives. Moreover, any one of these motives may play a different role in differently structured societies.

On the question of motivation, historical experience has quickly shown that reliance on the profit motive alone is not sufficient to guarantee industrial development. The profit motive is always coupled with other motives, and even Schumpeter could view the entrepreneur as moved by a variety of other desires, including that of founding a business empire, the will to conquer, and the impulse to succeed for the sake, not of the fruits of success, but of success itself. Moreover, the framework within which entrepreneurial activity takes place is not only that of private property and the furtherance of individual self-interest. Thus the family firm, often taken to epitomise the private enterprise ethos has been accused of being inimical to rapid industrialisation in France in the nineteenth century because, it has been claimed, the French family firm's concern for safeguarding the family patrimony made it cautious to the point of being non-innovational and even possibly anti-growth. On the other hand, as in Russia and Japan, nationalist and ideological motives may drive government officials to innovate so effectively as to give a country a high growth rate. Furthermore, the performance of customary social obligations may provide an adequate motive to succesful entrepreneurial action. This has been the case in Japan, where the reciprocal obligations between an individual and his lord typical of a pre-industrial society have persisted into the modern period in Japanese economic development.

What the historical evidence seems to suggest by way of a generalisation about motives in economic developments is that, since the drive for industrial development involves a fundamental change in society's whole attitude to life and work, it must be accompanied by significant ideological changes. By itself the simple pursuit of profit is not enough to produce the intense concentration of effort required to bring about sustained industrial change. It needs to be reinforced by belief that the people responsible for initiating industrial development are serving a wider cause. Whether this need is supplied by Calvinism, Marxism, Nationalism or, as in the United States, by an almost religious faith in democracy and free enterprise, some ideological motive force with its roots outside the economic sphere appears to be a necessary ingredient of a successful economic growth.

IV

The argument that entrepreneurial activity is not simply a matter of personal motivation alone is further modified by the fact that the supply of entrepreneurial services is also influenced to some extent by the prevailing social attitudes to such activities. It has been argued, for example, that unless the prevailing social value system is such as to bestow social approval upon the role played by the entrepreneurs, they cannot succeed, and modern industrial development will not occur or at the very best will be severely retarded. One of the difficulties with evaluating the importance of social approval for the emergence of entrepreneurs is that in many societies, stratified and complex as they are, approval by some groups of a given activity is paralleled by disapproval by others. Moreover, whereas the prevailing social values may debar some groups in society from undertaking certain kinds of entrepreneurial activity, they do not necessarily debar them from others. Thus, despite the existence of a seemingly rigid social code, there was no European country which did not experience at one time or another the phenomenon of aristocratic business leadership.[5] Even in countries where legal and other restrictions on the entry of the nobility into business activity existed, these appear to have been either disregarded or evaded in many cases. Often, however these prohibitions related only to retailing and handicraft production, which always left room for entrepreneurial activity in agriculture and large-scale industries, such as textiles, glassware, mining and metallurgy. Furthermore, where state enterprises were established, government officials, among whom were many noblemen, fulfilled entrepreneurial functions, while at the same time enjoying all the benefits and prestige associated with holding government office. Finally, it should not be forgotten that men of high social standing could often safely disregard adverse sanctions as did, for example, Hungarian noblemen such as Istvan Szechenyi in the nineteenth century.[6]

The importance of social factors in explaining the slow rate of industrial growth in France has been stressed by a number of economic historians. David Landes has argued that the pace and character of French entrepreneurship was set by family firms, owned and managed by blood relations, whose primary concern was safety, continuity and the preservation of the family patrimony.[7] These attitudes, it has been argued by others, were reinforced by anti-capitalistic and anti-competitive values on the part of the population as a whole and also by a value system that esteemed more honorific roles above business activity. Another failing of French industry, its unwillingness to make the best use of their technically-trained personnel, has been explained by the reluctance of French entrepreneurs to yield up family control of the business to any extent. Not surprisingly, these claims have all been subject to criticism. It has been argued, for example, that French business behaviour in the pre-1914 period was as effective as conditions allowed, that growth was more rapid than was commonly admitted, and that the French lag in technology, where it existed, came about because relative factor costs (scarcity of coal, high price of capital) provided less incentive for the adoption of the new industrial machinery. It has also been pointed out that some firms and industries in France, for example, the French chemical firm of Kuhlmann, owned their origins and success to technically-trained men. Perhaps the most effective criticism of the Landes thesis is, however, the point made by Kindleberger when he writes:

> ...the greatest weakness in attaching first importance to the nature of entrepreneurship in shaping France's...economic development is that the model is incomplete. What needs to be established is not

why business behaved as it did but, taking this for granted, why other firms did not come along and challenge existing enterprises.[8]

This criticism is all the more pointed because this is precisely what did happen in France in the banking field, where the rise of the Crédit Mobilier banks effectively challenged the banking practices of the 'old wealth' and forced the established banks to enter new fields of financial activity which they had previously avoided.[9] Why French industry lacked this dynamism is the important question.

The one country in which entrepreneurial activity does appear to have been at variance with the dominant system of values in the nineteenth century was Russia. In this country the traditional agrarian beliefs and deep attachment to the soil had survived fairly unchanged into the modern period and were accepted, at least superficially, by groups that were far removed from the peasant classes. Consequently, throughout most of the nineteenth century a strong and widespread disapproval of entrepreneurial activity was evident in the country. Divorced from the peasantry by reason of their occupation, Russian entrepreneurs remained despised and distrusted by the nobility and by the intelligentsia. Yet even in Russia the existence of widespread social opposition to entrepreneurial activity did not prevent rapid industrial growth from taking place in the 1890s. For this reason, the Russian experience is important not because of what it tells us about the significance or otherwise of social values as a determinant of entrepreneurial supply, but because it focuses our attention on what are the crucial questions concerning this relationship, namely, what is the degree of persistence in traditional values systems and what is their propensity to change in response to other factors. It is perhaps the case that a sociological or cultural approach to the analysis of entrepreneurship, emphasising as it apparently must the element of continuity and persistence in the values system tends to leave us with an impression that the resistances to change are more potent than the forces making for change. This is probably the reason why economists, with only a few exceptions, tend to be somewhat impatient with the findings of the sociologist and cultural analyst, and react to their conclusions by rating very highly the ability of the economic process, once industrialisation is under way, to compel modifications in social and cultural values consistent with further industrial development. The problem thus resolves itself into a question of the malleability of social and cultural traditions in the face of pressures, of varying degrees and kinds, for change.

V

Enough has been said for us to conclude that the emergence of a supply of entrepreneurs sufficiently numerous to ensure successful economic development did not depend on a high degree of malleability of the social and cultural traditions in any country. In Russia industrialisation was able to proceed even in the face of substantial social opposition to it, while in Japan it was the deposed Samurai who turned to industry and kept the social structure intact by the expedient of adopting vigorous young businessmen or taking them into the family through marriage. What the historical evidence strongly suggests is that the entrepreneur is not a fixed type, and that national, cultural and even personal characteristics intervene to shape the person and through him the institutional framework within which the entrepreneurial function is performed. Thus in Russia the quantitative and qualitative deficiencies of the local entrepreneurship could be alleviated by the importation from abroad of foreign entrepreneurial talent, although the overall extent of this inflow of business expertise should not be exaggerated. Even more importantly, the power of the state was used to protect businessmen and their interests from hostile social forces and the discriminatory laws these forces engendered. Later, when industrialisation in Russia was well under way, the use of investment banks, which had been pioneered in Belgium and France, and brought to the peak of their efficiency in Germany, provided a means of overcoming the problem of capital accumulation as well as the entrepreneurial deficiencies apparent in Russia at this time.

This Russian example only serves to illustrate the variety of institutional arrangements within which the entrepreneurial function can be performed. As we have already argued in Chapter 2, the successful spread of modern industrial technology depends not only on the existence of a set of conditions which are conducive to technical diffusion, but also on the existence of mechanisms capable of diffusing the new techniques between persons and through space. In so far as the entrepreneurial function involves activities directly bearing on the diffusion of technology, to that extent the mechanisms for diffusing technology—the firm, the investment bank, government— represent nothing more than the institutionalising of this aspect of the entrepreneurial function, although these institutions can perform a variety of other entrepreneurial activities at the same time as they are assisting in the diffusion process. While any of these institutions could, and did, assist in encouraging the international migration of technology, they were primarily instruments for diffusing technology *within* nation-states. It is therefore the purpose of the final section of this book to examine in greater detail these *national* mechanisms for diffusing modern industrial technology. Before doing this, however, it is necessary first to look at the *international* mechanisms for spreading technology between countries.

Notes

1. This is the significance of Professor Redlich's distinction between 'primary' and 'derivative' innovators. Whereas the former brings into existence something that never existed before, 'the latter introduces into his country, his region or his industry innovations existing so far only in other places'. See F. Redlich, 'Entrepreneurial Typology', *Weltwirtschaftliches Archiv*, Vol. 82, I (1959), pp. 150-66. Reprinted in F. Redlich, *Steeped in Two Cultures* (New York, 1971), pp. 112-32.

2. Even in Britain, the opportunity that existed for substituting domestically-produced cottons for imported Indian calicoes and muslins was an important factor facilitating the rapid expansion of the Lancashire cotton textile industry.

3. D.C. McClelland, *The Achieving Society* (Princeton, 1962).

4. Weber believed that the Calvanist ethic with its emphasis on work and thrift is a crucial element in accounting for the success of Western capitalist development. According to McClelland, the Weber thesis can best be understood as a special case, by no means limited to Protestantism (or religion), of a general increase in n-achievement brought about by an ideological change. Weber's thesis that the 'Protestant ethic' provided the basis for industrial capitalism has been under increasing attack in recent years as further historical research has provided counter-evidence to the Weber model, for example, the business success of Catholic enterprises. As an illustration of this, see D. Landes, 'Religion and Enterprise: the Case of the French Textile Industry', in E.C. Carter, R. Forster and J.N. Moody (eds.), *Enterprise and Entrepreneurs in Nineteenth and Twentieth Century France* (Baltimore, 1976), pp. 41-86.

5. The exceptions to this generalisation are Holland and Switzerland, in which feudal institutions never found a fertile soil.

6. As a landowner and entrepreneur—and also as a writer and statesman— Szechenyi played a very important role in the economic and political development of Hungary in the first half of the nineteenth century. Among other achievements, he helped to promote the Pest Steam Flour Mill Company, which began operations in 1842, using the new steel cylinder system of grinding wheat. A subsidiary company, set up to service the mill machinery, had by 1847 become an independent engineering concern under the name of Ganz and Company. By 1914 this Budapest firm was one of the greatest engineering works in Europe.

7. D.S. Landes, 'French Entrepreneurship and Industrial Growth in the Nineteenth Century', *Journal of Economic History* (May, 1949), reprinted in B.E. Supple (ed.), *The Experience of Economic Growth* (New York, 1963), pp. 340-53.

8. C.P. Kindleberger, *Economic Growth in France and Britain: 1851-1950* (Cambridge, Mass., 1964), p. 134.

9. See later, Chapter 13, especially pp 180-3.

Selected Reading

A. Gerschenkron, 'Social Attitudes, Entrepreneurship and Economic Development', *Explorations in Entrepreneurial History* (October, 1953)

H.J. Habakkuk, 'The Entrepreneur and Economic Development', reprinted in I. Livingstone (ed.), *Economic Policy for Development* (Penguin, 1971)

Kozo Kamamura, *A Study of Samurai Income and Entrepreneurship* (Cambridge, Mass.), 1974

C.P. Kindleberger, *Economic Growth in France and Britain: 1851–1950* (Cambridge, Mass., 1964), especially Chapter 6

D.S. Landes, 'French Entrepreneurship and Industrial Growth in the Nineteenth Century', *Journal of Economic History* (May 1949)

—— 'Religion and Enterprise: the Case of the French Textile Industry', in E.C. Carter, R. Forster and J.N. Moody (eds.), *Enterprise and Entrepreneurs in Nineteenth and Twentieth Century France*, (Baltimore, 1976)

G.P. Palmade, *French Capitalism in the Nineteenth Century* (Newton Abbot, 1972). See especially the Introduction by G.M. Holmes

F. Redlich, 'Entrepreneurial Typology', Reprinted in *Steeped in Two Cultures,* F. Redlich (New York, 1971)

J.F. Sawyer, 'The Entrepreneur and the Social Order: France and the United States', in W. Miller (ed.), *Men in Business*, (New York, 1962)

PART THREE: THE SPREAD OF MODERN
INDUSTRIAL TECHNOLOGY: MECHANISMS

11 THE INTERNATIONAL ECONOMY AND THE DIFFUSION OF MODERN INDUSTRIAL TECHNOLOGY

I

The international economy played a major role in promoting the spread of modern industrial technology in the period before 1914. The flows of trade, capital and labour which linked countries together were not only the means whereby the benefits of economic growth, in the form of higher *per capita* real incomes, could spread from country to country, but they were also the mechanism by which the technological and social innovations that are the essence of modern industrial growth could be diffused. In so far as the international diffusion of technology depended on the mobility of goods, people, money and ideas, it is apparent from our knowledge of the nineteenth-century international economy that mobility in this sense was greatly enhanced before 1914 by innovations in transport and communications and international finance. The result was a large-scale movement of goods, men and capital between countries. These international flows of economic resources were, in turn, important channels for the diffusion of the new industrial technology, since physical capital embodied it, immigrant artisans and entrepreneurs often possessed the required technical and managerial skills to use it, while imports, particularly of manufactured consumer goods and machinery and equipment, provided opportunities for adaptive imitation. Industrial growth of many countries came to depend as much on their ability to take advantage of the opportunities for trade and for the acquisition of new knowledge and additional factors of production presented by the international economy as on the quantity and quality of the economic resources domestically available to them.

II

At the beginning of the nineteenth century the total value of foreign investment was small, and its economic impact on both the borrowing and lending countries insignificant. It was business activity undertaken exclusively by a few privileged European trading and financial organisations with foreign interests. From the end of the Napoleonic Wars, however, foreign investment assumed a new character and an increasing significance. This change came about for a number of reasons. The establishment and growth of specialised financial institutions in both borrowing and lending countries, such as commercial banks (operating in foreign exchange) and investment houses, made foreign investment easier and less risky, while the accumulation of savings by a middle class willing to invest them abroad supplied the funds needed for an expansion of foreign lending. The international flow of funds was also facilitated by the appearance of more sophisticated financial instruments, such as credit money and bills of exchange. In addition, capital markets, such as 'the City' in London, became much more diversified in their financial dealings, thereby aiding the expansion of international trade and the growth of foreign investment.

Under these circumstances international lending expanded rapidly during the nineteenth century. From the end of the Napoleonic Wars until the mid-fifties, about £420 million ($2,050 million) was invested abroad. By 1870 the total value of these investments had more than trebled. But the great era of international lending occurred after 1870, with the international capital flow becoming a flood during the decade before World War I. By 1900 foreign investment totalled £4,750 million ($23,000 million), and it rose rapidly during the next few years to reach £9,500 million ($43,000 million) in 1914.

Britain was the major source of foreign capital supply during the nineteenth century, and France another foreign lender of substance during these years. After 1870, however, when the outflow of funds from the capital-rich countries accelerated tremendously, Germany and the United States became major lending countries and by 1914 together accounted for one-fifth of the total value of the assets owned abroad by all the capital-exporting nations. Belgium, the Netherlands and Switzerland formed another important group of countries willing to place large surplus savings at the disposal of other countries. Of the borrowing countries, Europe received the largest slice of this foreign investment (£2,500 million or 27 per cent of the total), since most European countries received some capital from abroad at one time or another during the nineteenth century. Next in order of size of capital inflow was North America (£2,300 million or 24 per cent). Two-thirds of this region's share went to the United States, the remainder going to Canada. Thus the two main industrialising regions of the world in the nineteenth century received just over one-half of the total foreign capital made available during those years.

A sectoral breakdown of this foreign investment is possible using the available British data. These figures impressively demonstrate the significance of overseas lending for the purpose of building the social overhead capital of the borrowing countries. This category, which includes transportation, public utilities and other public works, received almost 70 per cent of the British investment. Transportation, the largest industrial segment, obtained at least 46 per cent, and railways, its major component, 41 per cent of the total. By contrast, less than 12 per cent was invested in the extractive industries (including farming), and less than 4 per cent of the total in manufacturing. As would be expected, a similar picture emerges for the capital-importing country. Thus by 1914, $4,000 million (57 per cent) of the total United States foreign debt of $7,000 million was in the form of railway debentures held abroad, more than half of them by Britain.

While it is abundantly clear from the evidence that foreign capital did not *directly* foster the spread of industrialisation, its *indirect* effects on the diffusion of modern industrial technology should not be overlooked. Capital shortage, as we have seen, may hinder technological diffusion in a number of ways. For example, it will place limits on a country's stock of social overhead capital, especially transport facilities, with all that that implies for the growth of the market. Moreover, the fact that industrialisation in the nineteenth century was accompanied by population growth and urban development meant that there were heavy demands on capital in the form of housing, public utilities and the other facilities needed to service an expanding urban-industrial population. While in most countries the bulk of their capital needs were satisfied out of domestic savings, the availability of foreign funds to finance the construction of social overhead capital, meant that domestic savings could be used largely to finance the growth of manufacturing industry in borrowing countries without this expansion being threatened by inadequate transport or the lack of other ancillary services. In a few countries, however, foreign investment was also a critical element in the growth of the manufacturing sector. Italy and Russia were two such countries. In Russia the proportion of foreign capital in total capital invested in industrial undertakings reached startling proportions in the late nineteenth century, accounting for an estimated 26 per cent of the Russian total in 1890, 45 per cent in 1900, and 47 per cent in 1914.[1] No other major European state even came close to having a comparably significant infusion of foreign capital.

III

The spread of the new industrial technology throughout Europe was also assisted by an international movement of entrepreneurs and workers. The industrial revolution was not under way for long in Britain before British engineers, technicians and skilled workers were acting as direct, personal carriers of the new technology to other countries. The new textile machines were introduced in France and Germany partly by British entrepreneurs and skilled mechanics. John Holker, a Jacobite exile who settled in Rouen in 1751, founded a cloth factory at Saint Sever, where he introduced the latest cotton machinery and also brought over skilled operatives from Lancashire to train French workers in its use. After the Napoleonic Wars, English cotton experts, such as Job Dixon and Richard Roberts, helped to bring modern machinery to Alsace, while William Douglas and John Collier introduced new mechanical appliances for the carding, combing and spinning of wool and the shearing of cloth. Other new inventions and processes were taken across the Channel by British engineers. William Cockerill set up a plant for the construction of textile machinery at Verviers in Belgium, while his son John Cockerill founded the famous engineering establishment at Seraing, near Liège. British engineers and contractors also assisted in the construction of railways, such as the line from Rouen to Paris.

As Continental technology improved and the beginnings of industrialisation moved eastward and southward, countries such as France, Belgium and, later, Germany served increasingly as reservoirs of entrepreneurial and technical skills. French mining engineers, for example, supervised mines and factories, surveyed underground resources and introduced advance mining techniques into a large area of Europe. Most famous of these was Frederic Le Play, possibly better known as a sociologist and social reformer than as a mining engineer, who went to Russia in 1837 at the request of the Russian government to survey the coal resources of the Donetz basin, at that time totally undeveloped. Later, in 1844, he was persuaded to take over the technical direction of mining and metallurgical operations in the Urals. After the middle of the nineteenth century the governments of countries in southern and eastern Europe and the Middle East made even greater calls on French technical expertise to assist in the building of port facilities, roads, canals, bridges and railways.

The supreme achievement of the French in the industrialisation of Europe, however, was their development of the technique of investment banking and of managing the large-scale industries which they created. Under the Second Empire (1852–71) French financial innovators set up banks, railways, public utilities and mining and metallurgical industries throughout Europe, bringing French economic power and prestige to an all-time high.

One country which benefited considerably from immigrant skills during the early stages of its industrial development was Russia. In the middle of the eighteenth century, for example, cotton printing in the country was monopolised by the English manufacturers, Chamberlain and Cuzzins, whose factory was located at St Petersburg. Later, in the nineteenth century, German as well as British entrepreneurs and technicians were involved in the further development of the Russian textile industry. Indeed, by the end of the century, the cotton-spinning and weaving industry was dominated by L. Knoop, a German emigrant, whose firm for a long time was about the only channel for procuring cotton spindles and looms from Britain. Consequently, almost all the cotton mills of the central industrial region of Russia were constructed by Knoop, who quickly became the major shareholder of many of the mills. Apart from participating as a partner or shareholder in many firms, Knoop's company also owned its own factories, including the Kronholm cotton mill, near Narva, which, with more than 400,000 spindles was considered to be the largest in the world. Foreigners were also in evidence in other industrial fields in Russia. The Ukranian iron industry dates from 1869 when John Hughes, a British ironfounder, established an ironworks near Lugansk in the Donetz region. Apart from supporting the growth of the Russian iron and steel industry, foreign capital and enterprise was also involved during the second half of the nineteenth century in opening up Russia's coal reserves, while the Nobel brothers and the French Rothschilds played a prominent part in the development of Russia's rich oil resources.

In countries outside Europe industrial development was supported by an inflow of European migrants. As entrepreneurs and migrants they complemented and helped to make productive the capital which also flowed in from abroad. This European migration totalled some 44 million between 1821 and 1915. Although the bulk of the movement took place after 1880, with every decade the tide of population movement increased in volume, rising from an average of over 110,000 a year in the period 1821–50 to 270,000 in 1851–80, and to over 900,000 in 1881–1915.[2] In total some 11–12 million Europeans emigrated before 1880, compared with 32 million after than date, when industrialisation was accelerating rapidly in North America. Of the total gross immigration of some 51 million recorded between 1821 and 1915,[3] about 62 per cent entered the United States and 8 per cent Canada. Thus the industrialising region of the Americas accounted for around 70 per cent of the recorded immigration before 1915.

The essential economic function of international migration in the nineteenth century was to redistribute some of Europe's agricultural population to new primary producing regions overseas, where physical and social conditions enabled it to produce more per man than it would have done had it remained at home. Sometimes this result was achieved directly, but not always. Many immigrants, although drawn from largely agricultural economies, contributed to the development of new countries by taking non-agricultural jobs in them, thus releasing more of the native population to expand agriculture. A minority of migrants possessed industrial skills and were responsible for the introduction of new manufacturing techniques. But the chief contribution of immigrants to industrial development in these countries was to be found in the numerical addition to a country's population they made, first as newcomers, and later, through the high birth-rates they sustained, as parents. These growing numbers provided both the labour force and the large and expanding market so essential to industrialisation and large-scale production.

Whatever the occupational destinations of the migrants, there was a direct connection between immigration and economic growth in the receiving countries. Each inflow of population acted as a powerful force in pushing up the rate of growth of investment, income and employment. Whether these upsurges in economic growth caused the inflow of foreign population or whether immigration stimulated economic expansion—and there is evidence that both causal sequences operated during the nineteenth century—the contribution of the immigrants to economic growth was obvious. As entrepreneurs, they brought to the recipient countries the capital and knowledge that formed the basis of a wide variety of new manufacturing industries including, amongst others, textiles, furniture, chemicals, glass-making and brewing, and as artisans they supplied the technical skills necessary to make these new industries an initial success. A more characteristic contribution, however, was of another order. Often lacking even the minimum of skills, the bulk of the immigrants fed the construction industries with the manpower to build railways and other transport facilities, and to erect cities and equip them with public utilities, sanitation and other urban requirements. In addition, where, as in the United States, mechanised production was introduced on a large scale, immigrants provided the factory workforce necessary for rapid and sustained industrial growth.

IV

Given the opportunity for adopting new methods of production presented by the international economy, the spread of technical innovation also required an economic incentive. Probably the most effective stimulus to innovation is the market to be supplied: both its size and the rate at which it is growing. A large and rapidly expanding market creates an environment that is highly conducive to technological advance and to all forms of innovation, including the adoption and adaptation of foreign techniques. One important form of market expansion in the nineteenth century was to be found in the emerging international economy. Foreign trade is simply an extension of domestic trade, and expanding opportunities for the international exchange of commodities did encourage the spread of industrialisation. In Britain, industrialisation was initially based on a rapidly expanding export of cotton textiles, and later it came to depend increasingly on exports of iron manufactures and coal. In the United States before 1860, raw cotton exports played an important role in supporting early industrial development in the country, and industrialisation in Germany late in the nineteenth century was also closely tied up with an expansion of manufactured exports. Even in Russia and Japan, where governments created domestic markets for industrial goods through their own demands for military and railway equipment, the ability to develop an export trade, in wheat for Russia and in cotton textiles for Japan, was necessary to provide the foreign exchange needed to service the inflow of foreign capital or to purchase the foreign machinery essential to industrialisation. Whether the demand for industrial goods was satisfied directly through an expansion of manufactured exports, or whether it was created indirectly, through the growth of primary products exports leading to a rise in domestic real incomes, expanding foreign markets created an environment highly favourable to technological diffusion.

Of course, in its early stages, industrialisation tends to have an anti-trade bias because local manufacturing is of a largely import-saving character, being directed almost entirely toward the home market.

After saturation of the home market is achieved, and perhaps even before that point, the output of the home manufacturing industry tends to spill over into the export market, and there is a marked tendency for the share of finished manufactures in total exports to rise as industrialisation progresses. This is brought out clearly in Table 11.1. Although the statistics in the table cover only a relatively short period, what comparable data are available for earlier periods in the nineteenth century for the individual countries listed in the table are consistent with a rising percentage trend in manufactured exports.

Table 11.1: Share of Manufactures in Exports from Industrial Countries 1899–1913

	Percentage of total exports	
	1899	1913
Belgium – Luxembourg	46	45
France	55	58
Germany	70	72
Italy	41	45
Sweden	30	41
United Kingdom	64	77
Canada	7	10
United States	30	34
Japan	42	45

Source: A. Maizels, *Industrial Growth and World Trade* (Cambridge, 1969), Table 3.1, p. 58.

The spread of industrialisation before 1914 was encouraged by the growth of trade in those products which are complementary to the industrialisation process, such as capital equipment and semi-finished goods (or 'intermediate products').[4] Foreign trade in these products more than doubled in volume between countries which were industrialising rapidly during the nineteenth century, as Table 11.2 shows. These goods also formed a relatively greater percentage of the manufacturers' imports of already industrialised countries than of the other countries of the world, although the spread of railways to Africa, Asia and Latin America, and the acceleration of industrial development in these regions and in other parts of the world, meant that these goods were continuing to increase in relative importance in the foreign trade of these countries as well (Table 11.3).

Table 11.2: Distribution of Export Trade in Capital Goods and 'Intermediate Products' by Receiving Countries grouped, according to Level of Industrial Development, 1899–1913 (values at 1913 prices $m. f.o.b.)

	Industrial		Semi-industrial		Rest of world		Total exports	
	Value	%	Value	%	Value	%	Value	%
1899	749	66.2	169	14.9	214	18.9	1132	100.0
1913	1618	60.7	518	19.4	532	19.9	2668	100.0

Note: *Industrial countries:* Belgium-Luxembourg, France, Germany, Italy, Norway, Russia, Sweden, Switzerland, UK, Canada, United States and Japan.
Semi-industrial countries: Australia, New Zealand, the Union of South Africa, India, including Pakistan, Argentina, Brazil, Chile, Columbia, Mexico and Turkey.
Source: A. Maizels, *Industrial Growth and World Trade*. Tables A6, A8, A10 and A12.

Along with the expansion of world trade in manufactures which the spread of industrialisation gave rise to went significant changes in its composition. A decline in the share of textile manufactures in the total trade occurred, along with a rise in the share of metal manufactures, and a fairly general rise in the share of other manufactures (chemicals, paper and wood products, clay and glass products). These changes in the composition of the exports of industrial countries were partly due to industrialisation and the consequent changes in the structure of domestic output that accompanied it—involving a move away from primary production towards manufacturing, and within the latter a move away from textiles to metal manufactures, chemicals and

Table 11.3: Capital Goods and 'Intermediate Products' as a Proportion of All Exports of Manufactures to Countries grouped by Level of Industrial Development 1899–1913 (valued at 1913 prices)

PERCENTAGES				
Country grouping year	Industrial	Semi-industrial	Rest of world	Total
1899	36.3	23.1	24.2	30.8
1913	46.2	35.6	34.7	41.1

Source: A. Maizels, *Industrial Growth and World Trade,* Tables A6, A8, A10 and A12.

engineering products. They were also partly caused by the extension
of the international economy and the consequently greater international
division of labour, which applied within manufacturing activity as
well as between manufacturing and primary production.

V

What promoted these flows of labour, capital and trade between
countries? To a large extent they came about because of differences in
the relative prices of these resources in different countries. In the case
of both labour and capital, non-economic considerations, often
relating to religion or politics, exerted some influence on their
movement internationally, but for the most part it was differences in
wage rates and the rates of return on capital that prompted the flows of
factors of production from regions where earnings were low to those
where they were higher. With commodity trade, too, the exchange
was prompted by differences in the relative prices of the goods traded,
which reflected in turn differences in the costs of production in the
various countries engaged in foreign trade. In so far as the flow of
goods, capital and labour took place in response to differential
economic advantages of this kind, they acted as spontaneous or
'natural' carriers of modern technology and ideas. On the other hand,
specific and direct attempts were often made by governments and
other interested bodies to transfer technologies internationally. In
addition to sending students abroad to study the new techniques,
governments also encouraged the inflow of foreign skills and capital
through the use of subventions to immigrant entrepreneurs and
guarantees of dividends on foreign loans. Implicit in such policies was
the assumption that the diffusion of the new knowledge, either
nationally or internationally, was likely to be slow in the absence of
conscious efforts to encourage technological change.

   Apart from government, two other institutions emerged during the
second half of the nineteenth century capable of promoting the
international spread of industrialisation. These were multinational
business corporations and international investment banks.[5] The
branch factory and the foreign subsidiary company have become
increasingly important in the diffusion of technology during the
present century and provide both a direct injection of foreign
managerial and technical experience and a mechanism for the
transmission of the latest improvements from the parent company to

the branch or subsidiary. There is no question that the branch factory is a highly effective way of importing technology into a country. It usually provides, along with technical expertise, the capital that is not easily mobilised in the host country for new industrial ventures and the management experience it often lacks. This very power to break all the bottlenecks at once, however, can be the one thing about the multinational enterprise that the recipient country fears most, because it is achieved only by the foreign company supplying scarce factors from outside and charging a price corresponding to their scarcity. If the multinational enterprise demands high profits, salaries and wages for its foreign 'inputs', carries out little or no local research or new development, and makes little attempt to develop the technical and managerial skills of the local population, then there is certainly a risk that the branch plant may be an expensive and ineffectual way of injecting new technology into the economy.

By 1914, US direct investment in foreign manufacturing activities totalled around $478m. Most of this investment was in Canada and Europe, where 31 American companies had built or purchased two or more manufacturing plants between 1890 and 1914. In addition, there were another 24 companies with one or more plants in Canada only, and a further 9 companies with manufactories in Belgium, France, Germany and Britain.[6] Taken together, these companies covered a wide range of manufactures, including electrical engineering products, machine tools, chemicals, photographic equipment, motor cars, sewing machines and typewriters. The list is impressive, not only because of the 'newness' of many of the products it encompasses, but also because of the extent of the dispersal through investment of American technology abroad.

Britain's direct foreign investment totalled about £400m. in 1914, of which probably no more than £250m. was invested in manufacturing. By this date, 14 British firms had major manufacturing investments abroad, predominantly in light industries, such as food and tobacco, cotton thread, synthetic textiles, rubber, soap and glass. Only the Vickers Company, which built and operated armaments factories in Italy, Russia, Spain, Turkey, Canada and Japan in the years before 1914, fell into the heavy industry category. There were, or course, a number of other British firms which, in addition to the '14', had established manufacturing plants abroad by 1914. But the majority of these plants were extremely small, and some were little more than repair works which did a little assembly work on the side. Such firms undertook the manufacture of chemicals in Canada and the United

States, agricultural machinery in Austria and Russia, engineering products, including locomotives and textile machinery, in Canada, Germany, France and the United States, and food and drink in the United States.[7]

Out of a total of 17 Continental European multinational manufacturing companies existing in 1914, 9 were German, 4 Swiss, and the remainder were from France, Holland, Belgium and Sweden. The bulk of the foreign plants of these companies were located in other European countries, the only country outside Europe in which investment of this type was undertaken being the United States, where 8 of the firms had branch factories by 1914. Eight of the continental multinationals were based in the chemical industry, and 4 produced electrical equipment. The remaining firms were in food processing, metal, machinery and glass manufacture.[8]

Apart from being led in some cases by men with a global vision of enterprise, the European and American firms that had substantial overseas manufacturing investments by 1914 had all established strong oligopolistic positions in their home markets based on technical innovation. For many of these firms the shift into foreign production followed a common pattern. Saturation of the home market or the existence of surplus output capacity during periods of depressed domestic economic activity led to the growth of exports, and eventually to foreign production when export markets were threatened by local competition, tariffs, or some such other development. Examples of the connection between technical innovation, exports and subsequent foreign production are numerous and convincing. Innovative advantages, for example, appear intimately linked with the extraordinary export success of German electrical engineering firms— 48 per cent of total world exports of electrical goods in 1914— and their spread of manufacturing into Austria, Belgium, Britain, France, Italy, Russia and Spain.

The motives for switching from exporting to foreign manufacturing were many and varied. Tariffs and other trade restrictions, patent working regulations, subsidies, and other industry incentives, as well as the demands of governments for local production of goods purchased by the state, were some of the forces at work influencing business decision-making. Such nationalistic policies, for example, were responsible for American investment in the wood-pulp and newsprint industries in Canada, and Canadian patent regulations led to investment in the Dominion by American electrical firms. The spread of the armaments industry throughout Europe was also the result largely of government prompting.[9] Other forces at work included the threat to exports posed by the growth of local competition, and income levels in foreign markets, the latter being an important consideration for those firms producing income-elastic commodities, such as soap (Lever Brothers), photographic equipment (Kodak Eastman), sewing machines (Singer), and motor cars (Ford). Some American firms entering Europe during these years were influenced by the workings of the Sherman Antitrust Act (1890) in the United States and by the more lenient attitude long held in Europe toward cartels, mergers and other private business agreements. These firms entered into agreements with European companies covering such things as the exchange of technical and other information and the control of prices and output. However, those American companies with clearly superior products to those on offer in foreign markets generally avoided such agreements. Such companies, almost invariably with 100 per cent-owned foreign subsidiaries or branches, were to be found in the oil, aluminium, office equipment, motor car, fertilizer and farm equipment industries. The mixture of motives underlying investment in foreign manufacturing capacity obviously varied from company to company and between country and country, but overall by far the most important influence at work during the period after 1870 was the growth of tariff barriers and the need to jump them if foreign markets were to be retained.

What were the contributions of these multinational firms to the diffusion of industrial technology during the last quarter of the nineteenth century and the years up to 1914? First, there was the direct, and often substantial, technological contribution made by firms that were often in the forefront of their field. The fact that much of the technology used by these firms—chemical, electrical engineering, motor car assembly—was comparatively new is also important. Second, there was the demonstration effect provided by the factories themselves, often model plants, in their equipment, trained personnel and organisation. Thirdly, the foreign firms often obtained their supplies of fuels, metals and equipment from indigenous sources. Likewise, they hired local personnel, including people whose local knowledge made them better able to deal with local marketing, legal and labour problems, and government officials. The growth of multinational firms was still in its infancy, but even by 1914 these companies had exerted a profound effect on the development of manufacturing industries in countries like Canada and Russia.

The role of international investment banks in promoting the flow of industrial technology between countries during the period 1850 to 1914 can be touched on briefly here because it is dealt with fully in Chapter 13. Obviously, international capital flows on the scale recorded after 1850 could have come about only as a result of significant innovations in the field of international finance. During the first half of the nineteenth century, international investment rested almost wholly in the hands of private merchant bankers, such as Barings of London, Hopes of Amsterdam, Bethmanns of Frankfurt, and the Rothschild family which had financial houses in London, Paris, Frankfurt and Vienna. These bankers dealt mainly in government loans. After 1850, however, finance companies like the French Crédit Mobilier came to challenge the monopoly of the merchant houses. Being able to tap much wider financial sources than the private merchant banks, these companies became heavily involved in industrial investment of all kinds. By the 1870s, therefore, leadership in the field of international investment had passed firmly to the French and German joint stock investment banks, though these banks continued to draw on the knowledge and experience of the private merchant banks in conducting their business.

VI

Yet despite the existence of these natural carriers of technology on a scale previously unmatched in history, and despite the efforts made by some governments to reinforce the market influences determining the volume and direction of these trade and factor flows, the rate at which the new technology was diffused was slow, and the spread of modern industry limited. Thus, even in Europe and the United States, rapid industrialisation occurred only after 1870, more than a century after the new technology had emerged in Britain. Even more striking is the fact that by 1913 the spread of industrialisation was limited largely to western Europe, North America and Japan. To what extent therefore did this 'failure' in the diffusion of modern industrial growth reflect weaknesses in the functioning of the international economy as a mechanism for transmitting technology between countries? Unfortunately we are still far from fully understanding the detailed working of the international economy as an 'engine of growth' in the nineteenth century, and much research remains to be done to fill the gaps in our knowledge. We are, for example, still limited in our knowledge concerning the extent to which the economic growth of individual countries was dependent on the existence of the international economy, or how a country's dependence on the international economy may have changed over time, answers to which questions are obviously needed if we are to be able to weigh the relative importance of domestic and international obstacles to the spread of industrialisation. Because of our lack of knowledge in these matters, comment on the problem just raised is necessarily limited, but nevertheless a few general observations on it can be offered.

To begin with, if the diffusion of modern industrial technology was limited before 1913, it was partly because the supply of capital and labour available for international transfer was limited, and because not all of the countries desiring to import these productive resources were equally well-placed to attract them. For a number of reasons North America, and especially the United States, was particularly attractive for foreign investors and migrant labour, and western Europe, because of its compactness and its proximity to Britain, the seat of the industrial revolution, was also conveniently placed to take advantage of the new technology. The fact that these two regions received the lion's share of the economic resources that did shift internationally during these years meant simply that there were fewer of these resources available for other capital- and labour-importing countries, and their prospects for industrial development suffered correspondingly.

Part of the reason for the bias in the international flows of economic resources in the nineteenth century is to be found in a country's 'absorptive capacity', which may be defined as the amount of technical and capital assistance that it can effectively use. While it is not possible to measure exactly what the 'absorptive capacity' of an individual country is at a particular time, it is still possible to list certain conditions that are necessary for the productive utilisation of capital, whether of domestic or foreign origin. Absorptive capacity will be low, for example, when there are inadequate transport facilities, administrative and organisational bottlenecks, deficient qualities of entrepreneurship, a lack of complementary natural resources, scarcities of trained manpower, narrow localised markets, and so on. In respect of these conditions during the nineteenth century some countries, notably the United States, Canada, Australia, Argentina, Brazil, and a number of European countries, were better placed than others, for example China, India, Egypt and most of Africa. It is not surprising, therefore, to find that by 1913 almost two-thirds of the total foreign investment undertaken during the nineteenth century was to be found in the first-mentioned group of countries, whose capacity to absorb this capital was helped by the international flows of labour that accompanied these movements of foreign capital.

In some countries, moreover, primary production continued to be more profitable than manufacturing activities, in the sense that these countries' real income could be increased more rapidly by specialising in agricultural and mining production and exchanging their surpluses of primary products for manufactures produced elsewhere. As long as the real incomes of primary producers were sustained by the mounting demand for foodstuffs and raw materials of the industrialising regions at the centre of the international economy, the spread of industrialisation to peripheral countries was limited by the economic advantages accruing to them from the growing territorial division of labour which formed the basis of the expanding international economy of the nineteenth century. When, however, changing demand and supply conditions in the post-World War I period resulted in a downward pressure on primary product prices which reduced the real incomes of countries supplying these commodities, industrialisation programmes became a feature of many of these countries, as their governments endeavoured to diversify domestic economic activity by encouraging the production of manufactured goods previously purchased out of the export earnings of primary producers.

VII

The spread of industrialisation from Britain to the continents of Europe and North America was assisted by the functioning of the international economy. The flows of capital, labour and trade, which linked together the countries of the world, provided the channels through which modern industrial technology could be diffused between nations. If the extent of this technological diffusion was limited in the nineteenth century, it was partly because the stock of capital and labour available for international transfer was limited in the nineteenth century and partly because not all of the countries desiring to import these extra productive resources were equally well-placed to attract them. But what was an even greater obstacle to the spread of industrialisation was the fact that many countries, even when they received inflows of foreign labour and capital, lacked the internal flexibility necessary for them to take advantage of the changing technological opportunities that presented themselves. It was this weakness, rather than any fundamental deficiency in the functioning of the international economy as an 'engine of growth' that accounts for the limited industrialisation before 1914. To industrialise successfully, there had to be capital formation, technical change, reallocation of resources, as well as changes in social, political and cultural attitudes to economic activity. Since in many countries the forces of inertia were strong and deeply entrenched, the spread of industrialisation was necessarily a slow process.

Notes

1. J.P. McKay, 'Foreign Enterprise in Russian and Soviet Industry: A Long Term Perspective', *Business History Review* (Autumn, 1974), p. 340.

2. A.G. Kenwood and A.L. Lougheed, *The Growth of the International Economy 1820–1960* (London, 1971), Table 5, p.60.

3. The immigration statistics probably provide a truer picture of international population movements during the nineteenth century than those for emigration. Not all of the immigrants settled permanently in the countries to which they travelled but, owing to the lack of adequate information on the numbers returning home, the extent of the net movement is difficult to gauge.

4. Maizels, whose statistics are used in compiling the data in Tables 11.2 and 11.3 in the text defines 'finished' capital goods as machinery and transport equipment, though parts for assembling or for incorporation in machines are also normally included. Similarly, metals are considered as wholly 'intermediates', though a proportion of these would not in fact be further processed, e.g. steel rails.

5. The investment bank with foreign branches or subsidiaries is, of course, only another type of multinational corporation. The distinction between the two economic institutions is worth preserving, however, if only because, unlike the manufacturing multinationals, the investment bank is not *directly* involved in the diffusion of technology.

6. Mira Wilkins, *The Emergence of Multinational Enterprise: American Business Abroad from the Colonial Era to 1914* (Cambridge, Mass., 1970), Table X.3, pp. 212-3. American firms with heavy foreign involvement included Western Electric with plants in Canada and seven European countries; the American Radiator Company with plants in Canada and five European countries; and International Harvestor and the International Steam Pump Company, both of which had plants in Canada and four European countries.

7. See J.M. Stopford, 'The Origins of British-Based Multinational Manufacturing Enterprises', *Business History Review* (Autumn 1974), especially Tables 3 and 4, pp. 316-7, 324. British manufacturing investment was largely in Europe and North America. Only during the 1920s and the 1930s did an Empire preference become a predominant influence on location decisions.

8. L.G. Franko, 'The Origins of Multinational Manufacturing by Continental European Firms', *Business History Review* (Autumn 1974), Table 2, pp. 282-3.

9. For a discussion of the importance of this industry for Europe's industrial development, see Chapter 8.

Selected Reading

A.K. Cairncross, 'The Migration of Technology', in *Factors in Economic Development* (London, 1962)

L.G. Franko, 'The Origins of Multinational Manufacturing by Continental European Firms', *Business History Review* (Autumn 1974), pp. 277-302

A.G. Kenwood and A.L. Lougheed, *The Growth of the International Economy 1820–1960* (London, 1971)

J.P. McKay, 'Foreign Enterprise in Russian and Soviet Industry: A Long Term Perspective' *Business History Review* (Autumn 1974), pp. 336-56

N. Rosenberg, 'Economic Development and the Transfer of Technology: Some Historical Perspectives', *Technology and Culture* (December 1970), pp. 550-75. Reprinted in N. Rosenberg, *Perspectives on Technology* (Cambridge, 1976)

J.M. Stopford, 'The Origins of British-Based Multinational Manufacturing Enterprises' *Business History Review* (Autumn 1974), pp. 303-35

C. Trebilcock, 'British Armaments and European Industrialisation, 1890–1914', *Economic History Review* (May 1973), pp. 254-72

M. Wilkins, *The Emergence of Multinational Enterprise: American Business Abroad from the Colonial Era to 1914* (Cambridge, Mass., 1970)

——'The Role of Private Business in the International Diffusion of Technology', *Journal of Economic History* (March 1974), pp. 166-88

W. Woodruff, *The Impact of Western Man* (New York, 1966)

12 THE COMPETITIVE MARKET ECONOMY

I

All societies make choices of what to produce, how, and for whom, by means of various social systems. A market economy is one such system in which the basic economic questions are decided, not by tradition or by some central authority, but by producers and consumers acting in markets in response to changes in the prices of the things they buy and sell. The essence of the system is that goods are produced for exchange and that these exchanges are money transactions. All inputs and all outputs have prices that are set in the market by the actions of a host of competitors, each seeking his own advantage. Simultaneously these prices and their relationships to one another provide the guides for the direction of production into various channels, the selection among alternative production techniques, and the distribution of total output among various persons in society.

Given the nature of the functioning of a market society, it was not possible for it to coexist with a form of legal organisation which did not recognise the freedom of the individual to contract for employment as he wished. Nor could it exist without private ownership of property, which conferred on the individual full freedom to use and to transfer property as he chose. Indeed, economic growth requires that men, whether privately or as public officials, have access to resources and are free to buy, borrow or hire factors of production since, if a person may use only his own labour, land and capital, the advantages of specialisation and the economies of large-scale enterprise will not be realised. The organisation of production within such a system also requires a pattern of behaviour consistent with the new market environment imposed on society. This emerged in the form of a widespread drive to maximise one's income by concluding the best possible bargains in the market. Moreover, guided by the operation of the price mechanism, the drive for profit maximisation was a powerful tool for reallocating resources and bringing about the shifts in the occupational structure and in the composition of output characteristic of an industrialising society. Equally necessary for the success of such efforts to reallocate resources was an increase in the mobility of the factors of production. Increased factor mobility also led to an increase

165

in the degree of economic competition, since greater mobility meant any job or activity was now open to all comers. Finally since a properly functioning market economy presupposes exchange transactions involving the use of money and the operations of a price mechanism, the degree of monetisation of economic life is of vital importance. The operation of market forces is greatly limited in economies where subsistence activities predominate and where exchanges largely take the form of barter.

II

Market-directed societies are relatively new and, since their emergence was linked with the transition from a medieval form of economic system to a capitalist one, the growth of the market economy to its fully-fledged form took a long time. What were the main features of this transition? The institutional framework within which the economy operated in medieval times can largely be described in terms of feudalism in agriculture, the guild system in the urban economy, and absolute autocratic rule for the nation as a whole. In addition, mercantilism rapidly became the major economic policy of the government, with all its impediments to individual economic actions. Custom and regulation predominated in medieval society and social, religious, political and economic aspects of everyday life were very closely related. Changes did occur from time to time but they were slow in affecting the established order appreciably.

From the fifteenth century onwards, however, certain changes in the economic, social and religious conditions which had persisted for several centuries began to test the relevance of the existing institutional framework. The discovery and colonisation of the Americas, the establishment of new trade routes to the East, the appearance of new ideas, including those of a scientific kind, the declining power of the Church under the Reformation, and the acceleration in European population growth combined together to bring about significant and far-reaching changes in the institutional framework of European society.

The transition in agriculture varied in timing and speed from one country to another. In England, feudalism began to decline as early as the fourteenth century, as serfdom and medieval practices began to give way slowly to enclosure of the land, tenant farming and paid labour. These changes, combined with improved farming practices and increased agricultural productivity, led to the relatively widespread commercialisation of English agriculture well before the nineteenth century. On the Continent, the transformation of agriculture occurred much later, more rapidly, but less thoroughly than in England. By 1800, relations between lord and serf had changed only slowly, although in most parts of western Europe feudal obligations had been commuted into monetary payments. Serfdom disappeared first in the west, largely as a result of the French Revolution and its aftermath, and much later in the nineteenth century in eastern Europe. Whereas these changes did much to improve the social conditions in European agriculture, in those countries where peasant proprietorship predominated in the private ownership of the land, agricultural productivity remained low and the advent of a fully-developed competitive market economy was hindered as a result.

As with agriculture, the restrictions on manufacturing activities which pervaded Europe under the guild and mercantilist systems were relaxed only very gradually. In this process of change and decay, two developments were of particular importance. The first was the growth of small-scale cottage industry which developed out of what had been originally a purely subsistence operation. This new productive system was refined further when merchant-capitalists devised the 'putting-out' system of production and introduced it into such industries as textiles, woodwork, leatherwork and iron-working. The other development was the emergence in the sixteenth and seventeenth centuries of isolated examples of 'central shops', the prototype of the nineteenth-century factory. These shops, in which a number of workers performed their different tasks side by side, were introduced into such industries as silk, glass and chemical manufacturing, the mining of metals and coal, heavy metal manufacturing, shipbuilding and sugar-refining. As production units, however, these shops were not complete entities for they were still dependent upon home-workers for many of their inputs.

Wherever these developments took place, producers became more and more tied to the market and the competitive processes that this implied. They also reduced the importance of the guild system. In addition, the requirements of the state, especially as far as its growing military needs for standardised clothing and military equipment were concerned, could not be satisfied by the guilds' more individualistic system of production.

But perhaps it was the attack on mercantilist thought and practice by the emerging capitalist class, the growth of internal and external trade due to the spread of money throughout the economy, and the growth of the colonial system after 1500 which highlighted the inadequacies of medieval custom.[1] These influences paved the way for the elimination of restrictions on non-agricultural production, the introduction of competitive goods and factor markets, and the dismantling of controls limiting foreign trade. The failure of the institutional structure of the mercantilist economy to cope with the increasing demands of a rising population, the spread of the monetary system, and improvements in industrial techniques became apparent long before the first concerted attack was made on mercantilism in the eighteenth century. The rise of the merchant-capitalist led to the individual businessman who recognised only too well that a free market offered him a far greater scope for expansion of output and income than a regulated trade which stifled initiative. At the same time, the growth of economic liberalism made inroads upon the accepted absolute authority of the state, and the rights of the individual over those of authoritarianism were emphasised, for example in the English Bill of Rights in 1689, the United States Constitution of 1776, and the French Constitution of 1789. Consequently, when Adam Smith's attack on the restrictions of mercantilism and his advocacy of individual economic freedom appeared in 1776, his ideas affected political and economic thought profoundly and paved the way for the further development of a competitive market system.

III

The consequent upsurge of economic liberalism and the appearance of a number of important technical innovations in western Europe in the eighteenth and nineteenth centuries produced a combination of circumstances highly favourable to the growth of a market economy. While not all countries experienced these forces to the same degree or at the same time, it is nevertheless useful to describe briefly the foundations upon which the institutional structure of a market economy are based. These foundations can be expressed in the form of a number of 'freedoms', namely, freedom from state intervention, freedom to dispose of property, freedom of trade, of contract, of movement and of association. Inherent in all these freedoms were the ability of the individual to control his own future and the importance placed on the marketplace as a determinant of economic activity. Not all these features of the competitive (*laissez-faire*) economy were accepted in their extreme form, however, and it was necessary for the state to intervene in the functioning of the market to control or eliminate some of the worst excesses of the new system.

Many of the institutional arrangements which form the basis of a competitive market economy were highly advanced in Britain by the middle of the eighteenth century. The individual enjoyed a high degree of legal protection against arbitrary acts of the state, and freedom to dispose of property was highly developed. Internal trade was becoming freer as many of the mercantilist restrictions on economic activity became outdated and increasingly more difficult to enforce. The case for international free trade was being vigorously argued, especially by Adam Smith, but in the face of opposition from a protectionist agricultural class, complete free trade was not realised until the 1850s. Restrictions on the movement of labour were also easing, and the mobility of capital, particularly short-term funds, had been greatly encouraged by the introduction of the 'bill of exchange', which had become, by the beginning of the eighteenth century, not only a convenient way of increasing the money supply, but also a highly efficient means of transmitting payments to distant parts. Moreover, in the century after 1750, the degree of economic freedom in Britain was increased to an even greater extent with the removal of further restrictions on commerce and industry, and the market for goods and services. Freedom of association became legally recognised with the slow acceptance of trade unionism and the introduction of the limited liability joint stock enterprise, which permitted a greater degree of association among savers.

The industrial revolution in Britain represents the classic case of spontaneous economic growth brought about by the operation of a free market economy. How, then, did the market mechanism operate to diffuse industrial techniques within the country? The conventional textbook answer to this question is that diffusion would be achieved as a direct result of price competition in the market. Any successful attempt by a firm to introduce improved methods of production into an industry will, it is argued, reduce costs and thus make it possible for the firm to lower its price and thus obtain a greater share of the total market for the product. Profits will grow and the firm will be encouraged to expand production further. Competitor firms, on the other hand, faced with a loss of sales and revenue, will be forced to imitate the innovating firm or go out of business. Faced with this threat, no firm can afford to lag behind, everyone has a strong incentive to keep up with the leader or, if profits of innovation are great, to become one of the innovating firms.

Even in a highly-developed market economy this explanation of the process of technological diffusion is far from an adequate one. The existence of patent laws, for example, in the absence of a licensing or fee system which makes the new technique available to all firms, makes every innovator a monopolist, at least temporarily. Competition, therefore, often takes the form of developing a quite different innovation rather than of imitating the practice of other firms. In certain circumstances, moreover, the competitive response may be technical rather than imitative, in the sense that the effect of the introduction of a new process may be to stimulate efforts to reduce the costs of the old. Thus British soda manufacturers were able to survive the introduction of the Solvay process by reducing material costs, improving techniques and increasing efficiency, and because their by-product, bleaching powder, continued to command a good price in the market. Only after 1895, when a new and cheaper electrolytic method of chlorine production was introduced, did the Leblanc industry rapidly decline, the last British Leblanc plant closing down in 1920. The general implication of these observations on the functioning of the competitive market system and the diffusion of technology should be obvious. A crucial element in the spread of new technology within a competitive industry is the extent to which the innovation reduces costs and hence the price of the product. Where the reduction of costs is substantial and immediate, such as the Hall-Hérault process of aluminium manufacture (1886), which reduced costs over the older methods of manufacture from $10 a pound in the 1870s to 30 cents in the mid 1890s, the competitive pressures were overwhelming, and the firms had to take up the new process quickly if they were to survive. On the other hand, where the cost differential between the new and the old was small, because the new technique was only slightly superior to the old, the competitive pressures were muted, the response to change was slower, and the opportunities for combating the competition of the new process by bringing about improvements in the old more possible. In short, much of the history of technological diffusion can be analysed in terms of the degree of cost reduction achieved. Coke smelting of iron spread only slowly because it was only slightly superior to charcoal in certain circumstances of raw material supply, whereas puddling killed the older iron-refining processes much more quickly. Solvay only gradually established its complete ascendancy over Leblanc, but the discovery of synthetic indigo in 1856 destroyed the natural dye industry within a few years.

It must be noted that effective competition requires something more than the existence of a reasonably high degree of economic freedom in society. As one economist has observed, 'Competition presupposes knowledge and enterprise—even when enterprise goes no further than imitation . . . Poor communications, inaccessibility to ideas and information, and limited horizons of experience on the one hand and lack of enterprise on the other are the main obstacles that have to be overcome.'[2] In other words, the proper functioning of a competitive market system as a mechanism for diffusing modern technology not only depends upon the presence within society of a set of social, legal and political conditions conducive to a high degree of freedom in economic activity, but it also needs the presence in the economy of those demand and supply conditions discussed earlier—adequate markets, natural resources, skilled and semi-skilled labour, enterprise, and so on—which make the rational choice of techniques effective. Free choice in economic matters is worth little in the absence of the markets and resources necessary to make that choice effective. All the evidence suggests that in Britian in the late eighteenth century a high degree of economic freedom was associated with growing markets and a relative abundance of the resources needed for industrial innovation and for the rapid spread of the new industrial techniques. Consequently, Britain experienced a 'spontaneous' process of economic growth based on a relatively rapid diffusion of the new industrial technology.

In the second half of the nineteenth century, greater freedom of association led to the establishment and growth of the trade union movement in the labour market and to the establishment of the limited liability joint stock company. The association of savers on a large scale was facilitated by changes in the company laws of a number of countries and the large corporation became a feature of the iron and steel, chemical and other industries. While the legalising of such incorporation undoubtedly enhanced the spread of advanced technology, it also paved the way for some reduction in competitive forces by allowing a trend towards monopolisation in certain industries and the establishment of giant cartels, such as in Germany from the 1870s and their counterparts, the trusts, in the United States. Not surprisingly, the impact of large-scale industrial organisations on the process of technological diffusion was mixed. Given the need for a firm to maintain or improve the profitability of its large capital investment through holding or increasing its share of the market, innovation, product development and rapid imitation of its rivals' products and productive processes became increasingly important as we move into the twentieth century. As markets became increasingly oligopolistic, with price competition giving way to forms of non-price competition, such as advertising, the offering of liberal credit facilities, supply at short notice, and the provision of after-sales service, companies could ignore new technical and marketing developments only at the peril of their own existence. On the other hand, a firm's size and its use of monopolistic devices could also help blunt the impact of new competitive technologies. For example, apart from the reasons mentioned above, the British Leblanc industry survived for as long as it did partly because of a merging of companies to form the United Alkali Company, thus facilitating economies of scale, and partly by entering into price-fixing agreements with British Solvay producers.

The presence of trade unions in an industry could also inhibit the free functioning of the market mechanism so that the rate of adoption of a new technology was not dependent on considerations of cost-savings alone. Strong unions, particularly of skilled or highly-specialised workers, could, through industrial action, slow down the rate at which new techniques were introduced into an industry, and even 'unorganised' labour, through machine-breaking and various forms of industrial sabotage, could make the introduction of new technology into an industry a slow and expensive process. On the other hand, if, as Rosenberg has convincingly argued, strikes, or the fear of strikes, particularly of skilled workers, have acted in the past as powerful inducements to innovation and technical change,[3] then they must also have played their part in encouraging the diffusion of these techniques within the strike-affected industry.

As we have already seen, market forces operating through the price mechanism were also responsible in part for the spread of modern technology between countries as well as within them. In western Europe, the emergence of a competitive market economy and a greater degree of individual freedom were accompanied by a relaxation of impediments to international trade and commerce and international movements of labour and capital. The elimination of controls on foreign trade enhanced international competition and stimulated imitation in the industrial sphere. Thus the inflow of cheap cotton piece goods into Switzerland from Britain in the late eighteenth century led to the adoption or imitation of British machinery and methods of production by the Swiss cotton industry. Examples of this kind of response can be multiplied. At the same time, the greater degree of freedom in international labour and capital flows sustained international competitiveness by permitting a more varied response to changing economic circumstances. Thus countries faced with the threat of increased competition in their domestic markets from the exports of already-industrialised or industrialising countries could meet this competition in part through the import of foreign skills, capital and technology. On the other hand, modern industrial firms which developed foreign markets for their manufactured products, when faced with growing local competition or with the threat of tariff protection in their foreign markets, often set up subsidiary companies in these threatened markets, thus sustaining local competition and encouraging the more rapid adoption of the new technology.

While the price mechanism operating through international flows of trade, labour and capital helped diffuse modern industrial technology between countries, it must nevertheless be emphasised that the different factor endowments of countries which were reflected in differences in the relative price of land, labour and capital, were often critical in the selection of a technology, a fact that goes far to explain the observable differences in techniques employed between regions or countries. Between two countries as differently endowed as Britain and the United States in the early nineteenth century, we should expect the adopting country to adopt the new industrial technology in a highly selective fashion; that is, to adopt some techniques rapidly, others more slowly, and perhaps yet others not at all. At the root of this selection process was an economic mechanism operating through factor proportions and factor prices which determined the expected profitability of different techniques in a new environment.[4]

IV

Although the state was instrumental in eliminating or reducing the many restrictions imposed on the freedom of the individual in his economic life, and freedom from state intervention in economic affairs was a central tenet of economic liberalism, industrialisation under competitive market conditions tended to produce a number of undesirable trends which, on humanitarian grounds, even the firmest adherents to the *laissez-faire* economy could not completely ignore. Among these trends were the deplorable conditions under which the labouring classes had to work, the unacceptable living standards of the poor, the slums created in the industrial cities, the trade cycle, and the appearance of monopolistic practices in a number of industries late in the nineteenth century. Despite the adherence of national governments to the competitive market economy, all states found it necessary to intervene, in varying degrees of intensity, in the working of the free enterprise economy by introducing legislation to counteract the worst of the evils thrown up by the new economic system.

While many of the consequent improvements in the social and economic conditions of the working classes that followed from this government intervention in the economy helped to raise labour productivity, stimulate economic growth and thereby encourage the further spread of industrial technology, in those countries where the competitive market system worked only fitfully, the government had a more direct role to play in the industrialisation process. Investment banks were another means of diffusing technology in those countries where the market mechanism proved to be deficient for this purpose. Both investment banks and the state played important roles in promoting industrial development and thereby encouraging the spread of modern technology in those countries where, because of deficiencies of resources and weaknesses in the market system, spontaneous economic development under free enterprise conditions was considerably hindered. To the extent that they performed this function successfully, investment banks and the state were substituted for the free market system as a mechanism for bringing about industrial growth and development.

Notes

1. For a more detailed discussion on the relationship between the law and economic activity in England during the industrial revolution, see R.M. Hartwell, 'Two Services: Education and Law', a seminar paper which is reprinted in R.M. Hartwell, *The Industrial Revolution and Economic Growth* (London, 1971), pp. 226-61.

2. A.K. Cairncross, 'Migrations of Technology', reprinted in A.K. Cairncross, *Factors in Economic Development* (London, 1962), p.178.

3. N. Rosenberg, 'The Direction of Technological Change: Inducement Mechanisms and Focusing Devices', *Economic Development and Cultural Change* (October 1969), pp. 1-23. For example, 'Richard Robert's self-acting mule was invented in 1825 as a result of a strike on the part of the skilled and highly independent mule-spinners.' Rosenberg, 'Direction of Technological Change', p. 13.

4. See also N. Rosenberg, 'Selection and adaptation in the transfer of technology: steam and iron in America 1800–1870', paper presented at a conference sponsored by the International Cooperation in the History of Technology Committee, Pont-à-Mousson, France, July 1970; reprinted in N. Rosenberg, *Perspectives on Technology* (Cambridge, 1976), pp. 173-88.

Selected Reading

P.T. Ellsworth and J. Clark Leith, *The International Economy,* 5th ed. (New York, 1975), Part I

H.Heaton, *Economic History of Europe* (New York, 1948), Chs IV and XVI

A. Milward and S.B. Saul, *The Economic Development of Continental Europe 1780–1870* (London, 1973), esp. Ch. 1

F.L. Nussbaum, *History of the Economic Institutions of Modern Europe* (New York, 1933)

13 INVESTMENT BANKS AND INDUSTRIALISATION IN THE NINETEENTH CENTURY

While in Chapter 5 we noted that a reasonably developed financial market was an essential prerequisite for the appearance of modern economic growth in a country, one type of financial institution, the investment bank, became an important mechanism for spreading modern industrial technology in the nineteenth century. Established initially to assist national economic development, the investment bank was designed specifically to promote and finance industrial ventures of all kinds. It also played an important part in the international diffusion of technology, particularly in Europe.

I

For a number of reasons industrialisation in Britain did not require the development of specialised institutions for promoting and financing long-term industrial investment. First, the process of industrialisation in Britain was gradual. As a result, there was no great need for large amounts of investible funds at any particular stage in the country's early industrial development. Second, each enterprise was, at the outset, a relatively small concern with little demand for long-term funds and with the ability over time to finance additional investment out of retained profits. Third, in comparison with most other countries, innovating entrepreneurs were able to tap the financial resources of the nobility and gentry directly. For working capital, industrialists were able to obtain accommodation from local, generally family, banks, or from merchants through the medium of bills of exchange. Finally, the accumulation of capital proceeded rapidly, first in the trade sector, later in the modernising agricultural sector and, later still, within the industrial sector itself. Moreover, it was not until the second half of the nineteenth century that the average manufacturing firm increased in size and external financing became a major consideration. By then, joint stock banking had become widespread and such banks and other specialised institutions had become adept in the issuing of shares and debentures. There was little demand for the establishment of investment banks as such in Britain in comparison with Germany, for example, and although some were established after 1860 they did not assume the connections with industrial firms that became so pervasive in Germany, nor did they become important in the British financial sector.

On the Continent the situation was different. In the first half of the nineteenth century many European countries were economically quite backward, and even in the relatively advanced countries the gradual approach to modernisation, characteristic of Britain's experience, was impossible because successful industrialisation inevitably involved a process of 'catching up' with the leader. The adoption of the new technology and its adaptation to local circumstances meant that the development of both the industrial superstructure and the infrastructure of the economy in each country was telescoped into a period of a few decades. For example, whereas the spread of the railway across Britain followed that country's early industrial development by several decades and was thus financed without undue interference with financing of industrial ventures, on the Continent, railway construction preceded or coincided with industrialisation and thus added to the difficulties of financing development. The same was true of public utilities. While the typical business enterprise remained small during much of the nineteenth century, the needs of large-scale enterprises and of utilities for investible funds created a general scarcity which could have limited both the expansion of relatively small enterprises and the entry of new firms into the various industries. As with investible funds, there was also a shortage of entrepreneurial skills. Because the commercial banks were unable to satisfy the rapidly growing demands for long-term capital, it was inevitable that the movement towards incorporation of enterprises gathered pace. At the same time, the ability of the banking sector to provide long-term loans to industry was slowly being realised. Despite many attempts to set up banks to finance industrial ventures and a few successes, it was not until the 1850s that the connections between banking institutions and industry became a reality. Thereafter, investment banking became an important mechanism for accelerating the industrial development of several European countries.

II

For the most of the first half of the nineteenth century, the banking scene on the Continent was dominated by banks established by governments, such as the Bank of France, and by private, generally family, merchant banks, such as Rothschilds. These family banks relied largely on their own capital for investible funds. The only deposits they accepted came from a few wealthy clients who were unlikely to vary their deposits appreciably over time. Most of their investments were in the underwriting of government loans and foreign exchange dealings. As far as the latter was concerned, they accepted, discounted and cashed bills of exchange and thus facilitated transactions between merchants in different countries. Their private dealings were based largely on personal relations and the confidentiality of transactions. Their use of internal bills, however, was generally limited and thus discounting was costly and the availability of short-term credit much more limited than in Britain. After 1815, these banks entered into the lucrative fields of insurance and savings banking. Finding these avenues of investment highly profitable and relatively safe, the family banks found few attractions in long-term industrial investments (disapprovingly called 'industrial speculations'), although there is sufficient evidence to show that they dabbled in manufacturing ventures from time to time and that they were attracted to the financing of railways in the 1830s and later decades. Except for discounting facilities for working capital, however, industrial concerns, especially in France, had little call for large-scale external financing. The need for this kind of finance emerged only in the 1830s with the growing importance of railway construction and the increase in the size of manufacturing firms in such capital-intensive industries as metallurgy, coal-mining and glass manufacture. On the Continent, the mobilisation of investible funds to finance these types of industrial enterprises was achieved by changes in banking techniques.

The evolution of investment banking in Europe can be conveniently described in terms of three stages of development. First, there was the planning stage in which a number of these banking institutions appeared in Belgium and France. It was in Belgium, where the demands of the industrial sector for large-scale financing appeared early in Europe, that the first prototypes of the investment bank emerged in the early 1830s. Similar banks were established in France as a result of the activities of such bankers as Laffitte and the Péreire brothers. Confronted with the hostility of the established private banks and a very cautious government, few of the early French investment banks were able to establish themselves on a permanent basis. But where they existed, the aims of these financial institutions invariably included the acceptance of deposits, the discounting of commercial bills for short-term financing, and the provision of long-term funds.

The second stage, which covers the era of the *crédit mobilier* (1850–70), may be regarded as a transitional phase in the evolution of investment banks. It coincided with a rapid expansion of railway building in Europe and with industrial booms in a number of countries in the 1850s. Originating in France with the establishment of the Société Générale de Crédit Mobilier by the Péreires as a joint stock institution, the movement spread very rapidly throughout Europe either via the direct participation of the Paris institution in the banking activities of other countries, or via the imitation of that institution elsewhere. Between 1853, when the Därmstadter Bank was established with the aid of French capital and management, and the end of 1856, 15 such banks were founded in the Germanic states. In addition, in the 1850s French capital aided the setting up of *crédit mobiliers* in Austria, Spain, Italy, the Netherlands, Switzerland and Russia.

Although the *crédit mobilier* movement as a major force within the European banking field was relatively short-lived, during its existence it fulfilled a need which could not be accommodated by existing banking institutions. Apart from the ordinary banking business performed by the *crédit mobilier* as a deposit and discount bank, it also aimed to centralise the different credit operations required by large enterprises: capitalisation, issue of bonds, the provision of long-term credits, the most revolutionary feature of its operations. It was thus a 'mixed bank' involved in the mobilisation of short-term funds and in the immobilisation of some of its assets in long-term, 'speculative' ventures. In this respect, the new institution not only proved its ability to mobilise savings to meet the needs of large-scale investment in transport and manufacturing in France it also influenced the operations of the established private banks, *la haute banque*, most of which imitated the *crédit mobilier* by setting up their own similar organisations. The *crédit mobilier* also accelerated the movement of French capital abroad and at the same time, by financing ventures in other countries, it facilitated the transfer of French banking techniques and French technology and expertise to those other nations. Later, however, when Europeans found investment in industrial shares and bonds more acceptable and when deposit banking became more widespread, the need for such an all-embracing financial institution combining both short-term and long-term ventures began to fade. These developments, along with the discrediting of the *crédit mobilier* in France in the 1860s, following the financial collapse of a number of them, brought the movement to an end and led to their replacement by the great investment banks of *banques d'affaires*.

These *banques d'affaires* represent the third or 'highest' stage in the evolution of European investment banking. These banks were joint stock institutions which acquired shareholdings in the industrial companies they sponsored and issued securities through their associated deposit banks. Their development was therefore closely associated with the spread of deposit banking which began to gather pace throughout many countries in the 1860s. The two kinds of banks often shared the same directors. It was in this way that the functions performed jointly by the *crédit mobilier* became divided between the deposit bank, which adopted the short-term deposit-attracting and discounting functions, and the investment banks, which assumed the long-term financing function. In addition, the investment bank usually accepted some deposits but only from the firms over which it had some control. Outside France, many of the *crédit mobiliers* were remodelled into investment banks.

There was a close connection between the investment bank and the industrial firms whose shares it promoted and acquired and in the conduct of whose business it was directly involved. Having committed long-term funds to such manufacturing concerns, the bank had an interest in ensuring the continued existence and profitability of such enterprises. On the other hand, some investment banks were created or acquired by industrialists themselves, for example, Solvays and the Banque Générale Belge and the banks of the Wendels and Le Creusot. While several investment banks were established in France after 1860, French industry continued to distrust long-term bank aid and it was not until the appearance of several new industries that manufacturers were prepared to break with tradition by approaching these banks for long-term accommodation. On the whole, French banks were more active in foreign industrial ventures and were also instrumental in setting up investment banks in other European countries, Latin America, Egypt, China and Japan. For these operations, funds were obtained from the French deposit banks which had spread their branches throughout the country.

Unlike their German counterparts, however, the French banks were concerned principally with the *financing* of industrial projects and only rarely *took control* of such ventures. Indeed, in some cases the banks severed their connections with industrial firms once access to finance was no longer a major problem for such firms. It was in

Germany that the ties between the banks and industry were strongest and these connections went in two directions. While the banks secured representation on the boards of industrial companies and provided organisational skills and finance, industrialists were also represented on the boards of the banks and, in some cases, dominated their policies. As an example of the latter the connections between Siemens and the Deutsche Bank may be cited. Some firms, especially in the electrical industries, established their own banking organisations but, in the main, these operated outside Germany and were concerned largely with fostering the foreign operations of the German parent companies.

III

How did these investment banks affect industrial development in Europe and elsewhere in the nineteenth century? As already noted, the need for long-term investible funds appeared early in Belgium, where the Société-Générale de Belgique (established in 1822) and the Banque de Belgique (1835) became as heavily involved in Belgian industry as the German investment banks in German industry four decades later. They created and financed the operations of 55 joint stock companies with total assets of over 150 million francs (£6 million). These investments were spread across coal mines, ironworks, textile factories, engineering works, sugar refineries and glass works. By the end of the 1840s, Belgium's coal industry was the most developed on the Continent and her iron and machinery industries the most efficient. Much of the successful industrial development was due to the access to external capital provided by the two investment banks. They continued to aid industrial growth in the second half of the nineteenth century but on a smaller scale than before 1850. In the early 1870s, several new banks were set up to finance industrial development but, as manufacturing firms became larger, they moved progressively towards the self-financing of long-term investment projects, relying on financial institutions largely for working capital.

The links forged between the investment banks and industry were strongest in Germany. While the Darmstadt Bank had been operating on *crédit mobilier* lines from 1853 and the Disconto Gesellschaft from 1856, it was in the early 1870s that the number of investment banks rose rapidly. Among the new arrivals were the Deutsche Bank (1870) and the Dresdner (1872). These four banks became the most powerful in Germany after 1870 when they became concerned primarily with investment in manufacturing ventures. Indeed, the growth of investment banks and industrialisation were locked together more tightly in Germany than in any other country. Even in the 1850s, the early German investment banks were heavily involved in the industrial development of the Ruhr, unlike the Crédit Mobilier de Paris, on which they were modelled, which had little success with French industry at that time. The German banks and industrial firms shared common directorates. In some cases the banks controlled the manufacturing firm, in others the manufacturer controlled the bank. As one observer notes:

> The banks had very wide opportunities to serve their industrial customers—as issuing firms, as banking creditors as holders of large blocks of shares and as members of directorates. They accompanied them from the cradle to the grave. They floated them, issued new shares, gave credit accounts and manifold loans, delivered them of daughter companies, performed surgical operations in crises and provided for decent obsequies at the liquidation.[1]

This involvement was especially evident in mining, metallurgy, chemicals, the electrical industries and engineering. When new ventures required funds beyond the resources of any one financial institution, a consortium of banks was set up to provide the required funds. In this way the risks of such ventures were spread among the banks. At the same time, because these banks assumed risks in lending long-term to industry either by holding on to shares as an investment or until the shares could be passed on to others, they insisted on participation in the working of the firms they sponsored.

One of the outstanding features of the investment banks in Germany was their involvement in the setting up of giant industrial trusts which, through a process of vertical integration, controlled raw material sources, manufacturing, and often the selling of the final product. In some cases, the trust eventually outgrew the cartels in which its component parts had participated. For example, the mining of coal and iron ore, the manufacture of steel and iron and steel goods, railway and engineering materials, shipbuilding, and even the shipping companies, could all have been encompassed by a trust which was created and controlled by a consortium of banks. Such activities also produced a number of bank amalgamations during the period up to World War I.[2]

German investment banks set up and controlled by industrialists operated mainly outside Germany and became involved in the foreign operations of the manufacturing firms. A large part of Germany's foreign investment in the late nineteenth century assumed this type of venture and it was particularly evident in the international spread of the electrical industries. Plants to produce electrical equipment were set up in several countries including Austria-Hungary, Italy, Russia and Spain. At the same time, electrochemical works were established in Austria-Hungary, Norway, Russia, Spain, Sweden and Switzerland. All of these foreign ventures were aided by the German investment banks. Some also financed oil investments in Rumania. Taken as a whole, the foreign interests of the German banks were highly diversified. In addition to the financing of industrial enterprises, they provided funds for banking operations in Italy and elsewhere, railways in the Balkans and, under pressure from the German government, they advanced loans to a number of foreign governments. They were also active in promoting trade and commerce in the German colonies.

Both foreign and domestic investment banks played an important part in the industrialisation of Russia after 1890. While foreign investors in Russia came from France, Germany, Britain and a number of other European countries, the French assumed the leading role in encouraging the growth of the nation's manufacturing sector. As in the other newly-industrialising countries, these foreign funds were larely concentrated in the mining, metallurgical, electrical and chemical industries. At first, French banks, such as the Société Générale financed ventures in coal, iron and steel (it constructed large steel works—the Makeevka Company— on its coal deposits) and attempted, through the formation of a holding company (Omnium Russe), to co-ordinate efforts to expand coal and iron and steel production. In the 1890s in particular, both French and other European entrepreneurial skills went hand in hand with Western finance in promoting the spread of modern technology to Russia by assisting the growth of Russian industry.

In the 1900s, when another spurt of industrial development occurred in Russia, the financing of new ventures altered considerably. Russian investment banks, modelled on the German banks but using funds attracted from abroad, played a greater role in providing funds and entrepreneurial skills for local industry. At the same time, foreign bankers were content to finance the Russian banks and to expand the activities of companies with which they had already become involved in earlier decades. In Russia, therefore, as in Germany, the investment banks guided the growth of manufacturing during the critical stages of industrial development up to 1914. At the same time it was heavy industry which received the major attention of these banks. This emphasis on heavy industry was also a result of the efforts of the Russian government to steer bank funds towards manufacturing ventures with military potential, including the production of iron and steel, armaments and railway equipment.

Like Russia, Italy did not begin to experience rapid industrial development until the 1890s. Investment banking came to play an important part in the modernisation process that subsequently took place in this country. German banking techniques were introduced in the mid-nineties and later French and Italian banking interest added to the number of investment banks operating in the country. While the new banks spread their investments across the whole ambit of the manufacturing sector, electric power, chemicals iron and steel, engineering and textiles were distinctly favoured. As in Germany, the banks obtained administrative and entrepreneurial control of the firms in which they invested. For example, the Banca Commerciale Italiana, formed in 1894 on German lines, obtained effective control over the provision of electric power throughout the country and created the Society for the Development of Electric Firms, the sole purpose of which was to provide funds for the establishment of new firms within the electrical industry. But this is only one example of the manner in which investment banks shaped the growth of manufacturing industry in Italy where, because of the general shortage of investible funds, the investment banks obtained a hold over industry greater than in most other countries at that time.

The German influence was also evident in Scandinavia; the Danish Privatbanken was established in the early 1870s and was involved in later years in the formation of a number of industrial companies principally through the merging of smaller firms, while in Sweden the Stockholms Enskilda Bank influenced the growth of the mining and paper industries. The latter bank also participated in the development of Norway's electricity industry and in Russian telephone projects in the 1900s. In Switzerland, the Zurich Schweizerische Creditanstalt invested heavily in the local mechanical engineering industry and, along with French and other Swiss banks, aided the growth of the electrical industry.

Outside Europe, two other countries, the United States and Japan, experienced the beneficial effects of investment banking at a critical stage in their industrial development. In Japan, the combination of state encouragement and private attitudes in banking circles ensured a steady stream of funds into the emerging manufacturing sector. The Industrial Bank, which began operations in 1902 and which was modelled on the Crédit Mobilier, steered foreign portfolio funds into the iron and steel, shipbuilding, chemicals, machinery and electric power industries. The Hypothec Bank lent funds to the textiles and other, generally light, industries. As in Germany, some industrialists eventually formed their own banks to obtain control over the supply of funds available to them, but it appears that it was not until after World War I that major advances occurred in the Japanese investment banking field, that is, the formation of the *zaibatsu* banks, based on German lines.

From the 1820s on, investment banking activities evolved slowly in the United States through the development of private banking organisations established by former brokers, merchants or local agents of foreign banking houses. It was through the latter type of private bank that most of the British and Continental funds were transferred to the United States for investment in government loans, railway bonds and other private ventures. It was, however, the heavy government demand for loans during the Civil War in the 1850s that rapidly accelerated the growth of American investment banking and the emergence of several German-Jewish banks and some 'Yankee houses'. After the war, the major preoccupation of the investment banks was the expansion of the railways through the flotation of railway bonds. As in Germany, strong financial ties were forged between the banks and the companies they sponsored. The strength of the banks lay in their ability to mobilise large supplies of domestic and foreign funds and to direct them into the railway companies. In the late 1880s and the 1890s, it became necessary for the banks to reconstruct the capital and working operations of several railway companies which were experiencing financial difficulties.

The emergence of the large incorporated organisation in manufacturing in the 1880s and public acceptance of industrial shares, especially after the depression of the mid-nineties, appreciably enhanced the activities of the American investment banks. From the 1890s they increasingly turned their attention towards the sale of industrial shares and bonds and towards effecting mergers and other combinations. At this time, three other developments in their operations must be noted. First, the growth of life insurance companies ensured that the savings of policy holders became available to the investment bankers for investment purposes because of the attitudes of the insurance companies. Second, the needs of the investment banks for short-term funds ensured that close links were established with commercial banks, including the sharing of directorates. Third, the growth of 'syndicates' of investment banks to float specific issues of securities or to effect mergers became necessary when the resources required were relatively large or when the spreading of risks was deemed desirable. Such syndicates were involved in the establishment of trusts in a number of leading manufacturing industries towards the end of the nineteenth century.

From the Civil War to World War I, the American investment banks established themselves as powerful institutions in the nation's capital market. They aided the mobilisation and use of internal savings during a period in which savings were being accumulated rapidly, they tapped foreign sources of funds efficiently, they produced many mergers of industrial firms, they often saved companies from insolvency through their financial knowledge and, generally, they played an important role in ensuring that capital investment in the emerging manufacturing sector and in transport proceeded smoothly.

IV

Whereas investment banks were not the only financial institutions supplying funds to industrial enterprises in the nineteenth century, these banks are noted for the active role they played in promoting industrial development in a number of countries, especially after 1850. Compared with most other countries, Britain's industrial revolution was a relatively long-drawn-out affair and consequently the need for funds to finance long-term investment activity was not as pressing as in those countries that were latecomers to industrialisation, and in which there often existed an urge to catch up with the leading industrial nation. Moreover, whereas in Britain technological progress proceeded gradually, in the late developers industrialisation involved not only the adoption of previously-established modern techniques of production, but also the adoption of new production methods that emerged in increasing numbers in the second half of the nineteenth century. As a result, industrial development made more exacting demands on the financial sector of late-industrialising countries than it did in Britain during the early stages of her industrial development. Fortunately, however, investment banks were able to tap the savings of foreigners as well as domestic savers in their endeavours to accelerate the growth of the manufacturing firms under their patronage.

As the nineteenth century proceeded, it became increasingly more costly to undertake the introduction of modern industrial technology. A high rate of railway construction and the growing attractions of the economies of scale to be reaped in the production of coal, iron and steel, machine tools, chemicals and electrical engineering products considerably increased the demand for investible funds in Europe after 1850. These developments, along with the growing popularity of the joint stock company form of business organisation in European countries in which stock exchange markets were slow to emerge, created conditions favouring the growth of investment banking. The shortage of capital and of entrepreneurial and financial skills was particularly acute in those countries on the threshold of industrialisation. In these circumstances, the investment banks, in combination with other financial innovations of the time, became an important mechanism for mobilising savings and directing them into industry. So successful were these investment banks in mobilising capital and entrepreneurial skills that in a number of countries the attainment of industrial take-off was telescoped into a very short period of time of some two to three decades.

One must not, however, overemphasise the importance of investment banking and understate the role played by other forms of financing industrial ventures, especially self-financing from retained profits. The investment banks played an important role in the industrial development of Germany, Italy and Belgium. Their role was less important, but nevertheless a significant one, in Russia, Switzerland, the United States and Denmark. In France, the country in which this type of financial institution had its origin, the success of the banks was more limited. This resulted partly from a long-standing mistrust of banks among industrialists and partly from the particular manner in which French industry developed. French attempts at investment banking favoured other European countries more than they did France, not only directly through the movement of French capital abroad but also indirectly by providing the model for the investment banks that developed later. Moreover, the foreign investment activity of many of the European investment banks did much to assist the growth and development of international monetary relations during the second half of the nineteenth century. Finally, investment banks were more than just providers of financial services. Many of them were prepared to provide firms with entrepreneurial and organisational skills as well. To the extent that they did this, investment banks were even more influential in establishing the climate conducive to successful industrial growth through the adoption of modern industrial technology.

Notes

1. W.F. Bruck, *Social and Economic History of Germany from William II to Hitler, 1888–1938* (New York, 1962), p. 84.
2. Recent research suggests that in some respects the importance of the German investment banks in industrial development from 1880 to 1914 has been overstressed in the past, that often the role of the bank was passive rather than active and often the industrialists called the tune. In addition, many industrial firms had few involved connections with the *Kreditbanken* and, yet again, that the banks may have inhibited industrial development to a certain extent by concentrating their activities in heavy industry at the expense of other types of industries. More detailed research is still required. See H. Neuberger, 'The Industrial Politics of the *Kreditbanken,* 1880–1914), *Business History Review,* Vol. LI (1977), pp. 190-207.

Selected Reading

R. Cameron *et al., Banking in the Early Stages of Industrialisation* (Oxford, 1967)
B. Gille, 'Banking and Industrialization in Europe 1730–1914', in C.M. Cipolla (ed.), *The Fontana Economic History of Europe,* Vol. 3 (London, 1973), pp. 255-300
Jonathan Hughes, *Industrialization and Economic History: Theses and Conjectures* (New York, 1970), pp. 152-60
Tom Kemp, *Historical Patterns of Industrialization* (London, 1978), Ch. 6
D. Landes, 'The Old Bank and the New: The Financial Revolution of the Nineteenth Century', in F. Crouzet *et al.* (eds.), *Essays in European Economic History 1789–1914* (London, 1969), pp. 112-27
H. Neuberger, 'The Industrial Politics of the *Kreditbanken,* 1880–1914', *Business History Review,* Vol. LI (1977), pp. 190-207

14 INDUSTRIALISATION AND THE STATE

I

Today it is accepted by most people that the state has an important economic role to play in modern society. Whether the economy is centrally-planned, as in Eastern Europe or China, or whether its operation is the outcome of decentralised decision-making of the kind associated with private enterprise and the free market, as in most advanced Western countries, it has become a function of the government to maintain economic growth and to see that the benefits of that growth are shared by all members of the community. Whereas, in the past, governments have always had fairly obvious reasons for being interested in the economic health of the countries they governed, and for this reason were often prepared to promote economic development, in the early stages of the modern industrial era the philosophy of economic liberalism, with which it was associated, viewed the interference of government in economic affairs as likely to hinder rather than advance industrial development. This attitude was widespread in Britain and in the United States, where the philosophy of economic individualism held sway throughout most of the nineteenth century. Even in these countries, however, this *laissez-faire* attitude did not completely absolve the government from any responsibility for the state of the economy. Apart from defence and the maintenance of law and order, the government was also required to provide the legal and social framework necessary to a freely-functioning private enterprise system. Later, when growing wealth and rising real incomes sharpened the disparities between rich and poor, when rapid urbanisation gave rise to problems of poor housing, inadequate sanitation and a deteriorating social environment, and when trade depressions faced many workers and their families with the recurring threat of unemployment and possible destitution, the government, at least in Britain, was forced to interfere in the economy in an effort to ameliorate some the the worst features of industrial capitalism. In other words, if in some countries the government did not play an active role in initiating industrial development, it was certainly called upon later to play a more vigorous role in combating the economic and social ill-effects of industrial change.

On the Continent things were altogether different to what they were in Britain. In most European countries the state never fully relinquished its control over economic matters. Moreover, once industrialisation got under way in these countries the state was called upon, indeed even expected, to play its part in promoting change. There were several reasons for this. First, industrialisation in Europe and elsewhere in the second half of the nineteenth century was associated with a growing sense of nationalism. The reunification of Germany and Italy, the Civil War in the United States, and the threat of foreign intervention in Japan, were only some of the forces responsible for generating an upsurge of nationalist feeling at that time which tended to create a social and political climate amenable to state involvement in industrial development. In addition, the urgency of the desire to 'catch up' with the industrial leaders meant that some of the more backward countries, such as Italy, Russia and Japan, had to produce industrial change on a scale that made government support absolutely essential. Finally, the threat of competition from already established industrial nations was often enough in itself to convince industrialists in newly-developed countries of the need to seek the aid and support of the state in their industrialisation endeavours.

II

The state could use either direct of indirect methods of promoting industrial development. Direct methods used in the eighteenth and nineteenth centuries included the setting up of government owned and operated establishments, the payment of subsidies to selected key industries, and the purchase of manufactured goods, for example armaments and railway materials from domestic producers. Indirect methods of aiding industrial development included alterations to the institutional and economic structures of the country in the broadest sense. Some of the indirect methods used by the state in this period took the form of investment in social overhead capital, or public works, and education, the encouragement of the inflow of foreign capital and technological ideas, the promotion of domestic saving, the adoption of a commercial policy favourable to industrial development, and the implementation of numerous institutional changes affecting land tenure, business organisation and the provision of financial services.

There is a long history of state involvement in economic activity in modern times. Before the nineteenth century it was stimulated principally by the needs of the state for armaments and other goods and services of a military nature. Nevertheless, the pervasiveness of mercantilist philosophy throughout Europe ensured a long-standing state interest in industrial development and its stimulation by means of government subsidies and monopoly rights. Thus in France state-controlled enterprises had appeared by the late seventeenth century and monopoly rights and subsidies were granted to favoured private firms operating generally in the armaments, metallurgical and luxury industries. An additional incentive for state interest in the fostering of manufacturing ventures appeared late in the eighteenth century when the impact of the industrial successes being achieved in Britain was felt on the Continent. Thus, during this time, industrial firms in the Prussian textiles, chemicals, metals, coal and iron industries benefited from government patronage. In Austria and Russia, there were efforts on the part of the governments to encourage the entry of firms into mining and selective manufacturing industries.

But many of these ventures were sporadic, often short-lived and had a limited impact on the economic development of the countries concerned. The relatively small size of their operations, the backwardness of each country at the time, a shortage of investible funds, limited markets, the lack of cheap and adequate transport, and numerous institutional and other obstacles to growth ensured the absence of an economic environment conducive to the attainment of sustained economic growth. Moreover, it must be stressed that there was a complete absence of positive developmental planning. Whenever the state interfered in the market it did so either to meet its own particular needs or to overcome some obstacle encountered by private business firms at the time. This remained substantially the situation in most countries throughout the nineteenth century.

From the end of the Napoleonic Wars to 1870, direct state participation in industrial development was a more important feature of the early stages of industrialisation in Belgium, Prussia and certain other European countries. In Belgium in the 1820s, the Dutch government invested extensively in shipbuilding and manufacturing activities, particularly textiles, but after independence in 1830, the new Belgian government was more inclined to use indirect methods of stimulating the manufacturing sector. In Prussia, the state-owned ironworks, coal mines and the lead mines in Upper Silesia, increased production rapidly under the direction of the government. The Overseas Trading Corporation (the Seehandlung), a government-financed institution set up in 1772, had by the 1840s acquired additional financial interests in a number of Prussian manufacturing enterprises such as paper factories, machine-building works, iron and steel works, cotton-spinning and weaving establishments and worsted weaving sheds. The coal mines of the Saar continued to be exploited by the government of Hesse-Nassau, the Bavarian government operated mines and foundries in the Palatinate and the metallurgical works in Württemberg were favoured by government promotion.

By the 1850s, however, the need for state development of manufacturing in Germany was thought to be less pressing and many of the government undertakings were sold to private firms. At the same time, a decline in direct state intervention in industry was occurring in Belgium, Holland and France. Private savings, entrepreneurship and technical innovation were proving sufficient to support rapid economic growth in later decades and, consequently, the role of the state in promoting industrial development through the direct supply of capital and entrepreneurship became subordinated to the more indirect methods of aiding industry.

Such was not the case after 1870 in Italy, Russia and Japan, however. In Italy, the state granted subsidies to a number of industries, including shipping and steelworks, operated state-owned iron ore mines on Elba, and generally offered aid to firms located in the metallurgical and engineering sectors. On the whole, these efforts of the Italian government may have been somewhat limited in terms of long-run industrial growth. In Russia, the industrial ventures of the state were larger and more diversified in scope than those in Italy and perhaps more effective economically. Largely in response to the urgent need to strengthen the economic structure and military power of the country, the weaknesses of which had been brought home dramatically by defeat in the war with Turkey in 1877–8, the Russian government embarked on a policy of intensive state-controlled industrial growth which lasted from the mid-1880s until 1900. A second spurt of economic growth occurred from 1906 to World War I, but it was mainly in the first of these that the state played a major promotional role. As in Italy, direct state sponsorship of industrialisation involved the operation of state-owned enterprises and the subsidisation of others. It was also the technically advanced and heavy industries, such as iron and steel, metallurgy and machinery, which received most government support. At the same time, state contracts for military equipment tended to maintain a steady demand for the output of many manufacturing firms. By the mid-1900s, however, the need for direct public support of manufacturing was judged to be less critical than it had been in the mid-eighties. Thereafter, private enterprise proved to be more capable than in the 1890s of sustaining a high annual rate of growth until the outbreak of World War I.

In a few other European countries, state entrepreneurship was a feature of the development of manufacturing industries, for example, the Hungarian state-owned iron and steel works in Slovakia, copper works and a number of textile and flour mills.

Perhaps the most successful instances of state promotion of industrial growth among the latecomers occurred in Japan after the late 1860s. Faced with the collapse of its policy of isolationism and the need to prevent possible foreign domination of the country, the Japanese government embarked on a programme of rapid modernisation in the years immediately following the restoration of the Emperor Meiji in 1868. As part of this programme, the government actively participated in the development of a large manufacturing sector. By 1880 it had opened up new coal mines, established iron foundries, shipbuilding yards, textile mills, and cement, paper and glass factories, all along Western lines. The importance of these early ventures, which in the main did not require relatively large capital resources, lay in the example they provided private entrepreneurs of the profitability of manufacturing undertakings. Private firms very quickly emulated the example of the state and, by 1882, the government was able generally to allow private industry to take the lead. Thereafter, with the exception of the establishment of the Yawata ironworks in 1896, the most successful Japanese state enterprise before 1913 and a venture considered essential to the build-up of military strength, the Japanese government generally allowed private enterprise to develop the manufacturing sector, at least until the late 1930s.

In most modernising countries the government's demand for goods and services provided the state with a powerful means of stimulating industrial development. This was especially so in the second half of the nineteenth century when government expenditure as a proportion of national income tended to rise in most countries. In addition to the state's demand for construction materials for railways, schools and urban development, the growing government expenditure on military equipment also played an important role in the growth of several industries, especially iron and steel, shipbuilding and textiles.

The extent of the government's direct involvement in industrial development differed substantially from one country to another and, within each country, from one period to another. Direct state involvement in the industrialisation process was greatest in those countries that were latecomers to modern economic growth, and this may have reflected partly their relative backwardness, partly the inadequacy of private endeavours and partly the urgency with which the need for rapid industrialisation and the inherent transfer of modern technology from more advanced countries was viewed by the governments of these countries. To a large extent it was heavy industry, particularly coal and iron and steel, which attracted most government attention. After relatively short periods of large-scale intervention in the economy the state generally retired from exercising direct control of industry. Having provided through its own efforts the demonstration effects needed to stimulate the private sector to greater industrial activity, the government in most countries was prepared to leave further industrial development to private enterprise.

The state thus tended to promote the spread of modern industrial techniques from those countries in which the centres of invention and innovation lay to those more technologically and more industrially backward, and thus tended to accelerate what would probably have been a natural phenomenon in later decades. In some cases, such as in Western Europe and Japan, such efforts fell on fertile ground but, in others, in which the economic institutions, infrastructure and acceptance of new ideas were too immature at the stage at which state intervention commenced, the transfer of modern technology led to industrial complexes being established in a hostile and inadequate environment. Furthermore in such latecomers as Italy and Russia, the industrial structure which emerged gave too great an emphasis on heavy industry for the benefits of industrialisation to be spread throughout the economy.

III

An even more widespread phenomenon in the nineteenth century was the indirect state involvement in the industrialisation process. Apart from its generality, this involvement tended to be more sustained over time than most instances of direct state participation in industrial development. Of crucial importance here was government investment in social overhead capital and, in particular, its concern with the provision of adequate transport and communications facilities. In part, this concern stemmed from political or military considerations but there was often too a genuine concern for the promotion of economic progress. The state was often forced to intervene either because of the failure of private enterprise to provide services essential to the growth of the economy or because of the unwillingness of private entrepreneurs to enter comparatively unrewarding fields of economic activity. Moreover, because social overhead capital projects required large investment outlays, in many countries only the government possessed the ability to mobilise funds from domestic or foreign sources for such purposes.

The indirect promotion of industry by the state was most evident in the construction of railways. But even prior to the advent of the railways, financial aid was offered by a number of governments to assist in the development of other forms of transport, especially the construction of canals. On the Continent and in North America in the late eighteenth and early nineteenth centuries state aid, largely financed from loans obtained from abroad, ensured the development of a number of canal networks. The Erie Canal and several others built in the eastern states of the United States, and the Welland Canal, rebuilt by the Canadian government in 1841, were constructed in this way, while, in Germany, the waterways and canals became the province of the German governments and were maintained and expanded even when the major railways were being constructed.

State participation in and encouragement of railway investment arose out of a number of factors, some economic and some purely strategic. In other cases the fashionability of this mode of transport proved to be the determining factor. The degree of state participation in railway construction varied substantially from country to country, from almost complete abstention, as in Britain and the United States, to full control, as in Belgium, Sweden, Russia after 1881, Germany after the 1870s, and Japan after 1906. Often, however, the state took over the existing private railways to upgrade the services or to extend the system in conformance with general government policy. As a result, by 1914 there were very few countries in which the government did not exercise some control over railway operations.

The impact of railway construction on economic activity also varied from one country to another, depending upon the purpose for which the railways were constructed. While the emphasis was on profitability and/or the provision of external economies for other industries, the result of state investment was usually very favourable in terms of the stimuli provided for the growth of industry. Such was the case in Belgium, Germany, Russia, Canada, Sweden and the

United States. Belgium was the first continental European country to plan a national railway system, and its construction in the 1830s directly influenced the rapid industrialisation of the country. From the beginning of railway construction in Prussia, the government contributed by purchasing bonds in the private railway companies, by guaranteeing interest payments and by offering monopolies for specified periods of time. After 1850, the railway proved to be one of the major factors linking Germanic states economically and politically and it accentuated the importance of the rest of Europe to the growth of the German economy. After the formation of the German Empire in 1871, the state purchased many of the private lines in operation and constructed many others.

In Russia, the advent of the railway provided the means for linking previously isolated geographic regions together economically and boosted internal trade substantially. Government investment in railway construction complemented its ventures in manufacturing and facilitated the movement of raw materials from their sources to the areas of the country in which the industrial complexes were located. In addition, railway connection with western Europe provided the transport network for increasing Russian exports of agricultural products and for the importation of western machinery and other manufactures. The Trans-Siberian Railway, constructed between 1891 and 1905, opened up a vast subcontinent for settlement and from 1893 to 1913 some five million people crossed the Urals to tap the abundant agricultural and mineral resources of Asiatic Russia. Private and state co-operation in the provision of railways developed in a unique fashion in France after 1842. Capital investment was shared by both, the state's interest being concerned primarily with planning routes, obtaining the land and providing the permanent way. At the same time, the French government reserved the right to nationalise the railways after a certain period of time had elapsed.

But the contribution of the railways to industrial development was not always favourable, even when economic motives were uppermost in the thinking of the governments concerned. In Spain, for example, the rapid construction of railways by foreign (mainly French) entrepreneurs under government patronage did little for Spanish industry or, for that matter, for the financiers of the projects. The major beneficiaries tended to be the owners of the mines who gained rapid and cheap access to the ports. In the Balkans, on the other hand, the motives behind the large-scale railway expansion that took place there late in the nineteenth century were political and military rather than economic in nature. Spurred on by foreign governments, the foreign public debts of Greece, Romania, Serbia, Bulgaria and Turkey, expanded rapidly because of the construction of railways which provided few economic advantages to these countries in terms of economic development or the growth of their exports. In a number of respects, the foreign capital obtained from German, French and other sources reflected the political rivalries which developed during the last third of the nineteenth century in this part of the world, and the capital-exporting nations alone obtained the major benefits in the form of rising exports of manufactures to these countries. More favourable results occured in Hungary and, perhaps to a lesser extent, in Austria where a combination of state and private control of the railway system aided the industrial growth of these countries. In Sweden, too, as in many other European countries, the state-controlled railway system opened up many rural districts to trade following the upsurge of railway investment in the 1870s, thereby contributing directly to the growth of exports and indirectly to the spread of industry through the increased processing of primary products that resulted from the growth of the agricultural sector. Finally, whereas in many of the more economically-backward European countries, much, if not most, of the railway construction materials was imported, in Italy and Russia, state aid to the railway industry also involved contracts for materials from the local iron and steel industry.

Relative to the railways, other types of social overhead capital provided by the state were financially less significant in total even if many of them were capital-intensive in nature. But most of these forms of public investment became essential features of government economic activity in a modernising country. Such state ventures, generally at the local government level, as the provision of water and sewerage, streets, lighting and other similar services, became more numerous in several industrialising countries, not only because of the rise in *per capita* incomes but also because of the urbanisation of the population that occurred as industrialisation progressed. While state intervention in the promotion of improved transportation and communications and urban development was not always the result of enlightened government thinking, the role of the state in expanding market horizons and facilitating the spread of new ideas by means of the canal, railway, telegraph, cable and telephone, and the benefits to industry from harbour improvements and the favourable impact upon living conditions of public investment in urban services grew in significance as the nineteenth century proceeded. Investment in social overhead capital was necessary not only to promote industrial development but also to support it once it had taken place.

IV

Commercial policy, in the form of either the protection or the subsidisation of domestic industry, has always existed as a means whereby the state could encourage industrial development. Mercantilism was one such policy which incorporated a combination of protection of domestic industry from outside competition by means of a mixture of high import duties, quotas and embargoes and the state promotion of certain other industries by means of subsidies, the granting of monopoly rights, and so on. By the late eighteenth century, however, the mercantilist system in Britain was already under attack from the supporters of free trade, and the next 50 or 60 years witnessed the gradual liberalisation of Britain's foreign and domestic trade. On the Continent, mercantilism lived on longer than in Britain and, although a trend towards free trade was apparent in the commercial policies of most European countries from 1850 to the mid-1870s, this proved to be only a temporary departure from the normal practice of protecting domestic industry. During this liberal period, intergovernmental negotiations and agreements on railways, canals, rivers, the telegraph, and so on, were also instrumental in improving, international communications. In 1868, for example, the Rhine, a vitally important commercial link in western Europe, was declared a freeway for the ships of all nations and similar agreements were reached for the Scheldt, Elbe, Po and the Danube.

By 1870, trade within Europe was freer than at any other time during the nineteenth century, and international trade was responding to this stimulus. But the free-trade experiment was short-lived on the Continent, and from the later 1870s onwards there was a widespread return to protectionism. This came about for a number of reasons. What actually started the swing back to protectionism were two specific economic developments of the 1870s. One was the large inflow of cheap grain into western Europe from the United States and Russia; the other was the depression of 1873–9, the longest and deepest period of stagnant trade the world had yet experienced. Farmers and industrialists alike clamoured for relief, and the demands of this coalition of young industry and injured agriculture gave the initial stimulus to protection. Once started, this swing to protectionism was supported and maintained by the deeper forces of nationalism. Economically, this nationalism manifested itself in an increased desire for industrial development, and it was this desire and the competition engendered by successful industrialisation that was responsible for the growing demand for protection. Backing up the economic case for protection was the revival of nationalism in the late nineteenth century associated with the emergence of new nation-states, such as Germany and Italy. In addition to embarrassing foreign industrial competition, increasing tariffs provided the larger revenues needed to meet the rising expenditures on armaments brought about by the growing military rivalry between the states of Europe, as well as the increasing expenditures on education, public health and social services, which were in part social manifestations of the nationalist feeling. While nationalism and protectionism are not inevitably associated with one another, in nationalism we do have a force providing at least a predisposition towards protection. Taken together, nationalism and the lag in industrialisation made protection inevitable.

Germany adopted a system of moderate tariff protection for agriculture and manufacturing in 1879. Although a number of upward revisions of the duties on imports of grain occurred in later years, it was not until 1902 that much higher rates of duty on manufactured goods were introduced. Italy commenced the 1870s with a moderate tariff but new legislation in 1878 substantially increased the protection afforded by the government to manufacturing industry. Further increases in duties occurred in 1887. Switzerland imposed a moderate tariff from 1884 until 1906 when new legislation provided for high duties on food imports and large increases in duties on manufactures. Russia introduced high duties on manufactured imports as early as 1868 in an effort to promote domestic industrialisation. After several all-round increases in duties new legislation in 1891 gave Russia the distinction of being the most highly protected country in the world, and so high were the duties on coal, steel, machinery and chemicals, that the importing of these goods practically ceased. Sweden abandoned free trade in 1888 with protection for agriculture and later the manufacturing sector received similar benefits. Norway followed in 1897. In France, the demands of the industrialists for protection were hampered by the persistence of a strong free-trade sentiment and by the existence of long-term commercial treaties effectively pegging the tariff at a low level. But the addition of French farmers to the protectionist lobbies and the advent of a protectionist government in 1890 led to all-round protection in 1892. The tariff acts of 1910 predominantly favoured the manufacturing sector.

Countries outside Europe also resorted to a more protectionist policy after 1870. Canada adopted it in 1878. In the United States the trend towards freer trade in the first half of the nineteenth century was reversed in 1861, and the Civil War pushed up the rates of duty adopted in that year. In 1883, an across-the-board 5 per cent reduction of duties occurred but, thereafter, the American tariff level was pushed up twice in rapid succession. In 1890 the McKinley act raised the average level of tariffs to 50 per cent and, although the Democratic government brought about a downward revision of the tariff in 1894, lowering the average level to 40 per cent, the Republicans speedily reversed the trend with the Dingley Tariff (1897), which not only restored the McKinley rates but also raised the average level even higher to 57 per cent. Under the terms of commercial treaties entered into with Western countries prior to the Meiji Revolution of 1868, the Japanese government was prevented from introducing tariff protection until 1899. Although a policy of industrial protection was implemented in the latter year, the rates of duty were generally no higher than 15 per cent until the general upward revision of 1911.

A policy of protection offers domestic industries the opportunity of more rapid growth by reducing the competition emanating from their foreign counterparts in the home markets. It can thus promote industrial development in the form of import replacement production. On the other hand, the sheltering of home industries can place a brake on industrial development because it provides a situation in which the drive for highly efficient methods of production and the need for the adoption of new techniques as they become available in other countries becomes less pressing. Nevertheless, as we have already had occasion to point out,[1] two other features of the protectionist situation would appear to be conducive to industrial growth and technological diffusion. First, the erection of tariff barriers does appear to have stimulated direct foreign investment since one way in which foreign firms can overcome these barriers is by setting up branch factories in the protected markets. Once established, these foreign firms often acted as powerful agents for the diffusion of modern industrial technology. In Russia in the 1890s, for example, with the combination of high tariffs and the government's strategy aimed at attracting foreign capital, foreign entrepreneurs introduced advanced technology well ahead of that being used by Russian firms, particularly in the mining, metallurgical, electrical and chemical industries.[2] Protectionism may also have helped the diffusion of modern technology within countries by encouraging the growth of large-scale enterprises and the consequent domination of many industries by a very few large firms. Such was the case in a number of industries in Germany and the United States in the last third of the nineteenth century. One would expect, logically, that new knowledge and techniques would spread faster within a given industry the fewer the firms that have to be convinced of the profitability of their use.

It was in Germany and the United States that full advantage was taken of the tariff protection afforded to industry by sympathetic governments. Large-scale production, especially in heavy industries, was combined with efficiency, the adoption of the latest techniques and products, and the development of major centres of invention and innovation, and these two countries, in particular, became major exporters of manufactured products, despite the apparent shortcomings which the continued adherence to protection tended to portray.

V

There were several other ways in which the state could have helped to create the social and economic framework within which individual action could have initiated industrial take-off. A well-educated population, for example, eased the difficulties of industrialisation considerably. Thus Britain, and particularly Scotland, emerged from the eighteenth century with a much better educated population than that of any country on the Continent. This high level of educational attainment in Britain was not the result of state action in the field, however, but can be traced to the educational facilities provided by the various forms of religious dissent which had the result, broadly speaking, of making the Nonconformists the better educated section of the British middle classes. On the other hand when, from the early nineteenth century onwards, a process of catching-up occurred on the Continent, state financing of compulsory education became well established in a number of countries, including Germany, Holland, Switzerland and the Scandinavian countries. In Germany, in addition to compulsory primary and secondary education, a great deal of emphasis was placed on the provision of technical institutes, such as the Prussian Hauptbergwerks-Institut, and on the reorganisation of university education in favour of training in the scientific and engineering fields. By 1870, the German university system was the best in the world in these fields of learning, and the German educational system was imitated in a number of other west European nations. In France, the École Polytechnique provided important technical educational services from the early years of the nineteenth century. In the United States, too, formal education was comparatively common by 1850. The federal government had from its beginnings involved itself in elementary education and, after the Civil War, it broadened its involvement to include secondary schools. Using lands from the public domain to encourage the states to push local authorities into assuming the responsibility for establishing and supporting schools the federal government moved farther and faster in the educational field than the governments of the countries of Europe. Common school education for more and more children and technical education for advanced students help to account to a large extent for the rapid rate of industrialisation that occurred in the United States after 1865.

In a number of other countries the state's interest in education increased after 1870. This was the case in Britain where, after more than a half-century of neglect, the growing competition from newly-industrialising countries, such as Germany and the United States, forced the British government to review its attitude towards the provision of compulsory education. Much more alert to the needs of a modernising economy was the Japanese government which, from the outset of the Meiji era, gave a high priority in its expenditures to education in general, and to technical education in particular.

What is evident from this rather brief survey of the state's willingness to invest in human capital is that in most modernising countries in the nineteenth century the expansion of educational opportunities preceded industrialisation. Since this investment in education provided a growing supply of skilled and semi-skilled labour for industry, as well as entrepreneurs, managers and researchers, it is perhaps no accident that the countries with better educated populations were the first to import the new technology and were the fastest industrialisers. Higher levels of education also tended to make people more receptive to new ideas and to economic change. Finally, it must be noted that the provision of agricultural educational facilities aided the spread of more efficient methods of farming which, by raising agricultural productivity, provided a further support to a country's industrial development.

The state could provide further support to industrial development in a number of ways. It could do much to influence the financial environment of a country by encouraging the growth of a new and modern banking system through legislation and other means. Thus, while the Japanese government was prepared to advocate the development of a private, competitive, *laissez-faire* banking system, it was also quite willing, even anxious, to create special institutions to meet particular needs when these were not forthcoming in the private banking sector. The result was the establishment of such institutions as the Industrial Bank of Japan (1902) and the Hypothec Bank (1897), the latter, modelled on the French Crédit Foncier, lending primarily for land improvement and non-residential construction. The state was also instrumental in facilitating the inflow of foreign capital either directly by raising loan money abroad for its own developmental projects, thus allowing local capital funds to be used for domestic private ventures, or indirectly, by creating conditions such as guaranteed markets for output, guaranteed returns on investment, and so on, which were attractive to foreign investors.

The state could also assist industrial development by legislating into existence improved forms of business organisation. In the second half of the nineteenth century, the scope and nature of technological change and the growing desire for rapid industrialisation in a number of countries created a situation in which individuals and partnerships could no longer provide or attract the volume of funds required to finance large-scale capital-intensive business undertakings and the need for a corporate form of business organisation was evident. While the establishment of many such business units preceded modern industrial growth, the protection of shareholders by the provision of limited liability status was not common in the first half of the nineteenth century. Moreover, until the 1840s at least, the founding of joint stock companies was difficult and often costly. In almost all the industrialising countries the need for the large-scale organisation of certain industries after the 1830s, beginning with the railways, led to pressure being put on governments to pass legislation permitting joint stock company organisation with limited liability.

In France, as early as 1807 under the Code de Commerce, companies could be formed in at least two ways, the *société en commandite sur actions,* which required a charter and in which 'active' participants had limitless liability but in which the liability of 'sleeping' shareholders was limited to the extent of their shareholdings, and the *société anonymes,* a joint stock company with or without limited liability provisions depending on the constitution of the company. Because of certain restrictions on the latter it did not become as widespread in France as the former until free incorporation was allowed in 1867. The Code de Commerce became the basis of company law in Belgium, Holland, Italy, Spain and Switzerland. *Société anonymes* were set up in Belgium by the Dutch government in the 1820s and free incorporation in the following decade led to the establishment of up to 55 such companies by the Société Générale and the Banque de Belgique, both of which were themselves joint stock organisations. In Germany, the joint stock company emerged in the form of the *Aktiengesellschaft*, similar to the *société anonyme*, but free incorporation was not allowed until 1869. Limited liability joint stock corporations existed in the United States for much of the nineteenth century but until the 1870s a state charter was required for establishment and the states applied rigid controls over the functions of such enterprises. In Britain, although limited liability status was granted to joint stock companies in the second half of the 1850s, the growth of such organisations was slow until the 1870s.

Initially, the joint stock form of business organisation was most prevalent in transport and finance but, after 1870, it became much more common in the manufacturing sector. Government legislation in this field arose out of the necessity within the business sector for an improved method of providing investible funds to industrial concerns on a scale much larger than was required in previous decades. As a result of such legislation, important innovations were introduced in a number of industries including iron and steel, mining, metallurgy, electricity and shipbuilding.

Altering the legal framework within which businesses operated is only one example of the changes in the social and economic environment required by a modernising society. In a number of fields, old laws had to be abolished and new ones legislated. At the same time, new institutions had to be created, often with the aid of the state. Change was particularly necessary in agriculture, the predominant sector of the pre-industrial economy, if it was to play its crucial role in the early stages of industrial development. In most industrialising countries, therefore, governments were actively involved in promoting agricultural improvements by implementing land reforms, freeing serfs, establishing agricultural colleges and farm extension services, providing rural credit facilities, and assisting the diffusion of new agricultural techniques in a variety of ways. As a minimum, successful economic development depended on the government to ensure political stability and the orderly conduct of human affairs.

Finally, in several countries, there was an attempt by the government to reduce the impact of the worst features of industrial capitalism. Over time, one country after another began to legislate to deal with such problems as child labour, hours of work, working conditions relating to health and safety, overtime and night work, wage rates, sickness, old age, unemployment, and other aspects of economic welfare. Even in Britain, the closest country to the *laissez-faire* state, it was recognised early in the century that the state had to interfere in the working of the economy in such matters and a series of Factory Acts improved working conditions somewhat, reduced the prevalence of child labour and generally reduced hours of work for children and female workers. By 1913, some attention had also been directed towards minimum wages legislation, sickness and unemployment insurance, old age pensions and other improvements in the lot of the worker.

On the Continent, Germany adopted the most comprehensive legislation affecting the welfare of the labouring classes. By 1890, sickness, accident and old age benefits had been introduced and by 1913 a high proportion of the working population was covered by this legislation. Other countries followed suit in varying degrees of emphasis.

In general, however, one must not exaggerate the importance of this aspect of state intervention. In many cases, state regulation of working conditions was merely passing through the initial stages of welfare legislation and it was not until after World War II that vast improvements occurred.

VI

In conclusion, it can be said that state participation in the industrialisation process of the nineteenth century varied in degree and intensity from one country to another and from one time period to another within each country. It was in Britain that the closest approach to the *laissez-faire* economy was attained, but elsewhere state participation ranged 'from the decentralized and competitive promotional activities of state and local governments in the United States during the Jacksonian era to the highly centralized and bureaucratized activity of the

Russian state under Count Witte in the 1890s'.[3] It was generally to be found that the degree of involvement of the state in economic growth was highest in those countries which were 'latecomers' to industrial development and in those countries in which the degree of backwardness was the greatest.

While direct state involvement in the development of certain industries was not significant in the nineteenth century, indirect methods of facilitating and encouraging economic progress and the spread of industrial technology were widespread and in many cases the state made a positive contribution to the efforts undertaken to promote the growth of industry. Through the provision of social overhead capital, the willingness to dismantle all sorts of legal and institutional barriers to the mobility of economic resources, and to create the type of political, social and economic environment within which economic development could occur, the state acted as an important mechanism in the promotion of the spread of new techniques and ideas.

We must be careful not to overemphasise the role of the state in the nineteenth century, however. The developmental functions of the state were generally indirect in nature while, at times, state interference went against the long-term development of an economy. For example, concentration on heavy industry in some countries such as Italy and Russia led to inappropriate industrial structures at the time and created problems for further development in future decades.

Not all state actions were helpful, therefore, some were harmful. In addition, the replacement of private entrepreneurs by government bureaucrats was not always a wise move and may have often been costly. Furthermore, the rudimentary nature of whatever government planning that occurred did not always produce the correct economic decisions. Often, for example, military necessity placed a brake on economic development instead of fostering it. Having made this point, however, the fact remains that the state played an important, indeed vital, role in promoting industrial development in a number of countries in the period before 1914.

Notes

1. See pp. 61-2.
2. M.C. Kaser, 'Russian Entrepreneurship', *Cambridge Economic History of Europe,* Vol. VII, Pt 1, p. 474, citing J.P. McKay, *Pioneers for Profit: Entrepreneurship and Russian Industrialization* (Chicago, 1970).
3. Rondo Cameron, 'Economic Development: Some Lessons of History for Developing Countries', *American Economic Review* (May 1967), p. 321.

Selected Reading

Hugh G. Aitken (ed.), *The State and Economic Growth* (New York, 1959)
Tom Kemp, *Industrialization in Nineteenth Century Europe* (London, 1969)
——*Historical Patterns of Industrialization* (London, 1978), Ch. 7
A. Milward and S.B. Saul, *The Economic Development of Continental Europe 1780–1870* (London, 1973)
A. Milward and S.B. Saul, *The Development of the Economies of Continental Europe 1850–1914* (London, 1977)
Barry Supple, 'The State and the Industrial Revolution 1700–1914', in C.M. Cipolla (ed.), *The Fontana Economic History of Europe* (London, 1973), Vol. 3, pp. 301-57
A.J. Taylor, *Laissez-faire and State Intervention in Nineteenth Century Britain* (London, 1972)

15 INDUSTRIALISATION AFTER 1914

The diffusion of modern industrial technology did not end with the outbreak of war in Europe in 1914. In fact the continued spread of industrialisation was stimulated by both the war and the worldwide depression that occurred during the interwar years. Cut off from European sources of supply during the war years, manufacturing industry developed rapidly in a number of countries overseas and, although the return of normal peacetime production saw the collapse of some of these nascent industries, tariff protection ensured the survival of many others. After the war, industrialisation was rapid in the United States, Canada and Australia in the 1920s, and high rates of industrial growth were also achieved during these years in Brazil, Finland, India, New Zealand, South Africa and Japan. Relative to the newly-industrialising countries, the older industrial nations, like Britain, France and Germany, experienced declining rates of growth, and even the United States failed to attain industrial growth rates comparable to those of the newly-developing countries during the twenties. The world depression also fostered the spread of industrialisation, when the decline in world primary product prices and the growing restrictions placed on world trade in primary products in the 1930s, forced governments in a number of non-industrial countries to foster secondary industry behind tariff protection to safeguard living standards and expand employment opportunities in the face of growing rural unemployment. As a result, industrialisation in these countries proceeded with undiminished vigour despite the depression.

Despite the success achieved by some countries, the spread of industrialisation to new regions and nations during this century has been made more difficult by the growing complexity and the scale of modern technology. Since 1750 the world has experienced four great overlapping surges in technical innovation. The first great push—based on cotton textiles, iron and steam power—lasted until the middle of the nineteenth century or even later. Then came the second surge—based on railways and steel—lasting until the 1890s. The third innovational upsurge, involving electricity, the motor car and the aeroplane, got under way around the end of the century and probably ended a decade or so after the end of World War II. This period also witnessed the widespread adoption of the assembly-line method of production, which was first developed by Henry Ford as the means to efficient, large-scale, and therefore cheap, production of motor cars, but which was used later to mass produce a growing number of consumer goods, including washing machines, radios and refrigerators. The latest innovational push, which we have been experiencing since the end of World War II, is more difficult to label in a short-hand way, but its origin, in major scientific progress in nuclear and solidstate physics, organic and inorganic chemistry, electronics, engineering, the earth sciences, the biological sciences, and mathematics, is clear enough. Supported by invention and innovation, this scientific work has produced an ever-growing range of new raw materials, production processes, energy sources and production and consumption goods. The period witnessed the introduction of the transistor, plastics, synthetic resins, man-made fibres, new metals and metal products of aluminium and alloy steels, and whole ranges of antibiotics and other life-saving drugs. New production processes were introduced into most industries, including steel, cotton, glass, shipbuilding and construction. Prefabrication became a common method of production. Nuclear energy provided a new form of fuel for possible use in transportation and other industries in the future. Many kinds of electronic devices, including television and radar equipment, became objects of everyday use, while computers and transfer systems, which are the basis of automation and cybernetic methods, were more widely adopted. The list is far from complete, but it is long enough to indicate the nature of the far-reaching technological changes that have occurred since 1945.

The growing complexity and scale of present-day technology have tended to increase the impediments to its diffusion. This is apparent both in the 'lumpiness' of the investment in capital-intensive industrial plants, which puts them out of the reach of the unaided savings potential of many poor countries, and in the range of technical and managerial skills needed if the new technology is to be exploited successfully. Partly as a consequence of the changing character of twentieth-century technology, conditions in the already-industrialised countries have tended to diverge even more sharply from those in the non-industrialised ones than they did in the past, thus making the difficulties of technological diffusion between nations even more acute. Thus the new technology is increasingly dependent on ever-growing markets based on rising levels of *per capita* real incomes and relatively rapidly changing patterns of consumption expenditures. Financial institutions and other services supporting the development and use of this technology have become more sophisticated, while the educational facilities have responded by expanding greatly and becoming more diversified in most advanced countries. Moreover, to maintain and, if possible, increase the rate of technological progress, the advanced countries have been devoting an increasing fraction of their investment expenditures to research and development in recent years. Not unexpectedly, the technological developments brought about by all this R and D expenditure bears little relationship to the technical needs of the underdeveloped countries of the world. For all of these reasons, it is not surprising to find, therefore, that the technological gap between the advanced and the less developed economies of the world has continued to grow in the years since 1945, and that the effort needed to bridge that gap has become correspondingly greater.

If the obstacles to the diffusion of technology have multiplied in the twentieth century, the 'mechanisms' for promoting and supporting that diffusion have also not remained unchanged. Indeed, in line with our earlier analysis, one would expect new 'mechanisms' to emerge and existing 'mechanisms' to adapt and change in response to the new needs created by the changed circumstances. At the same time, two major political events in this country have served to promote the continued thrust towards worldwide industrialisation. First, following the 1917 revolution in Russia and subsequent revolutions in other parts of the world, communism emerged as a new ideological driving force in support of rapid industrial development. The second political development was the process of decolonisation which began some time after the end of World War II and which served to fuel an upsurge of nationalism that was partly manifested in an urge for economic advancement. The massive industrialisation drive, which became a prime objective of the Russian leadership, required a determined effort to hold consumption to a minimum and to transfer resources to capital-building, an effort greatly facilitated by the totalitarian political apparatus. In the absence of a free-market system, the required allocation of resources was achieved through the use of a central controlling and planning agency. In other words, a planning agency came to act as a substitute for the market. Whereas, in Russia, the adoption of central economic planning had considerable ideological significance, the use of planning in many of today's underdeveloped economies reflects more the institutional deficiencies of the existing market systems in those countries. Moreover, even in the advanced countries, economic planning of one kind or another at the government level has become necessary to ensure the demand conditions required to support the use of much of present-day technology. In short, the state remains an extremely important means for promoting the spread of modern industrial technology, and in economic planning it possesses a technique for development more powerful than any available to its nineteenth-century predecessors.

Because of a number of significant changes in the character of the international economy during the twentieth century, it has continued to function as an important mechanism for the diffusion of modern industrial technology. In the field of international investment, for example, an important feature of direct investment since 1900 has been the rapid increase in the importance of the multinational corporation. Although statistical data on the activities of these international companies are meagre, particularly for the first half of the century, a considerable part of the direct investment undertaken since 1945 is undoubtedly attributable to these international corporations, many of which have their origins in the United States. They cover a wide range of manufacturing industries, including chemicals, vehicles, oil, computers and foodstuffs, as well as raw materials' extraction. Obviously the entry of such firms into a country confers many benefits on it in terms of increased production, investment and employment, the introduction of new managerial and technical skills, and export expansion or import replacement. The diffusion of technology is also promoted. At the same time, however, the concentration of a number of these international companies in a country may pose serious problems for the government of that country, both in the sphere of political and of economic development. It is not surprising to find, therefore, that for 50 years or more, economists have speculated on how the economic benefits from the operations of foreign subsidiaries are distributed among 'borrowing' and 'lending' countries. Nevertheless, however the balance is struck in the case of individual countries, it does appear, on the basis of the available evidence, that the international corporation is a powerful mechanism for diffusing modern technology.

A feature of the post-World War II period of even more importance for the spread of industrialisation is the emergence of genuinely international institutions concerned with the problem of world economic and social development. One of the early simplifications of the process of economic development was the economists' model in which growth was a function of an increase in the rate of saving and investment. Given that economic growth in a large number of countries was limited by low levels of income and saving, a simple solution to this dilemma was clearly an infusion of capital resources from outside, which could be supplied either by individual donor nations or by a multilateral fund to which all advanced countries could contribute. The World Bank, which was set up very early to finance projects of a social overhead character in transportation, power and irrigation, has come increasingly to perform this function. In addition to the World Bank and its subsequent affiliates—the International Finance Corporation (1956) and the International Development Association (1960)—the United Nations has provided aid through a number of its organs in the form of technical assistance to developing countries, relief aid and investment in education and research. Technical assistance began with the setting up in 1950 of the UN's Expanded Programme of Technical Assistance (EPTA). At first, supplying capital and technical assistance were kept separate, despite their obvious relatedness. This gap was partially bridged in 1957 with the establishment of the United Nations Special Fund designed to perform those kinds of technical assistance particularly relevant to placing the underdeveloped countries in a position to utilise large-scale capital resources more effectively. The full integration of technical assistance and capital financing activities into a co-ordinated development assistance system has yet to be achieved, however, but substantial movement in this direction has occurred with the merger of the Special Fund and the Expanded Programme of Technical Assistance into the United Nations Development Programme (UNDP) and with the growing importance of the technical assistance activities of such capital financing institutions as the World Bank.

The relevance of these developments to the model of diffusion advanced earlier in this book should be obvious. In this century, industrial technology is spreading slowly to nations in which the obstacles to development are much greater than those that confronted countries that achieved industrial take-off in the period before 1914. Consequently, even stronger mechanisms for diffusing technology are needed if industrialisation is to succeed in these late, late developers. Government economic planning, the multinational corporation, and, in particular, the institutionalising of the mechanism for diffusing technology internationally in the form of a growing range of United Nations agencies, represent part of the twentieth-century response to that need. Finally, it must be noted that the importance of market considerations for the spread of modern technology has, if anything, tended to increase with the passage of time. Thus even in some advanced industrial nations the realisation that the size of existing domestic markets is inadequate to the output needs of some branches of modern technology has led to moves towards international economic integration of the kind exemplified by the European Economic Community. The need for international economic integration is likely to be even more pressing in the case of today's late industrialisers, given that, of the hundred-odd underdeveloped countries usually listed in this economic category, over 50 of them have populations of five millions or fewer inhabitants.

INDEX

absorptive capacity 162-3
Africa 162
agriculture: agricultural cooperatives
43-5; agricultural societies 42-3;
education and training 37, 45-8;
improvements in 32-4, 36-7, 38;
industrialisation and 31-2, 168;
labour supply 37-8; land consolidation 34-5, 36; land tenure
35-6, 41-2; machinery 38-40;
protection 48-9; state and 45-9;
see also individual countries
Argentina 162
Australasia 27, 162, 180, 184, 198,
209
Austria-Hungary 32, 61, 107, 119,
158, 191

banking 81-4, 90, 141, 142, 178-88,
204; and state 204; *Crédit
Mobilier* 84, 141, 161, 180, 186;
investment 15, 43, 142, 149, 157,
160-1, 177-89 *passim*; joint stock
80-2, 177; merchant 179;
syndicates 187; *see also* individual
countries
Belgium 17, 117, 129; agriculture 37,
43, 44; banking 83, 142, 179,
182, 188; company law 205;
entrepreneurship 151; exports 155;
foreign investment 149, 158, 159;
industrial concentration 119;
industrial growth 21, 24; labour
supply 107; state 192, 193; transport 59, 196, 197
bill of exchange 83, 170, 179
Brazil 162, 209
Britain 6, 10, 17, 25, 26, 129, 133,
134, 137, 167, 170, 172, 174,
177, 187, 190, 209; agriculture
34, 38, 41-2, 43, 44; banking 81;
capital accumulation 67, 69, 70;
education 106-7, 203; emigration
151, 152; export growth 53-4, 62,
154; foreign investment 149, 150,
158, 184; industrial concentration
119; industrial growth 21, 24;
inflation in 88; joint stock

companies 86, 204; labour supply
95-6, 98, 100, 103, 104, 206;
resource endowment 112; transport
57, 58, 59, 196

Canada 24, 25, 27, 32, 61, 149, 153,
155, 158, 159, 162, 196, 201,
209
capital: accumulation 65-74; and
saving 74-6; availability 124;
goods 128, 129, 155-6; markets
84-5, 149, 187
China 162, 181, 190
competition: and factor availability
166-7; and markets 169; barriers
to 172; *laissez faire* 170, 174,
190
cottage industry 168

Denmark 10, 17, 27, 44, 46, 81, 82,
117, 118, 133, 185, 188, 203

education 106-9, 202-3
Egypt 162, 181
emigration 151-3
England 86, 90, 106-7, 108
entrepreneurship 132, 133, 134-5,
136, 141-2

feudalism 167, 168
foreign investment 87, 148-9, 157,
158, 159, 160, 184; *see also*
individual countries
foreign trade 115, 117, 154, 155,
156, 163, 164, 168
France 6, 10, 17, 79, 129, 209;
agriculture 35, 38, 39, 43, 44, 46;
banking 81, 82, 83, 84, 90, 141,
142, 179, 181, 188; capital 67;
coal shortage 114, 135; education
107, 108; entrepreneurship 137,
138, 141, 151; exports 155; foreign
investment 149, 152, 158, 159,
184, 198; industrial concentration
119; industrial growth 21, 24, 25,
112, 140; joint stock companies
86, 204-5; labour supply 94, 100;
protection 61, 200-1; state 193;
transport 57, 58, 59, 197

214